25th /

G000300775

To Louise,

The most wonderful wife any man could ever wish for!

Edward xxx.

Dream Weaver

Dream Weaver

Elisabeth Furse
and
Ann Barr

CHAPMANS

Chapmans Publishers
A division of the Orion Publishing Group Ltd
Orion House
5 Upper St. Martin's Lane
London WC2H 9EA

British Library Cataloguing in Publication Data
Furse, Elisabeth
Dream Weaver
I. Title II. Barr, Ann
920

ISBN 1 85592 540 0

First published by Chapmans 1993

Copyright © Elisabeth Furse and Ann Barr 1993

The right of Elisabeth Furse and Ann Barr
to be identified as authors of this work
has been asserted by them in accordance
with the Copyright, Designs and Patents
Act 1988.

All rights reserved
No part of this publication may be reproduced,
stored in a retrieval system, or transmitted
in any form or by any means without the
prior permission in writing of the publishers,
nor be circulated in any form of binding
or cover other than that in which it is
published and without a similar condition
including this condition being imposed
on the subsequent purchaser.

Photoset by The Electronic Book Factory, Fife, Scotland
Printed and bound in Great Britain by
Butler & Tanner Ltd, Frome and London

To all those I loved and love.
Elisabeth Furse

Acknowledgements

This book owes an enormous amount to Eleanor Bentall, Barbara Meadowcroft and Neville Dent; and it has been greatly enriched by material from manuscripts by Henry Swanzy, Iain Finlayson and a taped interview by Nicholas de Jongh. Thanks are also due to many people who appear in the story, and for information found by Ariane Castaing, Bryony Edmunds and Stephanie Keil. Other people whose help is gratefully acknowledged include Rosemary Combridge, M. R. D. Foot, Jean and Catherine Gimpel, Harriet Griffey and Anthony Howard. Of many books consulted, the most drawn upon were: *Safe Houses are Dangerous*, Helen Long, William Kimber, 1985; *Turncoat*, Brendan M. Murphy, Harcourt, Brace, Jovanovich, 1987; *Des Capitaines par Milliers*, L. H. Nouveau, Calmann-Levy, 1958. The poem 'Reading *Notebook* by Anna Kamienska' on page 287 is © 1991 by Czeslaw Milosz, from his collection *Provinces* first published by the Ecco Press, New Jersey, in 1991; it is reprinted by permission.

Most of this story is true, but imagination and acting were the salvation of Elisabeth as an unloved child, a Communist party worker in Nazi Germany and a link in the MI9 escape route from Vichy France. I have checked the facts as far as possible, and I hope no one can reasonably claim to be treated unfairly.

Ann Barr

Contents

I

A Baltic Childhood, 1910–20

I came into the world in Königsberg on the Baltic, the capital of East Prussia, at midnight on 30 August 1910. I was named Louise Ruth Wolpert. My mother, born Ida Bloch, was German Jewish, my father, Paul Wolpert, saw himself as Russian because his family came from Riga in Latvia, part of the Russian empire. His father, Uri, moved to Königsberg in 1860, married there and had three sons and three daughters. In those days, sons were prized and daughters were an unwelcome responsibility. My father was deeply disappointed that his own firstborn was female.

My mother's relations, all Germans, were rich corn merchants from Lithuania. Her four brothers and three sisters, all of them tall, broad-shouldered, raw-boned and rigid, despised small, dirty, savage Russki and Polacki. I wasn't allowed to associate with my father's family or to speak Russian. To be German, a Baltic German, was honourable and clean and virtuous. To be German was to be automatically upper-class. But I did not want to be German. I felt Russian. Russian music and stories seemed to be my music and stories, Russian ways and warmth my ways.

My father had married my mother for her dowry, forty thousand gold marks. He wanted to be a doctor, but abandoned medicine when my grandfather, a broker on the wheat exchange, shot himself leaving gambling debts. My father had to go into business; he became a textile merchant and made a lot of money. He had a library and read many newspapers. I see him sitting in his big armchair reading, or looking out of the window reciting the *Odyssey* or the *Iliad* in Greek. Once, as I went to say goodnight, he said, 'You poor child, you can't understand Greek.' He would from time to time quote Greek to me. He could also recite Heine by the yard.

When he was not away on business, he would hold a *Herrenabend*, a men's evening. His friends came round for a cold buffet, samovar, vodka and gambling through the night. Next morning the rooms reeked of cigars.

My father had a passion for light opera and for opera singers, several of whom became his mistresses. I remember him setting out in his fur-lined coat with gold watch-chain, gold cigar-cutter, gold toothpick, gold pencil and gold nailfile. He smelt delicious, a mixture of expensive colognes and good cigars.

My father and mother took a great deal of trouble with their nails, hair and bodies, as was the custom then. Every morning a little sweaty, bearded man would come to their bedroom to give them each a massage, followed by a barber for him, a hairdresser for her, and a manicurist. Later, my mother trained one of the maids to do her hair.

My mother lived the life of the rich women of that time, travelling from spa to spa. In March it was Vichy and Vittel for the waters, then Taormina for the oranges, Marienbad for the sour milk, Merano for the grape juice to clear the blood. By the time she had finished with Merano it was October, and she came home for Christmas and to get ready for the skating and skiing of the winter months. I do not remember my mother's face. I remember only her hands and feet and her legs, which were heavy. On her heavy feet she wore very elegant shoes. Her hands were long and she waved them a great deal. She dressed well and expensively, but she had no imagination.

To my mother, a child was a nuisance. When I was four or five, she took me on holiday to the sea, with her sister and my nurse. I was on the beach with Nurse, who sat in the shelter of a *Korb*, a beach basket, when I saw my mother on the promenade. I ran up the steps and threw my arms round her legs. She pushed me away, saying brusquely 'Behave yourself.' I have never forgotten it. I was taken for walks in the town every day by my nurse, when she could meet other nurses. Königsberg had a drawbridge. We seemed to reach it always when it was opening. At night I dreamt I was clinging to it as it went up. My night nursery wallpaper had a pattern of tiny red roses with a large blank patch where I had stuck a turd to the wall and they had washed it off and punished me.

For four years I was an only child. Then my brother Max arrived, followed by another brother and a sister. Max had tuberculosis of the bone and was coddled by a special nurse. Though so much younger, he used to hit me. I found that if I got my foot in the right place, between his legs, I could get him down. Nurse said I would ruin him. My younger brother, Arno, would not eat, just filled his cheeks with food and refused to swallow: he was known as the hamster. I have a memory of my sister Gerda, ten years younger than me, being pushed in her smart white pram and the wheel coming off.

I never talked properly to grown-ups or ate with them. I had to kiss my mother's hand and my aunts' hands and make a *Knicks*, a curtsy, to everyone except the servants: my life was spent respectfully on the floor. Every Saturday I had to come to the drawing-room and recite a poem in my best sailor suit – white linen in summer, navy serge in winter – and was rewarded by a piece of chocolate. I wore big bows in my hair.

The nicest member of my father's family was Aunt Sonya, his cousin, who lived forty miles away in Reval, now called Tallinn, the capital of Estonia. She was gentle and doleful, with blue eyes and white curly hair. I was allowed to visit her, even though she was Russian. She talked to me and sang Russian songs, accompanying herself on the piano. She knew the beauty of nature, and would say 'Look at that flower,' and she was not angry when I blackened my face with blueberry juice. I wished I lived in Estonia with her.

My mother's family I remember with horror. Balts were tough people – they had to be. They had been walked over for a thousand years by the Germans, the Russians and the Swedes. The non-Jewish Balts were extremely anti-Semitic, because the Jews made good. The Balts were an agricultural people and poor, the clever Jews went into business and became wealthy. My German grandmother, Lena Bloch, was the toughest woman I have ever met. Everyone hated her, and her children feared her. Her sons told the story of buying her one of the early cars and rousing her fury: 'When carriages go without horses it will be the end of the world.' My grandfather, Meir Bloch, was a tease, and used to put his walking stick horizontally at the level of a child's nose and command 'Jump, jump.' But when he did it to me, I pushed the stick up and walked underneath. He was delighted, and said, 'She is as clever as a poodle.' I was known for a while as Poodle – in German, *Pudel*.

The name 'Lisl', which my old friends still use, was given me by Aunt Dora, my father's elder sister. She said, 'The child smiles like the sun.' In Austria the sun is called 'Lisl'. Lisl is short for Elisabeth, the name I eventually adopted.

My smile, and my attempts to reach out to people, were distrusted by the two women whose job it was to look after me, Nurse and my governess. In wealthy houses like ours Nurse was known as simply Fräulein and the governess as Fräulein Whatever-her-name-was. Different women held the governess's position over the years, but I did not love any of them. I hated Nurse, who came when I was about six and never left us. She was very jealous of her position in the household, and it was she who got rid of the governesses. She said to me, 'If there was nobody in the room, you would flirt with the furniture.' Every day she put me over the nursery sofa and smacked me with a hairbrush, 'Just in case you have been naughty.' I used to sit on the lavatory looking up at the box with the chain and thinking I might hang myself.

Nurse, whose real name was Fräulein Hirschberg, was the perfect servant. This is a type I do not trust, because they make their masters so dependent on them that they end up the masters. Nurse became my mother's personal maid and housekeeper. She had no family, and she was never not there. She threw a dark shadow over my childhood. She had a face like a parrot, with a sharp nose. That is why I have a dread of parrots.

One day, on a walk in Königsberg with Nurse, we saw a man with only one leg, hopping along on a crutch. When we reached home and she went to get our tea, I tied up one leg with a belt and hopped round. She came back into the room and beat me for making fun of him. I had only wanted to know what it felt like. That was the first time I was conscious of compassion. I regard myself as a Christian because I believe in the man who came to live and die for others. I see Jesus as my pal. That is at the root of my everyday faith. That I am by blood Jewish has made no difference to how I see myself.

When I was seven I got TB. Tuberculosis is a very poetic illness: you are not sick, you just cough. Everything money could buy I had. I was sent often to my grandmother's farm at Pilkallen in East Prussia, where my nose was squeezed every morning to make me swallow cod-liver oil and malt. My mother was ahead of her time in her interest in '*hygiène*' and diet. Every day I was given a fresh raw egg, still warm, pierced at both ends by Nurse, which I sucked through a straw, and three times a week spinach for the iron.

On the farm, I remember hearing the sound of the *centrifuges*, the churns, making the butter early in the morning. Later, the bedlinen was laid out on lawns and watered to bleach it. The outdoor servants, who slept in the stables, had red and white checked bedlinen, which was spread on one lawn, then there was blue and white for the indoor servants, and for us, white linen with monograms, embroidery and lace. The feather beds were hung up on clotheslines and beaten.

The feather beds in the guest rooms were used to warm the rising dough. Six or seven big rounds of yeast dough would be made and floured and covered with linen cloths, then slipped under the feathers. The smell was lovely. My childhood was all smell and taste, not touch. Nobody ever kissed me, nobody ever hugged me.

I grew up with four seasons. Everything changed with the time of year: food, clothes, what the horses pulled us in. In autumn we picked mushrooms. My nurse warned me not to touch the pretty ones – red with white spots or acid yellow – 'They are poisonous, like pretty people.' The best mushrooms were the colour of stone or earth. 'Ugly people are the best.'

In winter I loved travelling by troika, sitting warm and cosy in a fur bag and hearing the horses' hooves. Snow and ice have a music, and the crunch of one's own footsteps is each time a first experience. The smell of snow and ice is beautiful. The sea sometimes froze, so we could skate to the islands. There were ice flowers on the windows, and my nurse put apples and chestnuts to bake in the nursery stove. We ate blinis and stuffed cabbage, and never saw an orange – they were not imported. When I was quite small I was given my first skis, and told to hang on to the back of the troika and keep the skis together and straight. They moved apart inexorably, and I fell.

Then came the spring. I found snowdrops pushing through the snow with their little white heads. When it got warm the new leaves of the silver birches were intensely pale green, with a sheen, almost oily. The larches were brighter green, with red on those soft tasselled ends. When I saw moss I pushed my face into it, to get the freshness and the smell of the black earth. I still do. Whenever I go to the country I have to lie down with my face in the grass, wet or dry, and breathe it in.

We went to stay on the Baltic coast for two or three months in the summer. I remember a hammock. Hammocks were very important in my childhood, because children lived in hammocks, even grown-ups lived in hammocks when we went to the sea. The hammocks were slung between two pines, and surrounded by trees – black pines and white birch. My nurse put a bottle of ammonia under my hammock to keep the mosquitoes away. To this day, I can never smell ammonia without being reminded of the hammock with its cushions and the dunes, and the yellow sea; the cones falling from the pines, and the resinous tears of gum, like honey, sliding down the bark and dripping into the sea to slowly turn into amber.

In the woods I found chanterelles, which the Germans call *Gelbhähnchen*, 'yellow cockerels'. The little dark blue speedwell is *Männertreu*, 'men's loyalty', because it lasts only twenty-four hours. I liked the ferns, wide and fresh and full of dew. On the heath were wild strawberries, and later blueberries and cranberries. I loved the red squirrels jumping from branch to branch and tree to tree, and the busy ant-heaps. I could not understand how an ant could carry a big pine needle. I thought: I couldn't carry a tree on my back.

In summer there were iced fruit soups – redcurrant, white-currant, blackcurrant, and pale green cucumber, all topped with *smetana*, rich soured cream. And the cook made a wonderful jam, with plums. She broke the stones open and put the kernels into the jam and so much sugar that the jam was hard. My grandmother and aunts used to drink tea the Russian way, putting a spoonful of stiff jam on the saucer and scooping some up on a biscuit, then taking a sip of tea from the glass. Some vulgar people used to pour the tea into the saucer with the jam and drink from the saucer.

I can still taste the red fruit puddings and the smoked flounders. The smokeries hung their bronze flounders outside on a line for customers to choose. Flounders flitted and undulated around me when I threw myself into the tideless sea, that sea made golden yellow by soft sand. I learnt to swim very young and swam for hours. Flounders of the same yellow as the sand floated through the little sea dunes as I swam above. The sea was my friend. The Baltic is a sweet sea, with very little salt. The water does not carry you, so I had to become a good swimmer. It was a treat when it rained, watering down on me when I was swimming in the water.

When I was a child, all waters were safe and beautiful to drink, to wade in or swim in – seas, rivers, lakes. And the tap water was running happily into my mouth and across my body. The air was there to be smelt and breathed fearlessly, for the word pollution did not exist. All that grew on the earth was safe and lovely, and then came progress.

The summers of 1914, 1915, 1916 – I knew nothing of any war – were hot and dry, the winters icy cold. It was good to be busy, like the ants, collecting fruit and nuts, digging with a spade in the sand, letting the holes fill with water as pools for the tiddlers I caught in my net.

One summer, when I was about seven, two farm boys put me against a tree, pulled down my knickers and made pee-pee on me. I quite liked the warm wetness. It was my first sexual experience. They told me they had seen a calf born, and I think they expected I would shortly have a baby like that, with lots of blood and dirt.

I always wanted to have babies. I had many dolls: Lotti, Sonya named after my aunt Sonya, Anna after my aunt Anna, Baby. My dolls had porcelain faces and real hair, which I brushed. I loved them all, but what I wanted was a rag doll that had just come into the shops, called Käthe Kruse. Käthe Kruse was soft and had red wool hair and a sewn face. But Mother would not let me have one: rag dolls were unhygienic – *hygiène* forbade them.

All my pocket money was spent on books – I filled my mind and soul with them. I devoured the Red Indian romances of Karl May, *Uncle Tom's Cabin*, the *Heidi* books, and a shelf of stories by the Scandinavian writers Selma Lagerlof and Fru Marie Grubbe. I pored over Russian and Finnish fairy tales: these had my beloved trees, and foxes, and packs of wolves which sent shivers down my spine. I read Hans Christian Andersen, the Brothers Grimm, and Wilhelm Busch about the two cruel boys, Max and Moritz. I read the Greek myths, about Perseus flying through the air on his winged sandals, and Proteus the sea god, who could change his form and continually become someone else.

I discovered reading in bed. My bedside lamp was taken away, but Fräulein spent her evenings downstairs with the servants, so I stood with my book by the door, beside the light switch, and as soon as I heard her coming I pulled it and jumped into bed. I depended on books like a drug. They fed my fantasy life. People always accused me of lying. I was a natural fabulist. Fiction and fact were, nevertheless, quite separate in my mind – fiction was more real. Fiction lived with me, fed me, extended me. Facts could more easily be put aside, obliterated. I began to invent my life, which I respect myself for.

My father loved women to look beautiful – even me. He once told me my hands were old and ugly, which I found out later was true. He would bring me back dresses from a trip, and once a little hat with cherries on it. He believed in presents rather than legacies: 'Give with warm hands, not cold hands.' I can't think these gifts were the result of affection. Since he had wanted me to be a son, he resented me and called me 'The cuckoo's egg'. I had a low forehead and narrow eyes, so I was also called 'Eskimo'. One of his maxims was 'Watch how people walk and how they eat. If they walk and eat fast they will think and work fast.' I do everything fast – which is why I do everything imperfectly. But he said before he died, 'She's got my intelligence.'

He was a Social Democrat. I certainly have his interest in politics, but at the time I did not understand anything of what was happening in East Prussia and the Baltic states. During the First World War there were two revolutions in Russia. The first, in March 1917, ousted the Tsar and put in power a Social Democrat type of government under Alexander Kerensky, leader of the Mensheviks (they were the minority, *menshinstvo*, of the anti-Tsarists). The Bolshevik revolution in October 1917 (*bolshinstvo*, majority) gave the Russian Communists power, under Lenin, and the Bolshevik groups in our area began to make their own demands.

In February 1918, the German army marched into Königsberg and Tallinn, putting the Bolsheviks down. There was fighting in our street. I heard gunfire, then soldiers came into the house and shot from my nursery windows. Nurse made me lie on the floor. A return bullet knocked the corner off my marble washstand. Later, from the window, I saw a boot and sock lying in the road with the bloody leg still in it.

The Germans would have advanced into Russia, so Lenin was forced to sign the peace treaty of Brest-Litovsk with them in March 1918. By this treaty, Russia gave up the Baltic states, and Estonia eventually achieved independence. Russia took back the Baltic states after the Second World War, and Königsberg, renamed Kaliningrad, became a little Soviet state on its own.

Many Mensheviks and White Russians fled Communism through

the Baltic states into Germany. My parents moved to Berlin in 1920, to a large house in the suburb of Südende. My father's textile trading business, Wolpert & Bendix, was in Molkenmarkt, the oldest part of Berlin. My mother and her brother Adolf became property dealers. My uncles on my father's side emigrated to England or America. Some of them had to take their medical exams three or four times, in Russian, German, French and English. Others were linguists – Roman Jakobson was the greatest linguist in the world, and ended up at Harvard.

2

Berlin and Bergner, 1920–26

Our house in Berlin had a large garden, and my mother, with her country childhood, tried to make it into a farm. We had a goat for me and a cow to give milk for the other children (my mother knew that cows' milk contained tuberculosis germs). The goat used to wander into the house in summer. An Alsatian, Senta, lived in a kennel. We had a strawberry bed and an asparagus bed and walnut trees and pigeons. My mother had arrived home from one of her travels with a pigeon-house like a little Swiss chalet. I enjoyed seeing the birds flying in and out, until I was given pigeon pie. It made me sick, which was considered ungrateful rather than oversensitive.

The house was large, grand and heavy. The rooms were filled with Indian art brought back by Uncle Max, my father's brother, who worked in the East: Buddhas, and a fringed shawl over the Steinway. We had English Chippendale, fussy Italian filigree silver, silky shiny Persian carpets and horrible paintings of fleshy ladies.

A gymnasium was built for me, and I spent hours on the parallel bars, the vaulting horse and the rings, becoming very supple and strong. I was also given a bicycle, which meant more to me than my parents realised. I bicycled about the neighbourhood; that was the beginning of my travelling. I am a born traveller. I have to be free to set off any day without planning. To hop on the train and go is to me more natural than sitting at a table.

In April 1923, the German mark collapsed, leading to terrible inflation and a food shortage. A loaf of bread cost hundreds of marks. Thanks to my grandmother's farm, we had plenty, and my mother told me to take some to my music teacher. I remember furtively handing her a few eggs and some cheese and butter. Many businessmen were ruined, but to be corn merchants, like my mother's family, or have a cellulose factory, like my father's cousin in Tallinn, was to prosper.

My bedroom was Biedermeier, very chic then: pink, black and white, with a frieze of little black figures along the top of the wall, eighteenth-century ladies and gentlemen in wigs. I lay on my bed watching the reflection of the trees outside on the ceiling. I lived by those trees blowing on my ceiling.

Occasionally, if I was ill, my mother would let me sleep on a bed in her room. Her bedroom was full of mirrors: on the walls, on the doors, in the wardrobes. I was supposed to be asleep one evening when a friend of Father's, who often came to the house, was announced by a maid. Mother said to show him up, though she was dressed for bed and Father was away. When he came in he began to fondle my mother. In the glass I saw them embrace, she in bed and he more or less on the bed. My mother suddenly remembered me and tried to stop him: 'The child!' 'She is asleep,' he replied. They did some love-making. I was terribly shocked, though I didn't know what they were doing exactly. I watched and I listened, and from that moment my mother ceased to exist for me. I realise now that she had a deep dislike of sex and would not have allowed him to go far.

I would have understood more if I had noticed what was happening to the maids. My grandmother used to send us country girls from Pilkallen. They would arrive, pink-cheeked, strong and full-breasted, and my mother would choose one to be her personal maid, sending her to learn hairdressing. Others worked in the house and kitchen; but once they got the hang of the city, some took to the *trottoir*, the pavement. One cold winter's day I was on a walk with Fräulein when we saw our Ursula standing outside a department store wearing patent leather boots, a fur collar and smoking a cigarette – Ursula, who had arrived young and rosy from her parents' farm a few months earlier. I ran up to her, but Fräulein pulled me away. That was my first encounter with prostitution.

In winter I skated, skied, and tobogganed. My mother approved of any sport except dancing, which was not quite *comme il faut*. I was given a David harp, a guitar with ribbons, a mouth organ, my own piano and a lute. Nobody asked whether I wanted them;

though I did like playing the little harp. My piano teacher made me practise exercises, the *études* of Czerny – fingers up and down and up and down: no melody. In four years we did not reach the stage of playing music. The pedals were tied with string.

At Christmas we had a tree for the household, but there were no surprises or parcels to open. I was taken to the circus, and to the shops to buy my own presents. My mother would say to Fräulein, 'Go with the child and get her what she wants.' It was the same on my birthday. I knew that other children had a birthday table decorated with flowers, so the evening before my tenth birthday, I picked flowers from the garden and put them on the nursery table and wrapped the presents that had been bought for me. Then I went to bed. Next morning I woke up and went to look at the wonderful table and the exciting knobbly parcels and the garlands, and pretended someone had done it all for me.

A festive table has become a symbol in my life. I always try to provide feasts. Christmas means most of all. I give all the people I care for presents, things I know they need, such as a wooden spoon, woollen gloves, socks or nice tea, and I ask for white flowers for myself. All year round I collect presents at sales and markets. I like to have owned them for months or even years, so I am giving something that belongs to me. I am giving a piece of myself, like pieces of my skin.

All my childhood I was alone, because of my TB. My parents travelled a lot. My elder brother was often in a sanatorium in Switzerland. I don't remember having a single friend. I liked my Aunt Sonya and Aunt Dora. Otherwise I liked nobody. The family called me 'mad Lisl'.

I was fourteen when Fräulein Winter left and the next governess arrived: Fräulein Gertrud Crombach. Everything that could be wrong about her was wrong. Her skin was wrong, her nose was enormous and wrong, her mouth was crooked, her hair straggled. She was the ugliest thing imaginable; but to me she was the most beautiful. I loved the tinkling sound of her voice and the warmth of her dark brown eyes. She wore a coachman's green coat trimmed with black Persian lamb, and a Persian lamb beret. I called her 'Bächlein'. She led me out, drew me out, talked to me, listened to me and made me feel soft and willing to hear what she had to teach. She taught me everything. She led me from my childhood desert into green pastures. She was in love with teaching, in love with the theatre. She had studied theatre and drama but had become a governess to earn her living.

Bächlein took me from my world – my world of dreams, of fantasy, of introspection, in which I had become engrossed in colours and patterns, the patterns of trees against the sky, of leaves blown against the windows, of colours that exploded when I pressed my fists against my eyes – she took me from all that into her own world, and she could do it because she knew I had been dreaming. Through her I began to see, and smell, and respond, and to emerge from behind my books and my make-believe. I began to love, and love made me biddable and anxious to please and to learn, and I did it for Bächlein.

She lived with her parents and came to us every day. Her parents were working people who talked about things I liked, such as the phases of the moon. No one in my house ever mentioned the moon. The moon and stars had always been holy to me. My favourite song was by Matthias Claudius: 'Der Mond ist aufgegangen, die goldenen Sternlein prangen am Himmel hell und klar' ('The moon has risen, small golden stars twinkle in the heavens bright and clear').

Bächlein and I read Shakespeare, which improved my English. She also loved American literature – H. L. Mencken, Henry James, Sinclair Lewis, Upton Sinclair and Theodore Dreiser. Among Scandinavian writers, we read Sigrid Undset and Knut Hamsun.

Bächlein was writing a book about her hero Alexander Moissi, the Viennese actor, who had won the Iron Cross under the Kaiser but was to speak out against the Nazis. Moissi was famous for his voice, as Richard Burton was later, and Bächlein had a theory that he used it as though it were a musical instrument. Notating Moissi's voice was her secret work.

My mother's concerns were very different. One evening when she was going out she came into my bathroom to say goodnight, dressed in white fox. I was in the sunken marble bath. She looked at me and said, 'You are not beautiful nor are you pretty, but you have charm, good teeth and good legs. You may make it.' Perhaps she regretted the gulf between us. When I was fourteen she called me to her boudoir and pointed out that I was nearly grown up, so 'Now we can be friends.' It was too late for me.

Bächlein asked my mother's permission to take me to some of the plays we were studying, and surprisingly it was granted; *Richard III* was one of them. Then in October 1924 George

Bernard Shaw's *St Joan* opened in Berlin with the famous Viennese actress Elisabeth Bergner. I think my mother thought it was Schiller's *St Joan*: I don't believe she realised it was a new play by a rather shocking playwright. Bächlein was very keen to see it, particularly as Elisabeth Bergner was an old friend of Moissi's and knew Shaw.

In our box at the Deutches Theater we awaited the entrance of Joan of Arc. She came in, a thin boy-girl with a catlike tread. I found myself shaking from head to foot. Her voice, her movements, I cannot get over to this day. Everyone else might as well not have been there. Joan came and went. Her words resounded in my head. She was imprinted on my eyes, against the black and grey set. The interval arrived. Bächlein asked me what I thought of it, but all I could say was 'Who is she? Who is she?' At the end when the audience rose clapping and cheering I stood voiceless, weak at the knees, my arms hanging by my sides, only able to say 'Bächlein, my darling, Bächlein, my darling, what can I do for her?' over and over again. That night, I started to live.

In the theatre, I felt something hot rushing through me. When I got home I went to the bathroom and there was blood on my clothes. Nurse took my knickers and came back with clean ones and cotton wool wrapped in a cloth. She said, 'Now you are a woman.' Nobody explained anything. (Until I was fifteen I thought boys came out through the right breast and girls through the left breast.)

I pestered Bächlein about seeing Elisabeth Bergner again. She suggested I could take some flowers to the stage door. 'Just give them to her and say how much you enjoyed her acting.' I bought pink carnations with my pocket money. I thought them the very height of elegance and beauty – the opposite of my mother's orchids and cactus. It was a cold night. Bächlein took me to the stage door, and I stood with the crowd awaiting the star. Many fans held autograph books, and when Elisabeth Bergner arrived in a Hispano-Suiza they flocked round like fledglings thrusting for a worm. I was pushed against the wall. She was making her way through, her red hair flying and her nutria coat swinging open. Then she was walking towards me, and looking at that pathetic bunch of pink carnations I gripped as I stood paralysed. 'Are these for me?' Later she told me I pushed them at her and said, 'Do up your coat – you'll catch cold.' If I had asked for her autograph, I would have been just another fan, but she was struck by my thought for her. She said 'Who are you?' and I said 'Lisl.' 'Just like me,' she said. 'Well, come along,' and we went in together.

The next minute I was in her dressing-room. Her lovely fat old dresser, Lingenau, smiled a welcome at us. As I walked in, I started to live. I awoke, I became. I remember the warmth and the make-up and the scent. Lisl sat me down and asked me where I lived. I said 'Südende.' She said 'It's next door to me.' She lived in Dahlem. She asked whether my mother knew I was at the theatre. I said I was with my governess. I think I remember she called Bächlein in out of the cold. Then she kissed me and dismissed me. 'Now I must put on my make-up. Come again. Wait just a minute' – and she gave me a photograph, signed 'from L to L'. I floated home. All I had longed for, pined for, I had found. I can't tell you how moved I was by that play and by her. I had found the poetry of words, the voice of music, the contact that brought me to life. Bergner's feline grace, her erotic charm, her intelligence, had performed this miracle.

Next day I went on my bicycle to her address and rode round and round, much too shy to go to the door. For days I did that. I was not alone: teenagers were always arriving and circling round her house. But one day she must have seen me, because her *Zofe*, her personal maid, opened the door and called me in. I leaned my bicycle against the wall, my heart thudding. The house was light and calm. Elisabeth Bergner ordered coffee and cakes and asked me about myself. We talked about books. She advised me to read Thomas Hardy, Joseph Conrad and Rainer Maria Rilke. She questioned me about my parents, concerned that they might be worried. I lied vehemently. 'Yes, I *am* allowed out by myself.' I had climbed out of the window.

I loved her; I just adored her. Every day I bicycled over in the hope of seeing her. I told my mother I was going to my maths and science lesson: Bächlein could not teach those subjects, so I went to a Herr Barsch. She must have thought I had become very keen. Lisl sometimes asked me in. I became the envy of every teenager in Berlin.

Elisabeth Bergner was a big star in Germany. She had amazing physical presence, and was very beautiful, with huge dark eyes. She had spent her youth with the group of Viennese and Zürich intellectuals that included Gustav Mahler, Oskar Kokoschka, Tristan Tzara and Franz Wedekind. Mahler almost killed himself for love of her, and the Swiss sculptor Lehmbrück did, leaving a note to say so.

She was built like a boy and had a strange quality of lasciviousness. She often wore trousers on stage. Men, women, bankers, servants, children and dogs were in love with her: everyone was in love with her, except very normal heterosexual men like my father, who said her legs were too thin. She was a lesbian – she was bisexual, but more lesbian. She lived with a Swiss millionaire's daughter called Viola Bosshardt and a Great Dane called Boy. Lisl and Viola had their own silver with a special monogram, a big B containing a smaller E and V. Their silver grey Hispano-Suiza had red leather upholstery with a chauffeur, Giovanni, in a silver grey uniform with red epaulettes. Sometimes Lisl would take me with her while Giovanni drove her to the costume people or shopping. One day we were bowling along when a wheel came off and rolled down the road. Giovanni took both hands from the steering wheel, clapped them to his head, and moaned, '*La macchina! La macchina!*' Luckily cars went very slowly in those days.

Sometimes I went in to the theatre with Lisl, waiting in the dressing-room with Lingenau or watching from the wings or an empty box. The smell of dust and make-up and scent and lights is very erotic and pleasant in a play. One evening Marlene Dietrich, who had recently married, came backstage to see her friend Lisl. 'What is marriage like?' asked Lisl. '*Ich liege auf dem Rücken und zähle die Fliegen auf der Decke*,' said Marlene nonchalantly. 'Take the child out!' cried Lisl to Lingenau. I had not understood at all. I was wondering why she should lie on her back and count the flies on the ceiling. Dietrich was a very simple person, whose favourite occupation was cooking.

I made Lisl cushions, and spent every penny of my pocket money on her. I even stole to buy things for her – my mother always left money lying around. I never have a bad conscience because I am never conscious of having done wrong. I am amoral, in moral categories – a friend called me an amoral moralist. The newspapers printed reviews of Lisl Bergner's performances, which I pasted into albums. There were no cuttings agencies in those days, and fifty years later she used my albums for her autobiography *Bewundert viel und viel gescholten* (*Much Admired and Much Criticised*).

Lisl gave me presents, often books – Jens Peter Jacobsen, all Shaw's works. At last I was getting the surprises I had longed for. She gave me a gold snake necklace, and my first cashmere sweater, one of hers, sand-coloured and V-necked with a crocodile belt. I wore it all the time, like the typical girl in love. When I had my appendix out, Lisl came to the hospital with an almond tree covered in blossom. At Christmas I got her a little fir tree and decorated it with white candles and what we called angels' hair, in silver. I did the same for eight years. She received dozens of Christmas presents from admirers. A banker sent her a child's sleigh completely covered with mauve orchids. The waste shocked me, even then.

I studied Shakespeare with fervour – for she was playing Rosalind, Juliet and Viola. She also did *Miss Julie*, *The Lady of the Camellias*, Klabund's *Der Kreidekreis* (*The Chalk Circle*), and *The Constant Nymph*.

I was stage-struck. Lisl Bergner arranged for me to audition for her friend Max Reinhardt, the most famous German theatre director, and he thought I had the ability; but Lisl dissuaded me. She spoke seriously to me: an actress must devote herself to the theatre like a nun. A great actress can never have a man, a distracting love, or children. Lisl recognised that I wanted babies. 'You are born to be a woman, and to have a family. The theatre would stifle you.' I could not be a professional actress, but I am good at acting, which has been useful in my life.

My mother did not understand me as Lisl did. She went to my appendix surgeon, the fashionable Professor Ferdinand Sauerbruch (who was later used by Hitler), to suggest I should be sterilised. This was proposed not from cruelty but to keep me out of trouble and save me from what she considered a nuisance. My mother could not imagine anyone's life but her own – she had never noticed how I loved my dolls. Tubal ligation, tying up a woman's tubes, was quite a common practice in Germany at that time, and was believed to be reversible. When the professor broached it to me I screamed, and the idea was dropped. I started to read Kafka. I read Dante in French and the Russian novelists in German. I became a conscious human being.

Because Lisl's friend George Bernard Shaw was a vegetarian, I gave up meat. This attracted my mother's attention. Tubercular children were supposed to eat red meat regularly; she wanted to know why I wouldn't. I said Shaw didn't, and he was my hero. My mother, knowing my obstinacy, was afraid I would die. Bächlein offered a daring solution: that she should take me to London to talk to Shaw himself, who would dissuade me. She told my mother that friends of hers (she meant Lisl Bergner) were close friends of Mr and Mrs Shaw's and that she could arrange this; and that it would also be excellent for my education. My mother agreed, and Bächlein and I went to London, taking the boat from the Hook of Holland to Harwich, and stayed four days near the Shaws, who had a flat in Adelphi Terrace.

I had adored Shaw since that first performance of *St Joan*, and his beard and twinkly eyes came up to my expectations. Then he fell from his pedestal into the deepest abyss by saying cutting things about his family and friends and making fun of me. I do not think this was just to put me off vegetarianism. About that, he told me he had made a reasoned decision but I was just a copy-cat. He was a mean, cynical, conceited man who laughed at his own jokes and spoke unkindly of Bergner as St Joan. He said he preferred his two other St Joans, Sybil Thorndike in London, who evoked the suffragettes, and Ludmilla Pitoëff in Paris, who was closer to his concept of Joan as a French peasant girl. Shaw cured me of worshipping anybody because of their work or wanting to know them because of their fame. His work was brilliant, his name was famous, but he was mean and small. Ever since, the man has always meant more to me than the public person.

Back in Berlin, and no longer a vegetarian, I continued to haunt Lisl Bergner on my bicycle. I had a complete secret life for two years. Then my parents found out. I do not know who told them – I think it must have been Fräulein, jealous as always. She may have found Lisl's letters. There was a terrible row. Elisabeth Bergner was known as a lesbian, and my parents assumed she had seduced me. They consulted lawyers about bringing a case against her. I was taken to a psychiatrist. I told him the truth: she had never touched me. My mother summoned Lisl to visit her. Mother asked Lisl what she saw in a little girl like me, and she said 'I love your daughter.' My mother could not understand a bond of affection. All she was worrying about was the reputation of the family. Lisl said she would like to adopt me. My parents refused, but Lisl said she would leave the offer open. Lisl asked to take me on holiday with her. This also was refused.

My parents decided to send me to a finishing school in

Switzerland. Bächlein was sacked. I was broken-hearted, and so was she. We both wept and wept and wept. I was going into exile, far from my two life-givers. Bächlein's mission to educate me was cut off. She got a job as a governess in Greece. I did not see her again for fifty years.

3

Further Education in Switzerland, London, Paris, 1926–28

My mother took me to Les Hirondelles, near Lausanne, in the Vaud. The school was in a large château, with pretty furniture and girls from all over the world in a uniform of snowy white. It was presided over by Madame Mion, the directrice, who always wore black, with the rosette of the Légion d'Honneur.

We were fed on starch and more starch: pasta every day, pasta in every conceivable shape, smothered in horrible sauces. We all got fatter and fatter, lumpier and lumpier, heavier and heavier. We were taught English, French, Italian, music, flower arranging, gros point, petit point, painting on china: this was a cheat – we painted the flowers through holes in stencils, but the parents thought it was a wonderful skill. We were taught to change our dresses four times a day, how to do our hair, how to address royalty and the nobility, and the table manners and use of cutlery in four different countries. We were not allowed to learn to cook, but we were taught how to treat servants and how to train servants, including the butler.

When a new girl arrived, we watched to see whether she had a Mason Pearson hairbrush, which meant she was 'one of us'. Every night we assembled in evening dress and were taught ballroom dancing by the dancing mistress. Half the girls led, the others played the woman. It was interesting how already the dominating and submissive types were set in their roles. There was a lot of emotion, as there is at Eton. The atmosphere was full of *érotisme*. Each girl had her own bedroom. I had regular visits from Peggy Binder, an English girl, who fondled me and wept. She would creep into my bed just to be with me. She was homesick for her dogs.

We were taken by car to the opera in Geneva, where we sat in theatre boxes whose curtains were opened only when the lights went down and the stage curtain went up. We might have been in a harem. The opera intensified my longing for Lisl Bergner. Only one person was kind, our piano teacher, Miss Dawson, who was sixty and wore a wig of bouclé curls. She was tender to her girls, and to me she said 'Poor child'. I loved her for that, as I languished far from my idol.

In the winter we went skiing. The school took over a little hotel in the mountains of the Valais. All the other guests had to leave when we arrived, but Françoise, a very pretty French girl, managed to become pregnant by a handsome man during the changeover. She was proud of it, and told us all that he was '*très bien*' – a gentleman. She had been a virgin, but was tired of it – '*J'en ai marre.*' Her mother came and took her away for an abortion.

I was already called 'Lise la Sauvage'. One early morning I simply had to feel free. I put on my bathing dress, went out into the large park that surrounded the school and ran and ran and ran. But one of the gardeners must have been watching. They were the only men we saw, apart from the elderly coiffeur. I was back in time for morning Mass, and sat down as usual for breakfast. Madame Mion rang her bell. Her voice was high and penetrating. '*Mesdemoiselles, qui a fait la gymnastique toute nue dans le parc ce matin?*' Exercising naked? How shocking! It dawned on me that she meant me. '*Moi, madame.*' She had a short answer to that: '*Sortez.*' I spent three days in the punishment room on bread and water, reading the New Testament. When I was released, I learned that the girls had gone on hunger strike for a day in sympathy. I had caused a mutiny. My mother was asked to take me away.

I was sent to another *pensionnat pour jeunes filles de bonnes familles* near Geneva, owned by a dilapidated Russian countess who ran it along Russian Orthodox lines, unlike Les Hirondelles, which was Catholic. Madame had a Confessional, a table with two large candles. She sat at this table, ramrod straight, in front of a lifesize sculpture of Christ which hung against a purple velvet cloth and oozed pretence blood from gaping wounds. Here she forced us to 'confess' by the light of the flickering candles, which made her dark-set eyes and gaunt face all the more grave and ghastly. To get away from the bleeding Christ, we would have confessed to murdering our own brothers and grandmothers and pets. We were indoctrinated in the Orthodox rites, and impressed with the miseries of White Russian existence far away from Mother Russia. I had heard some of this from my father's family. We learned French with a Russian accent, Italian with a Russian accent and English with a Russian accent. Every morning, in chapel, we were supposed to give 50 centimes to the collection plate. Instead, I put in some metal buttons which made the same clinking noise. This lasted for five days before I was found out and sentenced to face the Christ, the candles and Madame for an hour.

I was desperate to get back to Lisl. I ran away and hid in a church, wondering how to travel from there to Berlin, but two priests found me and returned me to the school. Mother was asked to take me away. This time she decided to try London. She took me over, booking at the Ritz but moving on to the Milestone facing Kensington Gardens because it was nearer the family I was to stay with, a Sir something and Lady Grant in Onslow Gardens. I was enrolled at the Regent Street Polytechnic to improve my English.

I also learned about the English themselves. I remember the sound of the maids cleaning the grates in the morning. I had acquired a dislike for pasta at Les Hirondelles, and now I learned to dislike the taste and smell of haddock, the texture of soggy toast and the way it was cut into little triangles and stuck in toast-racks, and the flowery cheerfulness of chintz. Whenever I could I escaped into the streets. I remember iron baskets of red-hot coals in Piccadilly and at Marble Arch, glowing through the fog, and ladies in coloured raincoats, with sou'westers, blue or yellow, smelling of rubber. I thought people riding in open-top buses with their umbrellas up looked like mushrooms.

I remember, too, demonstrations by beaten-looking people asking for work, and the buskers who entertained the film and theatre queues – ex-servicemen, eyeless, armless or legless, collecting money in their hats or in tin cups. It was 1927, the year after the General Strike. I noticed the extremes of wealth and poverty. I walked around the slums of the East End, where babies were pushed in orange-boxes on wheels. I had seen Princess Elizabeth riding in a huge pram. I loved Lyons Corner Houses, where 'Nippies' in frilly aprons brought tea for a penny, currant buns for a ha'p'ny.

A friend of my mother's took me to the House of Commons to listen to Lady Astor, the first woman MP, neat and trim in a black suit. She spoke on the plight of women when there was so much unemployment. Her party, the Conservatives, was in.

Stanley Baldwin had been Prime Minister since 1923, except for nine months when Ramsay MacDonald formed the first Labour Government. I was asked if I knew which were the Conservative and which the Labour benches, and I guessed right. The men on the Labour side were shorter, with flat heads and hair shiny with oil. Some had bandy legs. Their trousers had no creases. The Tories had long legs and longer hair with no oil. Their trousers were well pressed, and at that time they wore brown shoes. But the two sides seemed to respect each other. Now that the people on each front bench are the same, they truly dislike each other.

All the time, I was writing to Lisl and saving up my allowance to escape to see her. She was playing in Munich. I took the night packet to Hamburg and a train south. My mother was told I had run away. My parents despaired of me. They consulted Lisl Bergner, and I was sent to Paris to study at the Sorbonne under the guardianship of her cousin Jean Bergner, a gentle young banker.

I lived in a little hotel and studied French literature and history. Jean Bergner did not know how to look after me, apart from not letting his wild friends meet me. He took me to Versailles (where I lost the lovely gold snake necklace Lisl had given me), and to museums.

For the first time, I was living on my allowance. I was only seventeen, and acted much more daring than I was, being still afraid of life, and of men. I walked about the city buying books on the quay and eating at little bistros. I decided I did not like the Mona Lisa, but I loved the pretty statue of the Virgin Mary in Notre-Dame, and went there every morning. I got to know the French writer Romain Rolland, author of *Au-dessus de la mêlée*, which had won him the Nobel Prize in 1915. He was a dear old man who loved music and practised a gentle pacifism.

Underlying everything was my longing for that other Lisl. I starved myself, and every few weeks went to see her. She was playing in Munich, Zürich, Stuttgart and Basel and I would suddenly pop up. I depended on her absolutely, as I have always depended on those I love. People see me as strong, but I have never been independent. I have always needed love. In 1928, I ran away to Berlin to be near Lisl.

4

Under Communism's Spell in Berlin, 1928-32

I was almost eighteen, living at home and looking for some purpose for my life. Lisl Bergner again asked my parents if she could adopt me (I was not consulted). They did not refuse outright; I had lost my reputation by mixing with theatre people, and Bergner was well off. She was now living with a man she called Bimbo – Dr Paul Czinner – who had directed her in the film *The Violinist of Florence*. He was a Hungarian who at the time made poetic, highbrow musical films.

One night in Lisl's dressing-room I met Hede Gumperz, an Austrian woman of about thirty who as a drama student in Vienna had met Lisl. Hede had an ugly face but a beautiful body, and a strong, almost aggressive manner. She asked me to her flat for lunch. She lived with a Marxist academic called Paul Massing, an agrarian – an agriculture expert – whom she married as her third husband.

I was fascinated by them both. Hede was kind to me, and Paul was witty and good-looking. They were a beautiful couple, and loved each other's nakedness. In their sunny apartment they would read, cook, listen to music with no clothes on. I remember Hede, bathed in sunlight, a pale wooden bowl between her thighs, shelling peas to Mahler's second symphony. They were free with their bodies, free-spoken, and made free love. I was shocked and enchanted.

Hede told me about her first marriage, to the famous Communist Gerhart Eisler (brother of Ruth Fischer, who had been a Communist deputy in the Reichstag but left the Party in 1926, and of Hanns Eisler, the composer). Gerhart was sent to China, where Stalin believed that the Chinese Communists could gain power from within General Chiang Kai-shek's Kuomintang organisation. Instead, Chiang turned on them and massacred thousands in 1926–7. Hede showed me photographs of the Chinese comrades being beheaded in the streets of Peking and Shanghai. Her second husband was a Communist academic and publisher, Julian Gumperz, who had been born in America and started the Malik publishing house in Berlin. While married to him, she acquired American citizenship.

Hede worked on my conscience. I had always felt guilty about being rich. In those days the very poor had no shoes, sometimes no food. I realised that the servants at home had been third-class citizens and remembered that they had been tender to me so far as they were able. No wonder they preferred selling their bodies to drudging long hours for low pay and sharing an attic bedroom. I had seen Käthe Kollwitz's passionate, dramatic drawings of working-class mothers, unemployed men, down-and-outs and starving children, and George Grosz's of tough, shaven-headed, overfed Prussian men.

Hede took me to the Café Zuntz, where Communist intellectuals met to talk. She weaned me from Lisl Bergner. I was perhaps subconsciously looking for an escape. I think my parents were going to agree to Lisl adopting me, but I did not want to be adopted – I did not want to remain a child. At Communist meetings, the speakers assumed that we were all warm, well-fed and well-off. Outside this comfortable hall, they told us, were men and women beaten down by unemployment, hunger, cold and despair. Back in the street, I would see the truth of the drawings of George Grosz – hideous profiteers smoking cigars and giving the butts to starving one-legged ex-servicemen. The Käthe Kollwitz children were before my eyes, begging for bread. I, the daughter of privilege, could and would fight for the poor as a devoted Communist. Being a Communist meant to be without nation, race, religion – I was freeing myself of all but compassion.

The act of joining the Young Communists – signing a paper – did not mean much to me. What did have meaning was the emotional commitment. I had joined those fighting for a better future for mankind. I now had the chance to be good, to be generous, to give love and take love. I could give and give and give. This was when I started to prove myself as a provider. I found tenderness, belonging and comradeship – everything I had been denied, everything I had longed for for eighteen years.

I was assigned the humdrum jobs of political activism, such as the printing and distribution of leaflets, and I went to meetings and demonstrations where quite often Communists clashed with the Brown Shirts (the *Sturmabteilung*). The Nazis had set up two private armies, the SA, bullying storm troopers in brown uniforms, and the more sinister SS (*Schutzstaffel*) in black uniforms, who had to swear allegiance to Hitler personally. Hitler used the SS to massacre the SA in 1934. The Gestapo (*Geheime Staatspolizei*), after it was created as a national force in April 1933, came under the SS. The ordinary military intelligence service was the *Abwehr*; they were nicer, if such forces can be nice.

It was my duty to study some aspect of Marxist theory, so I chose China and went to lectures on Chinese agriculture given by Karl August Wittfogel, a distinguished Marxist teacher, six and a half feet tall, who was a friend of Hede's. Madam Sun Yat-sen, Communist widow of the 1911 Nationalist Revolution leader who was succeeded by Chiang Kai-shek, was in the class. I was the only non-Chinese person except Professor Wittfogel and an English pupil, Humphrey Slater. I did not understand Marxist theory.

Lisl Bergner was angry, although she had been a Communist herself in the early 1920s. I was cut off at a stroke. She would not see me. She strongly disapproved of Hede's indoctrinating me. For my part, I was liberated from her and I grew up. I had discovered poverty, which is my natural element. I needed a faith to die for, and Lisl's personality was not enough. Hede's personality and what she was offering were more powerful.

I told the comrades I was the daughter of a grocer, and I left my family and my home. I gave up the Chippendale, the Gobelins, the Meissen, the Bohemian glass, the Persian carpets and my own room. I went out, literally penniless, into the world. My father very wisely cut me off. I was, and have remained ever since, a self-made poor. This is quite different from having been born into poverty or having been forced into it. I have no envy of the rich. I chose my condition with my eyes open, and by hard work and determination I have managed to remain poor when circumstances were against it.

My new life brought me some surprises. I hardly knew how to brush my own hair or polish my shoes and I certainly could not boil an egg. I also had nowhere to live. I moved in with married student friends, Frieda and Walter Löwenson, who had only orange-box furniture. They shared their bread with me and their bed with me – we all three slept in it. They would sometimes need to say 'Turn to the wall, please, Lisl.' That is the kind of friendship I have known and always stuck to. It is a comradeship people in Britain do not understand. The Löwensons were not Communists, but Zionists. Frieda was studying arts, Walter physics. He was a physicist in Israel after the war. (Walter is dead, but Frieda and I are still true friends.)

It was unfair to stay with them for long, so I went to the comrades and told them I needed a room. They found me a single garret room on the second *Hinterhof*, back courtyard. In Germany, apartment blocks are built on class principles: the *Vorderhaus*, front house, on the street is for the best people, then you go through a *Hinterhof*, and there is the back house, the *Hinterhaus*, with less light, for the poorer people. If you are really poor, you cross another courtyard to the second *Hinterhaus*, and there you live with very little light at all.

I felt fine about being in the second *Hinterhaus*. I sold my watch, took dogs for walks and did translations. I love translating: creeping into another mind and heart and soul. I ghosted for well-known translators such as Mrs Jacobson, whose husband was editor of the left-wing journal the *Weltbühne*, the equivalent of the *New Statesman*. She got me to translate *Dr Dolittle* into German from English for 60 marks, and *Winnie the Pooh* for another pittance. She was one of the hundreds in love with Lisl Bergner, which is why I got the job.

My parents had moved to a mansion flat in Landshuterstrasse in the centre of Berlin, near Professor Albert Einstein. My mother sometimes sent Nurse to my slum with food for me. I had got to know Einstein before I left home. He loved children, and used to buy us ice-creams. He had a boring daughter called Margot. He was a gentle little man, but I didn't think then, and don't now, that he had much intelligence: only that calculating machine in his brain that dealt so cleverly with numbers and concepts. He had published his Theory of General Relativity in 1915.

My heart and soul were taken over by the comrades. I acquired the regulation Young Communist uniform of dark blue shirt, dark blue skirt and a belt with hammer-and-sickle buckle. I was instructed to join a little group of people, a cell. I pictured this as being like a biological cell. There were twenty other comrades in the cell and we met in the back of a *Kneipe*, a pub. I was taught to walk into the meetings of other parties and pretend to be a sympathiser, so as to get information. The ability to pretend was essential in political work then.

Like Lisl, Hede was bisexual, and she tried several times to seduce me. She threw me on the sofa and said 'I must have you.' I thought it funny, and giggled. Then one afternoon when Hede was away, Paul asked me to go boating on the Wannsee. He took off his coat and put it round me and rowed us out into the lake. The boat capsized and we fell in. My first thought was not to lose the coat, because Paul was poor, and I kept hold of it. After we got to shore he took me to his flat, still wet, and laid me on the sofa. He seduced me very gently and very slowly, saying, 'How sweet you are. How sweet.' I was not in love with him, but it was nice, and did not hurt at all. He was tender. Most girls think losing their virginity one of the most important events in their lives, but it meant little to me.

When Hede got back, Paul told her, and she was furious. 'I wanted you,' she said to me. She told me years later that she consciously took me away from Lisl because she desired me, and also because she was jealous of Lisl and her fame. She did not believe Lisl was not having an affair with me.

What I did not know was that in 1929, after I met her, Hede was recruited as a secret agent by the GPU (which became the NKVD in 1934 and the KGB in 1954). She must have told her new bosses about me. One day, she asked me to meet someone in the Grünewald park. I was to carry a newspaper and wait for a man who would come up and say 'Do you smoke?' I would say 'Yes.' It happened just as she said. He was a dark square Slav who spoke with a Russian accent. The gist of our conversation was as follows. He said, 'We have a more important job for you than the one you're doing now.' Since I was a dogsbody, that wasn't difficult. He asked, 'Do you believe in Communism and the victory of the working classes?' I said 'Yes.' He said that I had impressed the comrades at a high level. 'There is more difficult work for you than labouring among the masses.' I said, 'What is it, comrade?' 'It's a job in what we call Intelligence. But before I tell you what it is, I want you to know that it will mean you have to disavow the Communist movement. You will have to say you are disenchanted, and repudiate your past with the Party. But in reality your life will be given to the Party, and for the job I am thinking of you will not be able to marry or have children.' I said I had misgivings, and he gave me a week to think it over.

We met again, and he described the job. I would pretend to be the niece or daughter of one of the European diplomats who was secretly working for Russian Intelligence. That would be my cover and my entrée to diplomatic parties. My aim would be to attract capitalistic diplomats, sleep with them, and learn their secrets. So I would have to remain single. I told him I was still not sure, because I wanted children. We arranged to meet a third time. At our third meeting, he asked if I had thought over how important private life was to me. I said I had, and 'I do want to have babies.' He said in that case I had better not do it. He was very nice about it, and the Party did not punish me. I realised later that he was in the GPU.

Paul Massing went to Moscow to work at the International Agrarian Institute, and Hede followed him. They came back to Berlin in 1931, but Hede dropped out of Communist activities and said she was disillusioned. I was too naïve to realise why.

Berlin in the late 1920s and early 1930s was exciting. The city was very free. I went to the political cabarets and discovered some of the transvestite clubs and bars. In one of them, Eldorado, all the men were dressed as women, but I merely thought they were theatricals. Until the end of the war, I didn't know about homosexual men. The comrades were not supposed to be homosexual. This ignorance led me into a mistake. There was a young, blond, very handsome comrade in our group, Fred, who liked me. He always blushed when I came near. I fell a bit in love with him. He didn't have another girl, and I waited, but nothing happened. I realise the reason now.

I was very retarded. I still enjoy life in a childlike way. Poverty taught me that an ice-cream is a treat and going to the cinema is a wonderful excursion. Everything is fun, even a bus journey.

One is born young or old, I think: eager or blasé, passionate or cold. I was always young and an enthusiast. Communism allowed me to lose myself in something bigger than myself, and I was happy. I was happy to starve, to rush around for the cause, to eke out a coffee with the comrades at a café for half the evening; whoever had money would put it on the table. We sometimes queued all night to get into the gallery, the *Olympia*, of a theatre or concert hall. I heard Menuhin playing as a boy of twelve. I went to see Beniamino Gigli and the Russian ballet.

I occasionally noticed my papa sitting in the front row with one of his mistresses, or in a box – but as I was up in the *Olymps* he did not see me. The première of Bertolt Brecht's *Dreigroschenoper* on 31 August 1928, with music by Kurt Weill, was extremely chic. Lisl got me a ticket. All the rich were there, and quite a lot of the old aristocracy. Communism was still a dream and the rich were not afraid of it. But then most of the rich were Jewish. All the universities had Jewish professors, and Jews dominated the theatre, cinema, literature and painting. The perversity and rebellion of the Jewish mind is what made Berlin's cultural life so rich. The Jews of only a generation back had been in the ghetto, but now they were free, and their minds raced. They created Communism and great art, until the Nazis turned on them. Life is like chemistry – action, reaction.

The three important men were Grosz, Brecht and Weill, the first two of them Communists. Brecht was the message, Weill the music and Grosz the eyes of Berlin in the late twenties and early thirties. They all left in 1933, so they only had a few years together in Berlin. Brecht, who was greedy, selfish, money-loving and had a Swiss bank account, created those wonderful songs about poverty. 'It must be possible for the poor to gain a slice of the loaf', 'Erst kommt das Fressen und dann die Moral.' Weill, although Jewish, mixed jazz and church in his composing. A lot of the music is church organ music.

The hiking movement flourished at the same time. For generations, young German men had gone *auf Wanderschaft* after their apprenticeship, picking up work as they journeyed. In the twenties and thirties, groups of both sexes went walking, and someone would play the guitar for their songs. They called themselves *die Wandervögel* – birds of passage.

I decided to visit the centre of my new faith, without telling anybody. I just went, like a *somnambule*, a sleepwalker. I stayed with Aunt Sonya in Tallinn and got a visa from the Russian consul there. My cousin Yuri (George) Makowski lent me the fare. He was in love with me and wanted to marry me.

In Moscow I went to the Lux Hotel, where all the Comintern people were. They welcomed the keen little foreigner. They gave me a room and let me translate the speeches of the English-speaking delegates to a Profintern (Communist trade union international) conference. But I went too far. I was translating a rather dull speech by a black American union leader and began making it more fiery. My sentences became longer than his. His reasonable arguments turned into blazing passion. The audience clapped me at the end. But it put me off platforms. Nobody who is good at face-to-face talking is good at public speaking. I am rather shy in most things. I am shy unless I have strong feelings – and then I am off. A conference is more satisfying than the theatre, because theatre audiences do not mingle and can't question the actors. In later life, I often went to political party conferences, summit conferences, film festivals and the Frankfurt Book Fair.

The Russians liked me and wanted me to stay on. They made up a song about me:

Lisa, Lisa, Lisaveta,	(Lisl, Lisl, Lislkin,
Ya tibia liubliu, za etto.	I love you for being you.
Yi za etto, yi za to,	And for this, and for that,
Lisaveta nitchevo.	Lislkin what the hell.)

After two or three weeks among them I missed my own comrades and went back to Berlin.

As the Party's odd-job girl I was kept busy. I did a great deal of translation, to and from English, French and German. I worked with Humphrey Slater, the young Englishman I had met at Professor Wittfogel's lectures, who was staying with the Wittfogels. Humphrey, known to the comrades as Hugh, was as ardent a Communist as me, and like me, he tried to talk and dress like a proletarian. He told the comrades his father was a tool-maker; he was really a bishop.

Humphrey and I became very close. The British aren't all saints – their bad apples can be very bad indeed – but for the most part they seem to have a quiet passion for what they call 'decency' and 'fair play' – words almost untranslatable into French or German. Even when the Nazis were conquering a country a month I could not imagine Hitler ruling that triangular island. The British are suspicious of anyone they say 'oozes charm': perhaps because this challenges me, I like pouring through their defences like the sea through a sand castle.

The British Communists, according to Humphrey, were infiltrating the trade unions and the Labour Party. 'We have to work as Communists within all the socialist organisations; they are too vast to be taken over from outside.' From him, I learned for the first time of the tactics of the Comintern in Britain.

Our main enemy in Berlin was not the Nazi thugs but the police, who wore helmets like flowerpots and carried out the orders of what was to be the last Social Democratic government, led by Chancellor Hermann Müller under President Hindenburg. When Humphrey and I were at a Communist meeting that the police broke up, we would ask them innocently what was happening, who were those people? An officer would escort us out politely, thinking we were young upper-class foreigners who had strayed into trouble. We thought ourselves very clever.

I acquired a nickname, 'Rote Lisl' – 'Red Lisl' – and was promoted to be editorial assistant on the paper the Comintern published for students. Humphrey Slater worked for it too, on the English-speaking side.

My supervisor, the editor of the paper, was the French Communist leader Jacques Duclos, then illegally in Berlin. He had had to leave France in 1928 for some months, after the President cracked down on the Communist deputies. I disliked him, partly because he was always trying to get his fat fingers on me. I had a yellow crocheted sweater you could almost see through that he ogled. Humphrey kept looking at it too. Duclos seemed to me a real butcher. My assessment was borne out at the end of the war, when he played a leading part in the Affaire Mathiau. The French Communist Party deliberately betrayed to the Gestapo a large group of foreign Jewish Communists, simply to show De Gaulle how strong the Communists were. It was one of the most sinister and dirty acts among so much that was unpleasant.

The Depression of 1929 added to Germany's millions of unemployed and helped the political extremists, the Nazis and the Communists. In the election of 1930 Hitler's Nazis (National Socialists) leapt from the ninth and smallest party in the Reichstag (Parliament) to the second largest, with six and a half million votes, while the Communists got four and a half million. The Catholic Centre Party was shakily in power.

Sometimes I would be sent to 'anti-Fascist' (Communist) conferences in other European cities to interpret. 'Anti-Fascist' was the cover word, as 'militant' or 'Marxist' were after the war. The 'demonstrations' of the sixties were in the thirties 'rallies'. We held many rallies, at which we marched, marched, marched and sang, sang, sang. There were barricades in the street, and a line of mounted policemen would ride towards us at a walk. We tried to unnerve the horses by shouting and waving flags, holding our breath until the police charged. Then there was a great sigh of relief. Every march is a provocation. One person walking is neutral, but even two people walking together begin to seem aggressive, and many people walking in step are like drums. Singing makes it even more menacing. We provoked the police, then called it police aggression. After the police chased us at one rally, I escaped into the Grünewald with a handsome blond comrade with sunburnt arms and a blue shirt. He pulled me down under a tree and ravished me. It was painful, but not because of the force he used – I was lying on an antheap. That was the last time I made love without giving my heart. I went also to Nazi meetings to listen to Hitler and his hordes.

The Young Communists were almost idiotically militant, and I was finding my work too theoretical. I wanted to do things for human beings. So in 1930 I joined the Rote Hilfe, Red Aid, for the relief and release of political prisoners. Every country's Communist Party had its Red Aid organisation. The German Red Aid was run from Berlin by Willy Koska, a Communist member of the Reichstag and a member of the executive of the Communist Party of Germany (the KPD). Willy was tall, fair, blue-eyed and good-looking. I am always attracted to tall fair men – I suppose because I am small and dark. Willy was also a beautiful human being. I had never come across such an example of the erudite working class; he loved music, nature, and his people. His father was a turner, his mother a cleaner, and both his father and grandfather were traditional Socialists.

I worked in the office, filing and typing with three fingers. I was paid my expenses only. At lunchtime, everybody stopped work to eat their sausage and bread or whatever they had brought. I just went on working, because I had no money. One day, I found a big sandwich in my desk drawer. Willy had noticed. I knew he had put it there, though neither of us said anything. Every lunchtime after that I found mine in my drawer.

Willy asked me to go to a Party meeting with him. It ended by being violently broken up by the Nazis, who wounded some Communists. Willy shielded me and hurried me out. We were both rather shaken. We walked and talked and stopped at a café for coffee and cake. He came back with me to my room, and we became lovers. Willy was my first great love, and we remained together for the next four years.

With Willy, I got to know Ernst Thälmann, the leader of the KPD, Wilhelm Pieck, its president, Ernst Torgler, the parliamentary leader, and Walter Ulbricht, Heinz and Margarete Neumann and Willi Münzenberg, all prominent Communists. Münzenberg was a Reichstag deputy who had set up International Workers' Aid, run from Berlin. Neumann's wife, Margarete Buber-Neumann, was the sister of Münzenberg's companion Babette Gross. They were two well-brought-up Potsdam girls who, like me, had embraced the class enemy.

In the early spring of 1931, Willy and I went skiing with Walter Ulbricht and Rose – his wife or girlfriend. Ulbricht was leader of the Berlin and Brandenburg County Communist party, and a member of the Central Committee. Ulbricht and Rose, a very nice, very plain French-Jewish girl, had a baby, Rosi, who came with us. We went to the mountains which divide Germany and Czechoslovakia. Ulbricht was a Saxon born in Leipzig, and his eyes were piercingly blue with a cutting quality – they softened only when he held his little daughter. I saw those sharp blue eyes later in Nazi faces and always thought of Ulbricht. He was a formidable man, much feared, but he was nice to me since I was with Willy who was his protégé. His nickname was 'the Saxon fox'.

Willi Münzenberg was the Communist propagandist. He was famous for inventing 'fellow travellers' (the English word was used) – people who sympathised with Communist ideals without being committed to the Party. Babette Gross wrote the biography of her lover, in which she says that it was actually a Communist called Alfons Paquet who invented 'fellow travellers', in 1919, but that Münzenberg put the idea into practice, beginning with the International Workers' Aid in 1921 (IAH in Germany and IWA in English-speaking countries). Münzenberg's genius was to see that idealists all over the world could be persuaded to help the oppressed if they did not know they were giving to the Communist Party. He invented 'fronts' to organise the help, privately calling them 'innocents' clubs'. In the autumn of 1931, he had a triumph with a world congress in Berlin to celebrate ten years of the IAH. Hundreds of foreign delegates came, including the American journalist Louis Fischer, then foreign correspondent for the *Nation*, whom I met. 'Solidarity' was often on Willi Münzenberg's lips – all those years ago.

My Willy, Koska, was not cynical at all. He was a profound believer, completely *rein* – pure. The liberation of his class was his creed and Stalin was his high priest. Once, when we were on a tram, he pointed at a rhyming advertisement with a slogan that said 'Stop eating butter. Eat margarine instead.' Willy said, 'That's capitalism for you, Lisl. Butter is better for you, but they don't want *us* to have it.' He was so handsome in his brown corduroy suit, and such good company with his talk and his singing and his guitar. He sang Schubert and folk songs, and revolutionary songs like 'Thoughts are free' from 1848:

Die Gedanken sind frei,	(Thoughts are free,
Wer kann sie erraten?	Who can guess them?
Sie fliegen vorbei	They fly past
Wie nächtlichen Schatten.	Like the shadows of night.
Kein Mensch kann sie wissen,	No man can know them,
Kein Jäger erschiessen,	No hunter can shoot them,
Es bleibe dabei:	I hold to that:
Die Gedanken sind frei!	Thoughts are free!)

The term of Field Marshal von Hindenburg, who was eighty-three, came to an end in 1932 and Hitler and Thälmann both stood against him for the presidency. Hindenburg won, Hitler came second. Germany seemed to be falling apart. There were three elections that year. In the streets, the Nazi Brown Shirts fought the anti-Fascist Blue Shirts, and many a night a Nazi or Communist was found with a knife in his chest. Violence increased as Nazis and Communists vied with each other to hold meetings and make inflammatory speeches. Hitler screamed and Ulbricht thundered, Goebbels squealed and Pieck mumbled.

At the same time, we were struggling within the Party – we had to identify and oppose the Trotskyists and right-wingers. We probably spent more time fighting among ourselves than fighting the Nazis. Stalin had sent an order forbidding the German Communists to work or vote with the Social Democrats against the Nazis. I now know that the Comintern decided to let the Nazis take power, reckoning that they would start a war and then Europe would go Communist. No doubt this was clever strategic thinking, but they had not reckoned with Nazi ruthlessness (learned from the GPU).

In June 1932, the Central Committee reviewed plans for going underground when the Nazis took over. Willy and I moved to a front room in a *Hinterhaus* in Beusselstrasse, in the working-class district of Moabit. I got a cover job as a filing clerk and typist for a lawyer, Dr Rabau. Safe houses were set up, meeting places organised, and in the summer of 1932 the cells were reduced to five people, *Fünfergruppen*. We hid the printing presses but they turned out information and appeals, distributed from loyal bars.

Lisl Bergner and Paul Czinner had seen enough to persuade them to leave Germany. They moved to London in 1932, where they married the year after.

5

Underground in Berlin, 1933

Hitler was pressing Hindenburg to make him Chancellor, and the old man gave in on 30 January 1933. The Third Reich had begun. On the night of 27 February, Willy came home very late, to tell me that the Reichstag was on fire. We both went to watch. There was the seat of government in flames. The police and Nazis were rushing about. Someone said, 'A Dutchman set it on fire – a madman.'

But, of course, it was not convenient that a Dutchman, a madman, should be solely to blame. The next morning the wave of arrests began. Not only the half-witted Dutch boy, Marinus van der Lubbe, was imprisoned, but Party members, intellectuals, leading anti-Fascists and anyone the Nazis considered an enemy. The KPD leader Ernst Thälmann, Ernst Torgler and Georgi Dimitroff, a Bulgarian member of the Comintern, were among them. Torgler was a dry stick, but Dimitroff was a lovely man, a latter-day Danton, with a bull-like head. He once tried to seduce me while I was teaching him German. Willi Münzenberg escaped to Paris, although he was *persona non grata* to the French government. Dimitroff became Prime Minister of Bulgaria after the war, but Thälmann was shot in Buchenwald in 1944.

The Communist violence and arson proved by the Reichstag fire (which of course the Nazis had started) enabled Hitler to persuade Hindenburg to sign a decree authorising the beginnings of a police state. There was another election on 5 March 1933, democracy's last gasp. The Nazis won, the Social Democrats were second and the Communists third. Hitler still did not have the parliamentary majority he needed, but by banning the eighty-one Communist deputies and many Social Democrats, he got legislation passed on 23 March which gave Parliament's power to himself and his Cabinet for four years. He had achieved a dictatorship.

The horror of dictatorship is that the least acceptable men in any country are on top – the power-hungry, the opportunist, the corrupt, and the little man who stamps papers and has it in for everyone. Dictatorship is being bullied by the suburbs. It frees the worst human emotions; decent people who are weak turn in the direction of such power. I saw many turn, and watched their moral acrobatics. On the other hand, dictatorship produces the bravest opponents.

Things were going according to Stalin's plan. I had hennaed my hair, and was called Elisabeth rather than Lisl. Political meetings were illegal, so we met in twos and threes in many places, even in telephone boxes. Cinemas were favourite spots to exchange messages. I once went to three films in one afternoon. Another good place was the zoo, close to the noisier animals: I saw a lot of the lions and the monkeys.

On 1 April 1933, the SA Brown Shirts imposed a boycott on Jewish shops. On 7 April a law came into effect which ousted non-Aryan and 'politically unreliable' civil servants. On 2 May trade union offices were ransacked by the SA and unions declared illegal. On 22 June, the Social Democratic Party was banned. Between 27 June and 5 July, all the other parties except the Nazis were dissolved.

To live in illegality, in *Illegalität*, became familiar in those years. People who had false papers, or whose right to be walking around free had been withdrawn, were condemned before they were caught. You felt hunted, or if not yet on the list, that you must stay hidden. You lived like a small animal, fearful of all that crept and walked and breathed. Your senses reached out to everyone, to detect informers or cowards – and the other sort, people who might help. Even in the military court, your senses stretched into the private life of the prosecutors, finding out what they were like in order to reach them. I creep into other people. I become them, and feel as they do and think as they do, and understand extremely well any Fascist, Communist, Freethinker, Quaker, Protestant, Catholic, Anarchist, killers of life and makers of it. I understand all forms of hate and love, but with me, *tout comprendre ce n'est pas tout pardonner*. Still, I do not think that I would have been alive today if I had not been able to understand all my adversaries, and often even sympathise with them.

Each of us hunted people was alone. Nothing mattered but our work and survival to do the work. You had to have eyes in your toes, eyes in the backs of your knees. At any moment might come the hand on the shoulder or the rat-tat-tat. We noted doorways or alleys we could slip into, and the exits from buildings. I used to feel that from miles away those who were searching for me were actually listening in, close by. It upset me; but it was also stimulating. The foreground of my life was the relationship between them and me. There is a kind of comfort in insecurity.

When meeting other comrades we learned never to be late, or early. With time I am scrupulous. I hate to take other people's time by making them wait: it is very uncivilised. In 1933, it could have meant detection and prison or worse.

Thousands of Communists, Socialists and Liberals were rounded up and bundled brutally into concentration camps. The Brown Shirts set up about fifty small ones, the Black Shirts of the SS had their own, including Columbia House – their Berlin torture chamber – and Dachau (in 1934 Hitler gave the running of all the concentration camps to the SS). The big ones were Oranienburg, later replaced by Sachsenhausen, north of Berlin, Buchenwald near Weimar in central Germany, Ravensbrück (for women) near the Baltic, and Dachau in the south, west of Munich.

Dachau had three thousand political prisoners. There was a saying: '*Lieber Gott, mach mich stumm, dass ich nicht nach Dachau komm*' ('Dear God, make me dumb, so that I don't have to Dachau come'). Beatings and terrible tortures were inflicted to make them talk – pulling genitals, burning their skin with cigarettes, almost drowning them. I passed reports, which victims or their relations had smuggled to us, to F. A. Voigt of the *Manchester Guardian* and Norman Ebbutt of *The Times*. We also gathered military information intended for the British government, as representing anti-Fascism: Mrs Ebbutt in London was in Intelligence. I will never forget the day I gave Norman Ebbutt a package of camp reports in a square near the Kurfürstendamm. The details were gruesome. He asked me if I realised we were risking our lives for very little. I answered something about freedom and civilisation. But he insisted on telling me it was useless. 'I will send these papers to London. And they will stuff them in a bottom drawer. In England, they think news of the concentration camps is exaggerated, most of it propaganda made up by the Communists or the Jews. *The Times* will not print it.'

Freddy Voigt was having the same trouble with the *Manchester Guardian*. He said, 'You poor young souls, giving your lives for a dream.' He was a gentle giant and a believer in Social Democracy, who hung in his flat the black, yellow and red flag of the Weimar Republic. If he had been German, he would soon have been arrested by the SS. I don't know what did happen to him. Norman Ebbutt was expelled from Germany in August 1937.

I was given the job of escorting political refugees across the border into Switzerland or France. There were two principal escape routes by land, one to Basel and the other to Lorraine by way of the Saar. The Friedrichstrasse main station in Berlin was always swarming with SS guards carrying 'wanted' photographs like a pack of cards. The parties that I escorted could be as many as eight people. My charges, each with fake papers, would go singly to a railway station outside the city at night and board a stopping train. They were told never to talk to or sit with another member of the party. We travelled towards Basel or Saarbrücken by way of several changes at small stations. When we changed trains, some of us would go into the station café and very loudly say we were taking a train we were not taking, in case the SS came in after we left. Everything had to be planned and deceitful. Every step could be life or death.

At Basel there was a special control point for 'foreign workers' – Germans who worked in Basel – and I pushed my eight carefully through, mingling them with the real workers, then went through myself. On the other side, a Swiss comrade called Willy Trostel would meet and take care of us. Always when we were clear of the control point, Willy hugged me and said: 'Safe at last!' He gave us all a meal, and then I returned to Berlin. Most of the others went on to Paris. The crossing at Saarbrücken into France was not a matter of stamping papers. We crossed by foot along secret paths, and each time we got through safely I heaved a sigh of relief that my charges were free, and so, still, was I.

We had made an arrangement with Walter Ulbricht that if Willy or I were arrested, the one who remained would telephone him with a coded message and then meet him in a telephone kiosk in Dahlem, the smart suburb where Bergner lived. One night in 1933 I did not sleep in our room in the Beusselstrasse, but stayed overnight with a friend. When I got home I saw that Willy had not been there either. I arranged to meet Walter Ulbricht at the telephone kiosk. He told me that Willy had been arrested, had managed to jump out of the police car, but had been shot in the testicles and recaptured. He was now in Columbia House, the SS torture chamber where men were beaten and interrogated, often as a first stage to being sent to Oranienburg or another camp. Walter also told me that I was next, and that there was a price of 100,000 marks on my head. 'You will have to leave.'

I said I would not go without Willy. Walter Ulbricht said it had been decided, and that the Central Committee was organising my escape. But I stood my ground. I told Walter that I would personally organise Willy's escape. I felt I could do it. I have always lived in a sort of trance. A friend in Berlin said that I jumped from icefloe to icefloe just ahead of the disaster I deserved. Since 1933 I have been what Germans call a *Tote auf Urlaub*, dead person on leave – living on borrowed time.

First I went to some friends who were not Jewish or political, and asked if I could use their address. They said yes, without asking questions, and arranged a room to look as though I had slept there. Next, I bought an engagement ring and had it engraved with the message '*WK und EW 1932 für immer*', 'for always'. Next I went to the Red Cross, to a doctor I knew, and asked for a certificate to say that I had tuberculosis, was very delicate and should not be upset. Then I slipped into my parents' house to change my clothes. From my former wardrobe I chose a pretty little blue dress, a white hat, shoes with heels, and gloves. I got the henna out of my hair, and curled it in the most conventional style.

I set off for Columbia House, and presented myself to the SS men at the desk. It went something like this. '*Was wollen Sie?*' I wanted to see my fiancé, Willy Koska. '*Nein*', and one of them looked at me in surprise. 'You can't want to see a man like that.' 'Oh, yes, I do.' 'No, not a young lady like you. He's a Red.' 'What's that? What do you mean, he's a Red? He's my fiancé!' 'He's a Communist.' 'Oh, no, he can't be. He's a lovely man.' 'You mean you didn't know? He's an important Communist, and he has a partner called "Rote Lisl", a very dangerous girl.' 'But I love him. I can't believe it!' 'You must not see him. He is dangerous and he is going to a camp. That will be the best place for him. He was probably led astray by that bad girl. We'll soon catch her.' I looked very shocked, and wept a little. 'Then of course I must see him. You are surely mistaken. He is such a good German, so loyal. I must talk to him.'

Germans are very sentimental about love, and by now I had their sympathy. I showed them my ring and my letter from the Red Cross, and said that perhaps it was my fault – I had not been able to see Willy enough in the last year because of my illness, and he might have got into bad company, but he could not possibly have done anything against the law, certainly nothing against Germany. 'I love him, I love him,' I kept saying, and they gave me a pass, touched to their souls by my devotion to this Red Communist criminal who had blatantly deceived me with a Red virago.

Guards sat outside the wards. There were two outside Willy's. I noticed, as I came into the long room, a large bin for bandages and dressings. I trotted past beds where lay men who had been tortured and beaten, and came to his. He was horrified. 'What do you think you're doing? They're looking for you. Get out as fast as you can.' 'They're looking for Red Lisl, not for Fräulein Wolpert. I've come to get you out of here.' 'But I can't walk.' They had shot off one testicle and damaged the other. 'When *will* you be able to walk?' 'In a week or so.' I told him I would come back in seven days and leave a parcel of his clothes in the bandage bin.

Succeeding with something like this is luck, almost magic. Always when I am about to venture, I wonder: will I manage it or won't I? I look for signs like the rain stopping or a bus driver's smile, then – I'm on. I had to think where to hide Willy until we could leave Berlin. Lisl Bergner and Paul Czinner were in England, but her house and servants were there. I went to see her maid. This nice woman knew the sexton in the Dahlem Protestant church, whose priest was Pastor Martin Niemöller. Niemöller had welcomed Hitler, but was soon disillusioned, and a year later, in 1934, became the leader of the Protestant clergymen who got together to oppose Nazism, calling themselves the Confessional Church: Dietrich Bonhoeffer was a very active member. The sexton offered to hide Willy in the belltower. I asked, 'Does the priest know?' He said '*Der Pfarrer is mit uns*', the pastor is with us.

When the week was over I went back to my SS men at Columbia House. They were amused to see the poor little fiancée again. 'Don't worry, Fräulein. We're hot on the trail of Red Lisl. We'll get her soon.' They didn't seem to mind the parcel, which I said was a present for Willy. In it was a shirt, trousers, shoes and money. I managed to dump it in the bin, under some old dressings. I murmured to Willy that he would have to try to walk out, but that I would have a lorry waiting nearby to take him to the church. He implored me to leave while I could.

I trotted away, smiling to the ward guards and the men at the entrance desk. 'Did he admit it?' they asked, with little smirks. 'No,' I said. 'It's not true. He doesn't have a girlfriend, he loves only me.' They looked pitying, and off I went to arrange for the lorry. It parked near the torture building once or twice, but nobody came. Then two days later, Willy suddenly appeared at the church. He had found the clothes, walked to the lavatory, got out through a window, and made his way to Dahlem. It was an extraordinary feat for a wounded man straight out of a hospital bed, but people are not normal when they are fighting for survival.

That night Bergner's maid came to tell me he was there, and I went to him. He said he felt fairly safe, but the bells shook the tower and hurt his wound. Luckily they rang only once a day, since the church was Lutheran.

I met Walter Ulbricht again at the telephone kiosk, and told him Willy was out. He could hardly believe it. It seemed almost a dream to me, too, but I was born to save people and can do it. Some people are mascots, and I have always been a mascot.

Walter organised papers and a crossing into Switzerland for Willy and me. We said very grateful farewells to the sexton and set off, using the slow trains I had taken so often. But this journey was worse. We were to walk over the Swiss border – it was impossible for two such wanted people to pretend to be migrant workers – and I had developed an inflamed boil, a carbuncle, on my leg, which gave me a high temperature. It hurt more and more until I could not walk, and Willy had to carry me, in spite of his own wound. At a town near the frontier, Willy left me at the station to look for a monastery or convent. We always went to religious houses for medical help, because they did their duty as Christians and would not betray us. He found a convent and carried me there. The nuns lanced my boil, disinfected it, bandaged my leg and gave us a meal.

We had already missed two of the time points Walter had given Willy Trostel. In this sort of work you give at least three time points, but must never wait around for your contact. For the border crossing, we had been given two alternative places, too. So the Swiss had to be there to try to find us. It sounds complicated but it was the way we worked. Willy, barely able to walk, and I, stumbling on one leg, hobbled and hopped by night, in near blackness, across the frontier between Germany and Switzerland. There, on the other side, was loyal and loving Willy Trostel. He took us to his flat, found a doctor to look at our wounds, and allowed us to stay with him and his wife and son until we were fit enough to cross by night into France.

In Berlin, 'Rote Lisl' had been identified, and SS officers called at my parents' flat. My father was away, but my mother behaved very well, telling them that she only wished they could find me for her. After they had gone, my mother warned my young sister Gerda not to say a word about me. My sister told me this after the war.

Lisl Bergner was furious that I had got her maid to help me. She said I could have caused the Nazis to confiscate her house. After the war broke out, Michael Powell and Emeric Pressburger asked her to be one of several stars in *49th Parallel*, shot in Winnipeg, so she and Paul Czinner went over to Canada in 1940 in a ship taking child evacuees. He took the train to Hollywood, and she joined him there without finishing the film. The Germans had invaded the Netherlands and she must have thought she would be safer in the United States, which was neutral.

Her cowardice made me angry. In her autobiography she does not admit to running away. She writes that her plan was to give a series of lectures to be written by the German intellectuals Thomas Mann, Lion Feuchtwanger, Bertolt Brecht and Franz Werfel, who were all in America, to try to bring the Americans into the war.

Lisl's Dahlem neighbour Pastor Martin Niemöller was arrested in July 1937 and sent to Sachsenhausen and Dachau, where he spent seven years before being liberated by the Allies in 1945.

6

Underground in Paris, 1933-34

After Willy and I got into France in 1933, we reached Paris and made our way to the comrades at the Red Aid. The president of the French Red Aid was comrade Cordier, a railwayman and prominent trade unionist we had met before at international meetings; he was expecting us. False papers were organised, and we were boarded with comrades in the Buttes-Chaumont district in the eastern part of the city.

We were now under Willi Münzenberg, propaganda director of the Western Bureau; its political director was Walter Ulbricht. Ulbricht moved to Paris that autumn. The office was hidden inside the innocent-sounding World Committee for the Relief of the Victims of German Fascism. Willi Münzenberg had founded this 'committee' in the spring of 1933, soon after he moved to Paris, making sure that no Party official was known to be connected with it. He got the idea of harnessing the international rich after the success of his Comité Contre la Guerre et le Fascisme, founded in Amsterdam. He had travelled from Berlin to a conference they held in Paris in September 1932 (Humphrey and I went too) which was brilliant with intellectual attractions. Henri Barbusse presided and Gorky sent a message. The audience's wild enthusiasm, which even upset the Paris police, showed Münzenberg that it would be easy to set up an international network of the well-known, well-off and gullible.

Willy Koska was given a job organising Party activity in Germany and I was put on propaganda. For safety, Willy and I had to split up. I went to a small hotel in the Place de l'Odéon on the Left Bank and he moved in with fellow Germans. I asked to continue to escort political refugees from Germany to France and Switzerland – perhaps I had come to believe I was uncatchable – but the Committee decided I was *brûlée*, burnt out. I did have the job of writing reports on which comrades had come through on the underground railway and where they were sent. I had no idea the reports were for Moscow.

Another of my tasks was to take round manifestos and petitions, trying to collect famous names. The French intellectuals were committed to the fight against Hitler. Most of those I visited seemed to me very wise – compassionate and honourable. I was well treated by the writers: Romain Rolland, whom I had known before, and Henri Barbusse, and I adored André Gide. These three were leaders: Sartre did not exist as a writer in 1933, neither did Beauvoir nor Camus.

I suppose André Gide must have been the best-known novelist in France, but he was wonderfully nonchalant the first time I brought him a petition, and signed without reading it. He and his wife lived in style in a flat near the Observatoire. The Gides took one look at me in my cheap little dress and fed me several times, both at home and in restaurants. They called me '*la petite*'. Mrs Gide was interested in Buddhism – which was a good thing, because Gide always had several boys visiting him, all good-looking, who spoke beautifully about poetry. It was rather mediaeval: the master with his pupils. Apart from his wife, I was the only woman there. I had no idea Gide was homosexual. His flat was beautiful, the food was delicious, and Gide himself was sensitive, decent and charming.

I was very young for a long time. It's not that I never grew up, just that I never lost my enthusiasm and my trust. Old people do not trust – they become suspicious. To me, these well-known people were either *sympathique* or they were not. I was not dazzled by fame – I hardly knew what the writers had written. I had read a great deal until I was eighteen, but at that time I was reading nothing – I was too busy. I always did everything to excess, always have and always will.

Another writer I met in Paris was Thomas Mann, and his children, Klaus and Erika, who were very close – some said incestuously close. Klaus and Erika were generous, and always gave us the best food and drink. When they were broke, they went to Papa for money. Once, his children told us, Papa turned off the supply, but they managed to turn it on again by an amusing accident. They were on a visit to the family house in Switzerland (Mann left Germany for Switzerland in 1933, before moving to America) when Klaus noticed a push-button in his father's library. He thought it might be for the light, and tried it. The wall moved away, and behind it were shelves of pornography. After that, the money never dried up. But Klaus might have invented that. I also met Thomas Mann's brother Heinrich, a more committed socialist writer.

Most of the painters, including Picasso and Tanguy, signed everything, except Braque, who despite being very anti-Fascist was cautious and always asked what party or organisation was behind a petition. Léger signed now and again, but Matisse refused. I learned a great deal about human nature as I got to know the artists. Picasso, for all his generosity and genius, was horrid, sexist and vain. Braque was wholly delightful. He dressed formally, like a bank manager, and worked at his painting from nine to five like any clerk, in the rue du Douanier Rousseau where he lived with his elderly wife. He did not talk about art as something special, but as a job, '*mon boulot*'. Fernand Léger was a disappointment. His paintings are so beefy and brilliantly coloured, but in person, he seemed insipid, pale grey. Alberto Giacometti was much younger: nobody liked him, he was unhappy, and he had a hunched back and a sinister-looking brother, Diego.

Through meeting those people I learned that the more important the work of a man, the less weighty his personality. The people one meets who seem full of living personality are usually the second-raters: the big makers spend their free time relaxing with sex or hobbies, not in impressive personal displays. And great men are often extraordinarily weak with women – they just do not know one woman from another; their minds are too busy elsewhere.

I approached the dancer Isadora Duncan and her lover Edward Gordon Craig, the producer and stagecraft writer, son of Ellen Terry; he was very handsome and conceited. Isadora would sit on the floor and hold forth, scarves and draperies in constant floating motion about her. Nobody took her very seriously – we called her '*la folle Americaine*'. I went to Georges and Ludmilla Pitoëff, who ran a small theatre company of Russian refugees. It was Ludmilla's St Joan that Shaw preferred to Bergner's. She had nine children, and I saw her play Juliet when she was eight months pregnant. They were a lovely couple and fine actors, and of course they signed. Among film actors, two were very *sympathique* – the beautiful Danielle Darrieux, with her long, soft chin, and Jean Gabin, who really was as he seemed in his films, the tough with a heart of gold.

And so I got to know them all, and they got to know me. They treated me as one of themselves and wanted to hear more about me. I told them I was a student at the Sorbonne. I didn't tell them I was working for the Western Bureau – I wasn't allowed to talk about that. But in a way I also belonged to them: my loyalties were as much with them, these brave generous friends, as with the Party. And after all, what I was doing was in a good cause. I had no doubts about that.

I began to visit London, as liaison with the British section of the World Committee for the Relief of the Victims of German Fascism. The main task of the British members was to raise money, which I collected from them and took back. Our usual meeting place was the Grosvenor Hotel, next door to Victoria station, so I could go straight there from the boat train. I met Mrs Lang, who was the wife of the Archbishop of Canterbury, Mrs Ebbutt, married to Norman, *The Times* Berlin correspondent, and the Labour peer Lord Marley, the international president, but the two I saw most often were Rebecca West, who had joined the Fabian Society in her teens, and her fellow writer Carmel Haden-Guest, author of several novels. Carmel was the left-wing wife of the former and future Labour MP, Leslie Haden-Guest.

They collected quite a lot of money in cheques, in cash, even in jewellery. Sometimes the committee members would come to Paris. I remember Carmel and Rebecca sitting on my bed in the tiny hotel room and asking questions. The money was intended to keep open the escape routes, the 'rouble road'. Much of it actually went towards propaganda, especially into producing the news sheet *Inprekorr*, meaning International Press Correspondence, a leaflet printed on the thinnest paper imaginable and reeking of printers' ink, which was sent to every country in the world. I can still smell that ink.

Once when I was in London I met H. G. Wells through Carmel Haden-Guest, who took me to his house in Hampstead. He and the Haden-Guests had been friends for thirty years, since Leslie supported H. G., as everyone called him, against the Webbs and Shaw in a Fabian Society struggle. His relationship with Rebecca

West was over. I thought him a quirky, ugly, witty little man. His son Frank came up the garden path with a girl, and Wells remarked, 'Here comes my daughter-in-lust.'

H. G. struck me as a petit bourgeois. He smelled slightly, and his skin was unpleasant. One can feel the physical quality of the petit bourgeois with some people – they might be born higher or lower and have a marvellous mind, but you can touch and smell the petit bourgeois in them. Wells made a contrast in my mind to Shaw – Shaw was dislikable, but absolutely classless. I have a deep and passionate hatred for the petit bourgeois mind – people who are careful about appearances, greedy and hard. I cannot bear in-betweens in class or anything else.

Not all the money the British gave for escapes and escapers was spent even on propaganda. It was when I saw where some of it went that my faith began to crumble. I remember the first twinge. Otto Katz, Münzenberg's second-in-command, was a Czech, and very smooth. He always wore fine, well-cut suits, and one day I noticed that he also had a new gold watch. Buying a gold watch: this was *wrong*. I thought of all the comrades I had helped over the frontier, who were living out of sight in the poorest quarters, dressed like tramps, starving themselves for the cause. Then I saw the presents Katz and Münzenberg were giving their mistresses, the cars they bought, the clothes, the scents. I was handing the little comrades 10 francs while the leaders spent twenty times that on a luxury. Münzenberg, was, I realised, even worse than Katz: he was working-class, very good-looking and totally cynical. Among the leaders, I felt I was living a life that only six years before I had renounced. The top Communists, who had money and frequented the grand houses of left-wing sympathisers, had come to despise the ordinary comrades.

The leaders liked me, and needed me. I could easily have touched that money and lived as they did. But I was young, and an idealist, and it disgusted me. Our motto, the end justifies the means, did not seem to mean this. Some of the other French leaders were men I would have avoided if they were not my superiors in a worthy cause. Maurice Thorez, head of the French Communists, was rather like his German counterpart Ernst Thälmann, but duller. André Marty, the sailor who had led the famous naval mutiny in the Black Sea in 1905, was a legend, but almost inarticulate; yet during the Spanish Civil War, two years later, he was responsible for executing hundreds of members of the POUM – the

Trotskyist organisation whose suppression by the Communists George Orwell wrote about in *Homage to Catalonia*. As in Berlin, the enemies hated most fiercely weren't the Fascists but the 'heretics' (Trotskyists, Anarchists and Anarcho-Syndicalists) on the left and the Social Democrats in the middle.

I knew Willy was in touch with Germany, but we were not allowed to tell each other the details of our work. Everybody knew only the minimum, so that they could not talk under torture – as we had said in Berlin, 'make me dumb, *dass ich nicht nach Dachau komm*'. Even today I never ask anything I do not need to know, although whatever I know now is not dangerous. Our life was dangerous: we were surrounded by death as other people are surrounded by air.

The way the leaders were living at the expense of the comrades gnawed at my mind. Willy was not immune to this corruption: he was in exile, far from his home and his people – I saw him slipping, going under, condoning the behaviour of his colleagues and unconsciously adopting their attitudes. If he had not been embittered by his wound, he might have resisted, but he had lost confidence in his masculinity and that sapped his morality. He had been a very proud, male man, but now although he could just manage an erection occasionally he could not father children. He became obstreperous and disturbed. We were not getting on well. He took me for a trip to the south of France to try to mend things, but the comfort made me uneasy. I felt that a holiday, a hotel and good food were wrong when the comrades were slaving and starving. I was always a boring moralist.

At the same time, Paris was becoming increasingly dangerous for anti-Fascists like us. Although the Communist Party was legal in France, various rightist groups had emerged to fight it, including the Croix de Feu and the Cagoulards or 'hooded men', the French Fascists who killed the shady financier Alexander Stavisky, which led to the bloody riots of *l'Affaire Stavisky* in Paris on 6 and 12 February 1934. The Nazis were pressing right-wing sympathisers in the police, Intelligence and the government to hand over the anti-Hitler Germans living in France.

I expected all the time that someone would shove a card in my face and say 'Follow me' in any language, not necessarily French. Sure enough, early in 1934, there was a knock on my door, and two men walked in with police identity cards showing them to be Deuxième Bureau. Their message was roughly this: 'The Germans are asking for your immediate extradition, and have given us plenty of reasons. You have one week to leave the country. We are not interested particularly in helping the Germans, but if you have not left by then, we shall have to arrest you and hand you over.'

French Intelligence was in two minds – they were under pressure to send German Communists back; on the other hand, the Communists provided them with German military information, since we had infiltrated Nazi organisations and the forces. Probably that is why I was given a breathing space. I now know that I had been sentenced to death by a Nazi court soon after I rescued Willy from Columbia House and we escaped from Berlin: the Germans wanted me in order to execute me.

I told Willy and Walter Ulbricht, and they discussed it. For me to leave France would not suit the Party: I was too useful. They called in another comrade, the gold-bedecked Katz, and went over the options. There seemed only two. I could change my name and continue to live in Paris with a new set of false papers, or I could contract a *mariage blanc*, a marriage in name only, with someone who was not German and whose wife would have the legal right to live in France. If I chose the false papers, I would have to dye my hair and go totally underground. I said I preferred the marriage. The leaders asked if I could organise one. I telephoned my old friend Humphrey Slater in London.

Humphrey rang me back next day to say he had arranged it. I went over to London and met Albert Coker, called Bertie, a loyal Communist Humphrey knew who was willing to marry me for the cause. He was a tall young journalist in spectacles, a science specialist for Newnes. While we were getting the licence, I stayed with Leslie Wolff and his friend Agnes Gillott in Brunswick Square in Bloomsbury. She came from a Quaker banking family and was a lovely girl and a devoted Communist. Bertie Coker was also idealistic and nice, a typical British Empire boy, born in Cairo. He visited me at the Bloomsbury flat, where we lived off tomato sandwiches and cheese sandwiches. We got on well during the short time we knew each other. Leslie and Agnes were the witnesses at our marriage, which took place at St Pancras Register Office on 15 March 1934. I then applied for a British passport; Dudley Collard, the Communist Party's solicitor and an old Wykehamist, signed the form as my sponsor. I knew several British Communists: Harry Pollitt and Molly Bramley and David Springhall, the Intelligence man, whom we called 'Springy'; I did not like him.

When my passport came through, I went back to Paris as Louise Coker, and checked into another hotel in the sixteenth arrondissement. I then registered as a student at the Sorbonne. My *carte d'étudiant* is stamped 21 April 1934. To test my new papers I asked my Communist bosses to send me on a courier trip to Berlin. Dressed as a young lady of substance I took the train from Paris, travelling by night, always by night. I led a group of political refugees across the border to Switzerland and returned to Paris. I was apprehensive the first time I used my new passport in Germany, as it gave both my maiden name and place of birth. But all went smoothly. Then we heard I was under sentence of death for helping Willy to escape from the SS, and the leadership decided I should not go again.

European agents of the Party were being called to Moscow. There were rumours that German Communists were being handed over to the Nazis by the Soviets. There were also rumours of a terrible famine in Russia. Willy and I were summoned to Moscow.

I was beginning to have doubts about Stalin, but I was still loyal to the faith he represented. I respected the sincerity of the young German comrades, and of men like André Malraux, whom I sometimes saw and heard talk in the Flore – brilliant, handsome and noble. If such a hero was a Communist, there could not be much wrong with Communism. I tried to discuss it with Willy, but he would not. The Party was all he had. I realised that Communism had come to resemble the Catholic Church. We were the monks and nuns vowed to poverty, chastity and obedience, and the bosses were the cardinals. For Willy to criticise Stalin was as unthinkable as for a priest to criticise the Pope.

I must have been falling out of love with Communism for Viola to have such an effect on me. Viola Bosshardt, Lisl Bergner's girlfriend, turned up in Paris, and it was as if that whole past life bloomed again in my mind. I became aware that existence without the Party was possible. She had married Laszlo Benedek, Paul Czinner's film editor, who became a director, but he had just left her for a Hungarian girl called Ziza. (He went to Hollywood, where his big success was *The Wild One* with Marlon Brando and Lee Marvin.) Viola lived in great luxury in a suite in the Hôtel Celtic in the Champs-Elysées. She often told me to come to her if I needed anything. While I was in trouble in my mind over Communism, she must have helped it with her care and intelligence: that partly corrupted me.

I accepted Viola's invitation to go to Le Lavandou on the Riviera for a few weeks. During our stay, she seduced me. She was very tender, and I loved her as a human being; I had known her for so long. Basically I am not a very sexual person. We were two women, both utterly female – we didn't dress in trousers or smoke cigars, and we didn't hate men or want to get away from them. It all happened very naturally, and seemed natural.

I am glad I did it, for the experience. I have told my daughters about it when they talked about lesbianism. I said: 'You can't tell me anything, I know it all.' That affair washed a lot of terrible things away. I had been feeling pain about leaving the Party, and Viola felt pain about Laszlo. At Le Lavandou, I had time to think. Viola asked me to stay with her, but I knew I had to strike out on my own.

When I returned from the Riviera, I had decided not to go to Moscow. I did not want to go on working for the Paris office either. I talked over my decision with Willy, and we agonised over whether Communist leaders should ever award themselves money and privileges. Finally, he said, 'I think you're right.' But he himself had decided to go, to learn the state of things at first hand.

There was another factor in my decision. I assumed that the comrades who were called to Russia were from then on Moscow-based, without freedom to travel – since we did not see them again. And freedom to travel, to go from city to city and country to country in Europe, is essential to me. I did not know that Stalin was calling in many of the comrades to liquidate them. He had become suspicious of everybody, particularly foreign Communists. Willy went to Moscow. Poor Willy – poor idealistic, loyal Willy. He was executed in 1937; so I was told after the war.

I told the Paris leaders that I refused to go. This was equivalent to leaving the Party, supposedly a terrible act. But Walter Ulbricht took it rather well. I think he attributed it to my worsening relationship with Willy. That was that. There was nothing official: they just let me fade out. Viola Bosshardt invited me to share her suite in the Celtic. Suddenly I was surrounded by fashionable, intelligent people, not Party zealots. I had slipped back into the life I thought I had left for ever.

* * *

I wondered what to do. Perhaps I should go to London. I had hopes of a country which contained people like Humphrey Slater and the idealists of the World Committee for the Relief of the Victims of German Fascism. But I loved my new life in Paris – friends, concerts in the Salle Pleyel, the satirical journal *Le Canard Enchaîné* mocking both Right and Left (*'Plan – Plan – Rataplan'*), the fragrant coffee from São Paulo in Brazil, the novelty of Bulgarian yoghurt, which was said to produce centenarians, even the bright lights advertising DUBO-DUBON-DUBONNET and BYRRH, and the rhyming advertisement for a chain of café-restaurants – *'Chez Dupont tout est bon.'*

It was a holiday before what I knew was coming. In July 1934, the Austrian Nazis murdered the Austrian Chancellor, Dollfuss. A week later, on 2 August, President Hindenburg died and Hitler became head of the German state.

In December 1934, Stalin arranged to have his supporter Kirov, the Communist leader in Leningrad, murdered. This gave him an excuse to purge the Party. Literally millions of Communists were executed by the NKVD, many after phoney 'trials'. Walter Ulbricht went to Moscow, but survived all the purges to become head of the East German government. He died as such in 1973.

Willi Münzenberg refused to go to Moscow, and met a mysterious end. In May 1940, the French interned him as a national of the country they were at war with. In the camp, Chambaran, about 70 kilometres south-east of Lyon, were several other German political refugees who knew their likely fate if the Nazis captured them. On the night of 20 June a hundred internees, including Münzenberg and a red-headed German who had recently joined the group, broke out and set off south towards Marseille. Münzenberg's friends lost sight of him in a wood. In October 1940, his body was found under an oak tree with a rope round its neck. The French police assumed suicide, but it seems probable that the NKVD had executed him. His consort Babette Gross escaped to America. It turned out that Otto Katz had been watching Münzenberg on behalf of the NKVD. After Münzenberg broke with Moscow, Katz left him and allied himself with the Stalinists, but it did not save him. He was 'tried' in his native capital, Prague, in 1952, forced to sign a lurid confession of his and Münzenberg's acts of Trotskyist treachery, and hanged.

Paul Massing, in Berlin, had organised a group of anti-Fascist academics, and in 1933 the Nazis arrested him, tortured him in

Columbia House and sent him to Oranienburg. He was released at the end of the year, and he and Hede got out to America. Hede was still working for the NKVD, and made good contacts in the State Department. The Russians were pleased with her work, and very displeased when in 1937 both Massings announced they were withdrawing from Soviet Communism. They were summoned to Moscow and went, against Hede's better judgment. The NKVD interrogated them threateningly for seven months, while holding their passports. By luck, Hede met some American friends visiting Moscow; she telephoned the NKVD and said that she had American witnesses to her demand that they be allowed to leave immediately; if not, she would go to the US Embassy and publicise their case. Four hours later the passports arrived, and they went back to New York.

7

Working on Films in London, 1935-36

I was offered a job in London by a Russian actress called Anna Sten who arrived one day at Viola's. She was on her way to England to star in a film, *A Woman Alone*, from a Russian novel by Fedor Ozep. A young millionaire, Robert Garrett, had put up the money. Anna was charming, small and blonde, a devotee of the Stanislavski method. Oddly, she was a friend of my mother's, despite my mother's dislike of actresses. She didn't speak English well, so she asked me to go with her as an interpreter and companion.

So I moved to England, and into another *tranche* or slice of my life, which has been lived in *tranches*. I have many times left a whole existence behind and started again in another place. This is like my ancestors: my people for generations were rich, were poor, gained, lost, remade and relost, until giving up and moving on became normal; but for that kind of accepting – from which much of our mellowness stems – you have to have been through the mill for a very, very long time. Wars must have swept over you and hordes of strangers overlorded you, to accept losing and losing and losing and maybe winning again.

Anna Sten took an apartment in St James's and we settled in. Almost everything that could go wrong did go wrong with the film (which was called *Two Who Dared* in America). If the 'angel' was Robert Garrett, the devil was Klement the producer, a Hungarian Jew. He was a foretaste of another Hungarian I hated working with, Gabriel Pascal. Thirteen script-writers were summoned from all over Europe and Klement made paper darts out of their drafts. He booked the Russian ballet at colossal expense. They came for a week to dance in the open before a specially built Russian village, and it rained every day. I was the only one who did well out of it, although I narrowly escaped being ravished on the roof of the Dorchester by the male star, Henry Wilcoxon, a tall handsome American. I suppose I was silly to accept an invitation like 'Sunshine, come on the roof and I will show you the stars.'

My change of fortune came when Anna said, 'Lisotschka, watch that continuity girl who works with the director. If you want a job, you could certainly do it.' The continuity girl's work was to note all the details of the actors' clothes, what they were carrying, their hair, what was in the set, and what they had last said, so that fragments of scenes shot at different times appeared to the audience to have continuity. I watched her, and one day she did fall ill. I got the job, and I am proud to have one of the earliest membership numbers, 35, in our trade union the ACT, Association of Ciné-Technicians. It was founded in Soho in 1933 by Captain Matthew Cope because the working conditions were so bad: there was no overtime, no transport, no nothing. The first general secretary was George Elvin, who was paid £3 a week. We used to visit him in his little office in Shaftesbury Avenue. In 1956, the union became the ACTT, the Association of Cinematograph, Television and Allied Technicians.

After Anna Sten left London, I took a flat on the river in Putney and went to the studios every morning. Few females worked in film-making, only the actresses, dressers, hairdressers and continuity, also called script girls. The continuity girls in the union with me were Tony Rowe, Angela Martelli and Tilly Day. I loved being the only woman on the floor behind the cameras. The men nicknamed me 'Sunshine'. Everyone was a real comrade and there was little one-upmanship. A motto was stuck on the staircase wall: 'Be nice to people on the way up. You may meet them on the way down.'

The studio was the most classless society I have ever come across. The chippies, sparks, props, masons, painters, special effects, designers, dressmakers, architects, make-up people, hairdressers, camera, sound, the director, the producer, the actors and actresses and little me, continuity – needed by everyone and blamed by everyone – were all working for the film. It was like building a cathedral in the Middle Ages – crafts and arts, technicians and artisans, thinkers and labourers, dedicated to one edifice.

There were many Communists in the studios, including Ivor Montagu, a former foreign editor of the *Daily Worker*. They dominated the union for years – and they knew something about my defection; some resented it. But my old friend Humphrey Slater forgave me. He invited me down to Bermondsey on the south bank of the Thames, where he had been drafted by the Party. It was a working-class district with a lot of unemployment. Battersea North, also on the south bank, had returned Shapurji Saklatvala, the second Communist MP to Parliament, in 1924 (J. C. W. Newbold got in for a year in Scotland in 1922; he held it intermittently until 1929, the sole Communist member). The Party had put up W. H. Hannington for Bermondsey West in 1931, and although he got only 4 per cent of the vote, losing to the Labour incumbent, Dr Salter, the Communists hoped to increase Party membership without fielding a candidate in the 1935 election.

I found Humphrey in a little house, in the usual revolutionary garb: tweed jacket, Stonehenge tie, corduroy trousers, white socks, crepe soles. As usual, it was a woman comrade who brought us tea. Humphrey and some of his well-connected friends had taken over the front rooms (the parlour) in several comrades' houses. Fires blazed in grates, and the comrades' wives toiled to do their visitors' washing and cooking. Humphrey's band was living very cosily while they indoctrinated Bermondsey with Communism.

One of Humphrey's friends was David Haden-Guest, the son of Carmel from the Committee for the Relief of the Victims of German Fascism. David had the odd habit of eating everything with his fingers, and bought his clothes from his younger brother because he felt a Communist should not have new ones. Most of his money went on the cause. He was a pure Marxist, utterly abstract, the only undergraduate among the founders of the first Communist cell in Cambridge in the summer of 1931; and he subsequently ran it. (The cell was set up after a visit by Clemens Palme Dutt; the Cambridge enthusiasts did not know he was a GPU agent, or that their cell was to be used by the GPU to spot talent.) David Haden-Guest was at Trinity, and knew his contemporaries Philby, Burgess and Maclean. In Bermondsey, I was tactful to Humphrey and his friends about the problems of the Comintern.

Dr Salter held Bermondsey West for Labour in the election and was its MP until 1945. The Conservatives won, and Stanley

Baldwin became Prime Minister again, ousting Ramsay MacDonald (the Communists got one seat).

During the Spanish Civil War, Humphrey Slater and David Haden-Guest went out with the British battalion of the International Brigade and Humphrey became their chief of operations. He got typhoid in Spain and spent some of his convalescence in France. I visited him while he was ill, but we quarrelled over politics, and he called me his 'little Fascist hyena'. 'Fascist hyena' was the fashionable insult then.

One day in the spring of 1935 I was walking through the studio when I heard a voice calling 'Lisl! Lisl!' It was Carmel Haden-Guest. I had been half expecting to see her, because we were filming her novel *Children of the Fog*, about working-class London during the 1910 slump and the Great War. Barbara Gott was the star and John Quinn the director. Carmel was delighted to see me – she did not seem to know about my abandoning the Party. She invited me to Sunday lunch at her house in Sloane Street. She said her younger son Peter, who was at Oxford, would be there – 'such a beautiful boy'.

Carmel had grown up at the court of King Edward VII – her mother was said to have been one of his mistresses. Her father was an Equerry, Colonel Goldsmid. When Carmel's nanny took Carmel and her sister into the drawing-room, people used to look first at rosy little Gladys and say hello before turning to dark little Carmel. Nobody liked clever, gauche Carmel very much; they preferred charming, sunny Gladys. Gladys married a very rich peer, Lord Swaythling of the Montagu banking family; Carmel, being the rebellious sister, married a divorced doctor, Leslie Haden-Guest, who became a Labour MP, then stood as a Conservative, then became a Labour MP again. The Haden-Guests were separated. They had three children: David, Angela and the apple of Carmel's eye, Peter.

At lunch, Peter walked in, fair, good-looking and elegant. Carmel said, 'Isn't he *handsome*?' He offered me a cigarette. His cigarette case held both Turkish and Virginian, and he had a lighter. Since he did not smoke, I thought this very suave. He was reading English at New College, but he wanted to be a ballet dancer. He was twenty-two. After lunch, Carmel suggested we go to the cinema, and we went to see the Marx Brothers in a fleapit in Charing Cross Road. Carmel was very short-sighted so she sat in the front row.

Peter and I sat somewhere in the middle. After ten minutes of the film (I can't look at the Marx Brothers ever again), he whispered in my ear, 'Where shall we go for our honeymoon?' I said, 'Italy.' He said, 'No, Spain. How many children shall we have? I think four.' I said, 'No, six.' A few minutes passed, and he leaned over again. 'I'm serious. I intend to marry you.' I said, 'Do you mean you want to sleep with me?' Peter said, 'Oh, no, I'm much too tired. I already have two mistresses.' I was again impressed. I said, 'I don't sleep around,' and he said 'I do.' I said, 'You're a man.'

After the film we went back to the house for tea. Carmel said, 'Now, darlings, you go and play; I must get on with my book.'

Peter took me into a large room which he used as a dance studio, and put on a record. He played Beethoven, Mahler and ballet music. We talked, and he did some exercises at the barre. He said, 'Will you spend the night here? I promise not to touch you, but I want to be close to you.' So I did, and he was as good as his word.

We both appeared at the breakfast table, and he told his mother 'I'm going to marry Lisl.' Carmel did not change her tone. 'Don't be silly, darling. She could be your mistress.' 'I mean it.' 'Then I'll stop your allowance.' It was said pleasantly, they were quite *dégagé*, something I had not met before.

He was a happy playboy, always. That's one of the reasons I loved him. I had come from heavy, drab underground work into the life of a light-hearted, charming Oxford boy. Peter was *the* Oxford boy – the eternal Oxford boy. Our attraction to one another was the attraction of opposites. He wrote about me: 'She embodied in my eyes the fearless qualities of European anti-Fascism – she was also exotic and attractive to the nth degree.' He brought me back to elegance and fun and life. With him, I relaxed completely, and suddenly everything was light after being dark, and we danced.

Peter left Oxford with a fourth class degree, and took me to stay with his father in his cottage in Essex. He was living with Edith Edgar, who worked for the BBC; they married at the end of the war, after Carmel's death.

Leslie Haden-Guest was always known as 'the Doc'. He had been a notorious womaniser in his youth and when Peter was out of the room he pinched my bottom and said, 'You're much too good for my son.' I was told that he had visited the Soviet Union in 1920 with a Labour delegation, including several trade union officials and Bertrand Russell, and that he and Russell had decided that Communism wasn't working. In Lord Russell's memoirs he wrote: 'Haden-Guest was a theosophist with a fiery temper and a considerable libido.'

While Peter was at school in London, he had had several years' ballet training from Princess Serafine Astafieva at the Pheasantry in the King's Road. She had taught Markova. He got a job with the newly formed Markova-Dolin ballet company for a three-month tour of Britain. His stage name was Peter Michael. Ballet had been very chic in Britain since Diaghilev brought his company over in the twenties. Colonel de Basil's Ballets Russes still came to London every year. Peter's Oxford friends were all in love with ballerinas: Donald Hodson was in love with Margot Fonteyn and James Monahan with Beryl Grey. James ended up as director of the Royal Ballet School.

In those days the ballet girls were very modest, very egalitarian. Young ballerinas like Margot and Beryl and June Brae would dance at the front one night and at the back the next. Everyone knew that Margot had something special, not so much her dancing but the dramatic quality; her presence was the strongest on the stage. Beryl was very good technically, and June was brilliant, but Margot had that *je ne sais quoi*. My life had changed completely from Communist work to being part of the ballet entourage, but the ballet world has much in common with Communism – the same obsession and devotion. I felt at home then, but after the war I didn't, because they had the star system.

That autumn, Peter and I went with the Markova-Dolin troupe to Birmingham, Leeds, Glasgow and Edinburgh. I remember how cold it was, but I was delighted by the theatrical digs – guest houses which looked from the outside dingy and miserable, until you were welcomed by the warmest-hearted landladies. Everyone in the troupe had the same salary, £7 a week, and I learned to cook large meals for five or six people on a gas ring beside the coal fire. A pot of soup, precariously balanced, was quite likely to tip, and there went our dinner and out went the fire.

Two important dancers in the troupe were Diana Gould (who later married Yehudi Menuhin) and Algeranoff, who had the loveliest disposition, all modesty and gentleness. He was a Christian Scientist, and when he strained an ankle he refused to see a doctor, but sent a telegram to his adviser who had been trained by Mrs Baker Eddy herself. Back came a telegram telling him to look up a certain New Testament verse, and sure enough, the ankle recovered. I put it down to his will-power.

I found I was pregnant. We could not get married, because I was already married to Bertie Coker. It took four years to get a divorce by the law as it stood then. I wanted a baby very badly, having already had three abortions while living with Willy. Carmel wanted me to have a termination and Peter said, quite rightly, that we were not yet ready for a child. Broken-hearted, I went to Dr Cecile Booysen in Kent. Dr Booysen performed abortions because she believed in it, and charged very little (Carmel paid). She and another woman doctor founded a birth control clinic in Finsbury. The actual operation never worried me. It was less serious than having a tooth out.

We lived with Carmel in Sloane Street, and I was working harder than ever. I did a musical, *The Street Singer* (which came out in 1937) with Margaret Lockwood and Arthur Tracy. Margaret Lockwood's voice was small, but she had looks. She was very common: she and Tracy were what we called 'the walk-on boreds' – small-time actors and actresses.

I worked on Carol Reed's *A Girl Must Live* (1938), which had Margaret Lockwood and Lilli Palmer in it. Lilli Palmer was not a bored. She had come from Germany and was a good performer and a good painter, though always depressed. This serious, intelligent actress had an obsession with Lisl Bergner, and even copied Bergner's kittenishness. Bergner disliked it – actors hate their style being copied. The strange thing was that Bergner was working on a nearby set, where Paul Czinner was making *As You Like It* (1936) with Laurence Olivier.

On 18 July 1936, I realised another baby was coming. I know the exact date, because of what also happened that day. We were at Covent Garden, in the gods of course, watching Colonel de Basil's ballet company. Between *Cotillon* and *Firebird*, I was taken ill and went out. I suspected I was pregnant. In the street, the newsvendors were waving their papers and shouting 'Revolution in Spain'. I went back to my seat and whispered to Peter, 'I think the war has started.' As soon as we got home, we switched on the wireless. Franco and his troops in Morocco had risen against the new Spanish Republic.

I see my past before my eyes like a film. But Peter Haden-Guest has a different version. He says he met me not in the spring of 1935 but on 29 December 1935, when he was already a member of the Markova-Dolin ballet, having left Oxford in 1934. He had gone on a six-week tour of England with them starting in November, followed by a twelve-week season in London ending on 7 March 1936. He says the company then had a holiday – he and I went to Le Lavandou – before a tour of England and Scotland, during which I visited him several times, and Anthony was conceived.

British people may claim data to be right, but truth is not made of data – truth is what you transmit to others. I try to feel guilty when I am told my facts are wrong, but I feel nothing but a rising pride for having done what I did and helped others as I did. How can anyone who is Protestant, middle-class, white, and never had to fear for their very life because of any of these adjectives understand even that bad man Robert Maxwell, who ruined his firms and robbed their pension funds and drowned mysteriously from his yacht in 1991? Maxwell would have always been a chap on the make, but his ruthless pursuit of material security was based on his boyhood in Hitler's Europe, when he had to lie and lie and lie and cheat and cheat to survive. After that he was emotionally crippled for life – dispossessed forever, a foreigner among locals forever. Even nine children could not give him security.

Little do Anglo-Saxons know of the subconscious fear of being killed and before that tortured for nothing but your racial belonging: killed because you dropped your trousers on order and were seen to be circumcised. And do Anglo-Saxons know what fear does to people? Can they creep under the skin and into the souls and minds of people who were threatened twenty-four hours a day, and day after day, with death for just one stigma? You had to change your birthmarks. I changed mine even though I expected to die for what I believed in, in the fight against that evil called Hitler. I expected to die, but I decided to die fighting and never to become a victim. What people call 'lies' are substitutes for basic rights. You lie, sure you lie, you might kill to stay alive, women might sleep with men to stay alive (they did in the camps) – you might betray your best friend, your closest family for your own survival. I am glad to be able to say that I never did.

The British believe in fair play. People who play fair have

covered themselves in every way, and they have also excused their lack of passion. Fair play covers a lack of involvement – they tie themselves, and will not get involved in fighting for right or wrong because fair play sets up rules. When you're really fighting, there's no fair play.

8

Mother and Son, Paris, Alps, Pyrenees, 1936-38

Peter wanted to go to Paris to study with Alexander Volinine, who had been Pavlova's partner, and we moved in November 1936. Our income was £3 a week from his mother, some fees from his private ballet pupils, and any money I could get as a translator and continuity girl. We starved beautifully that winter, on onion soup and spaghetti, in a cheap little hotel in the rue Chevalier de la Barre at the bottom of the steps up to Montmartre.

I needed to find a flat before the baby came. An emigrée friend let us hers in Passy, the fashionable quarter by the Bois de Boulogne. The Latins always treat you as sacred if you are pregnant: there was a lovely little woman from Normandy who sold eggs, butter and cheese, and she let me have them cheaper. In the markets I bought herring, and once a week we had minced meat. I think I was born for poverty, born for struggling, born for helping, born to live for others. I still spend all my energy going to market and waiting until the last moment so I get the peppers with a few pennies off.

I registered to have the baby at the Russian hospital, the Clinique Mirabeau in the rue Narcisse Diaz – I wanted to be with my own people. The birth began in the local cinema, where I started to lose the waters. Our son was born on 2 February 1937. He was an enormous baby, 11½ lb, and friends scurried around getting baby clothes. We called him one name only, Anthony, after Peter's childhood friend Anthony West, the brilliant, prickly, illegitimate son of Rebecca West and H. G. Wells. We made Anthony West his godfather (though he was never christened). We registered his birth as Anthony Coker. He was always smiling and never cried. I was deeply thrilled to have that fat little baby lying there at last, after dreaming of babies all my life.

Wheatie, the nurse I had after the births of my other four children, said she could tell a child's character in its first month. She knew whether it was lazy, defensive or gentle from the way it took to the breast and slept and moved. I know that Anthony was greedy, and bit my nipples. He had to go on a bottle at six weeks.

David Haden-Guest had gone to Spain to fight with the International Brigade. Shortly after Anthony was born, we heard that David had been killed only forty-eight hours after he arrived. It was during the Republican offensive across the Ebro – apparently a sniper spotted the newspaper he was reading. Peter was terribly upset. The brothers were very different: David had seemed to me so abstract as to be almost a machine, not interested in human beings at all. Peter liked people, and attracted them by his wit and charm.

We, the young angry dreamers, listened alertly to the news from Spain. We almost felt we could hear bugles across the Pyrenees. Carmel Haden-Guest and the other members of the Committee were deep in the Spanish struggle. Angela Haden-Guest, Peter's sister, had gone to Spain as a nurse. Their cousin, Ivor Montagu, went out to make a film, *Defence of Madrid*, with Norman McLaren as his cameraman.

Carmel felt that to fight Franco was even more her sacred duty. She visited us in Paris to rally us. She wanted me to become a courier again, leading groups over the Pyrenees – political refugees out of Spain and Republican reinforcements in. I said that instead I would do what I could in Paris. Carmel was glad to be reunited with her son: 'Look at him! So beautiful.' She loved blond, blue-eyed men, as I do. Poets were her speciality: she adored Stephen Spender. She took Peter out to dinner at the PEN club in his tails and white tie, leaving me with Anthony.

Carmel was on the British committee that had been set up to help the Republicans. They asked me to approach well-known artists for pictures or sculptures to be auctioned in London for the cause. Braque, Picasso and Matisse gave. Artists are always generous, that is what I love about them. Picasso, a Spaniard himself, used to give drawings and say, 'Take what you like; take something for yourself too.' I said, 'No, I don't like them,' and he kindly said, '*Je te comprends.*' He was nice then, much nicer than when he became rich and powerful. Those art auctions were very successful in London. I went to one, and saw how Rebecca West's new husband, Henry Matthews, a banker, watched to see she was all right. The prices paid turned out to be bargains – a Picasso drawing might have gone for seventeen guineas.

Peter and I moved to a larger apartment on the fourth floor in the rue La Fontaine in Passy. This had a studio where he practised and a bathroom and tiny kitchen in the gallery overlooking it. We had no cot, so Anthony slept in a basket in the bath. We eventually hired a girl to look after him, so that I could go back to work.

Renée was a real country girl, with red cheeks. She slept uncomplainingly under the kitchen table, and could make meals out of practically nothing. We lived on rice with onions and garlic, *riz annamite*. Then she met a butcher's boy, who slept with her under the table, and we ate meat. But one day she came in weeping: '*C'est fini, c'est fini,* there will be no more meat.' She had given him a gold signet ring which was only gilded, he bit it and said he was finished with her.

I had no labour permit, so could find work only if a film team asked for me. As a continuity girl in Paris I earned the equivalent of £5 a week. For a while I did subtitling on the English version of Jean Renoir's *La Marseillaise* (released in 1938), about the French Revolution, with his brother Pierre as Louis XVI. Jean Renoir was human and very intense. Like his father must have been, he was a peasant, not complicated. Pierre was nervier and more artistic, but basically they were like Auguste Renoir's pictures, sunny and open. They had had a happy home.

The French units were more democratic than the British: the director would ask your opinion. The British units were reserved, and everyone had titles. It was satisfying being with these French people who loved their craft and worked as members of a team: they reminded me of the comrades. The hours were very long and we were paid no overtime; we were lucky if we got a sandwich at one o'clock in the morning. But that was what I liked, and was used to.

I was not a very good mother. I loved babies, but did not know much about them. When I noticed, occasionally, that the colour of what Anthony did in his nappies was wrong, I rushed to Mayfield in Sussex to consult practical Joan Ogden, the wife of Peter's friend Ronald Ogden. Joan adored Carmel Haden-Guest and had called her first two children after Carmel's: David and Angela.

Peter and I were on the party circuit: the cocktail party had come over from America. We were invited out a lot and we had a lot of people in. They had to tiptoe to use the bathroom, because of the baby in the bath. One guest turned the bath tap on, I don't know why, and I found Anthony in his basket bobbing on the water like Moses. Another night we went to a party, and I forgot that Anthony was outside on the balcony. There was a storm, and when we got back we found the fire brigade there, saving him from the downpour. People had gathered in the street and when they saw me they shouted '*Mère dénaturée!*', barbarous mother. Peter was very angry with me.

At the beginning of 1938, my lungs ached and Anthony was coughing. He had caught a touch of TB from my milk. The doctors said, 'Mountain air! And separate mother and child.' The best place for children's lungs was then thought to be Arosa in Switzerland, so I rustled up some money from Ronnie Emanuel, an Oxford friend of Peter's, and set off with Anthony by train.

We arrived at Arosa under the Weisshorn in the evening. It was snowing, bitterly cold, and I had very little money. I left the travelling cot and the pram and my luggage at the station and set off with Anthony in my arms. The hotel nearest the station was obviously expensive, but in I walked and asked for a maid's room for the night. The Swiss, when they are wonderful, are more than wonderful. The manager produced a large room and a bath, and a porter was sent to bring our things, and more porters put up Anthony's cot. I was charged so little for all this.

Next day I found the local midwife, and she took Anthony in for a very modest fee. I paid her two months' *pension*. Then I set off for a different mountain top, Obergürgl in Austria – much cheaper to live in than Switzerland. I knew about it from a French writer friend of Peter's, Jean Rouvier, who went there every winter. The village could only be reached from the railway station on foot, or by sleigh – but for that one had to pay. So I climbed and climbed with my rucksack, and finally reached the lovely, tiny little place nestling in the mountains. The villagers were all from one of two families. I hired a cheap room in the post office and bought bread and sausage and cheese and milk, and got myself some skis, and proceeded to breathe deeply and slither over the snow.

Two other girls were staying in the post office, and a young doctor had rented a surgery there. The girls were Flavia Blois, from an old Suffolk family, and Monica Forbes, whose parents were Americans living in Europe. They were both good skiers and had come to Obergürgl for an important race. My life became entwined with the Forbes family because of what happened during the race. Monica reached the finish, then news came on the intercom that someone was badly hurt. It was Flavia Blois, who had hit her head on a rock and impacted her skull. She was brought down on a stretcher and the young doctor gave her a local anaesthetic and operated in the post office, assisted by Monica and me. There was a great deal of blood and a lot of scrunching as he reset the skull; I saw the grey brain.

Flavia could not be moved, and Monica could not reach the Blois parents, who were abroad, so Monica stayed in Obergürgl until her sister Eileen arrived to take over so that Monica could go back to the London Theatre Studio. Monica says she remembers me sitting cross-legged on her bed 'like a funny little gnome, very bewitching', telling her that anyone can do anything they want – they must just do it. Monica and her sister were both very good-looking and besieged by young men, but they had not thrown themselves into life as I had.

Eileen Forbes, not Monica, was Flavia's great friend. Their bond was a love of painting. Eileen had studied at the Byam Shaw in London and Flavia at the Beaux Arts in Paris. I got on very well with Eileen, as I had with Monica. Eileen was interested that I was living with Peter Haden-Guest – her sister Iris had been at Volinine's with him. Eileen adored babies, and when I told her about Anthony in Arosa she said we must have him in Obergürgl. So I went to fetch him. I carried him in my rucksack all the way up from the railway station with the cot coming by horse.

I remember us sitting at tea by candlelight in my fresh-smelling pinewood room. I made a cake and sandwiches and laid the table. I have always done that, prepared a table and food – not drink, I cannot afford that, I ask people to bring their own. Even when we were living on *riz ammanite* we always asked people to meals.

I carry within me a parcel of ethics deriving from my Russian background: hospitality is a religious law – dining-room door never closed in case the Messiah or Christ comes; a *couvert* always laid for him; food taken to your hosts in case they go short letting you share their table. Having people round my table has been my life. They come in tired, looking grey from work, perhaps wondering why they are there, and I make them comfortable, sitting not standing. After some food and drink they feel good and when I see their faces light up, I am happy. It is chemistry, like so many things in life. The secret is discrimination – inviting the right people, people with hearts and minds who feel and like to discuss things. I love to see their affection for one another. Perhaps they will afterwards be nicer to other people. Remember that Christ had supper with his followers: they did not just sit and twirl their thumbs and talk, they ate together and drank together.

Eileen Forbes was very good with babies, and she became devoted to Anthony. She was staying in the annexe of the hotel. Sometimes after Anthony was in bed, I left him in the care of the Frau Postmeister and went over to sit with Eileen and Flavia (who was getting better) and we listened to the little band.

Then everything tumbled down. It was 13 March 1938, a Sunday. Just before midnight, the band stopped playing except for a single drummer, and the leader made an announcement. 'Today the Führer has reunited Austria with the German Reich. From now on we are one great German country. Heil Hitler!' He gave the Nazi salute.

We were stunned. War must be very close. Eileen urged me, for Anthony's sake and mine, to marry Peter as soon as possible. I had to go to London to join him, but she offered to take Anthony to her mother's house in the Pyrenees. Mrs Forbes had rented a hunting lodge near Pau, a centre for English and American hunting people because it had a pack of hounds. 'Our old nanny has nothing to do, and the air would be so good for him.' It seemed the best thing. Eileen sent her mother a telegram: 'All well. Arriving train late Monday or Tuesday with Flavia.' She did not dare mention a baby. We left next morning. Eileen said, 'Lisl, I'll look after Anthony. Can you check the luggage?'

We had thirteen pieces, one a very smart pigskin suitcase with the then new zip-fastener, a present to Eileen from her beau. In it she had put her pearls and her silver fox stole. When we got into the train, I counted the thirteen cases in the luggage van. The train was packed with skiers leaving in a hurry. At the German border it stopped, we got out and the cases were put on the platform for the customs men to go through with Nazi intensity. Then the luggage was put back and we travelled on. An hour later, Eileen said, 'Let's count the cases.' We could only find twelve, and of course it was the pigskin that was missing. My heart stopped for a moment, and Eileen went white. I began to grovel; but I saw Eileen pick herself up, and she cut me short. 'No,' she said, 'it's my fault entirely. I shouldn't have left you with the responsibility. It was my case, and I should have looked after it.' With those few words, Eileen gave me the greatest gift for my future: the lesson that one must take the blame oneself if things go wrong. I am glad to say that the suitcase was found on the platform by some American girls, who brought it to Paris and got in touch with its owner. So Eileen did get it back, but she had decided that I was irresponsible, and she was not a girl who lightly changed her mind.

Peter was at Victoria station to meet me. In the taxi, he said lightly, 'Darling, it's wonderful to have you back. I've been absolutely pining for you. Guess what? I've just had an affair with Joan.' I felt something crack in my heart. Joan Ogden, my friend. Joan, to whom I had rushed if anything seemed wrong with Anthony. It was a terrible shock. But we were modern, we were Bloomsbury. I answered with his own lightness, 'Oh, really, darling?' Peter said, 'I knew you wouldn't mind; she's always been in love with me.' Tears were running across my heart. It didn't break, but it had cracked, and could not be mended. I went quite still, and closed off all feeling like a wounded and frightened animal. It was as if I had painted a mask over my face. Things were never the same again between us. Our love ended as it had started, with a nonchalant exchange.

Soon after I came back, Peter got a job as a dancer and choreographer with the Ballet Intime, started by Molly Lake and Travis Kemp. We found a little house in Raphael Street in Knightsbridge, number 12, and moved in in April. Margot Fonteyn lived near us with her mother. Margot's real name was Margaret Hookham, and her mother was formidable: we called her the Black Queen. The Black Queen did not like me – she said I had kissed the Blarney stone. One of Margot's admirers was Warren Tute, who later wrote books about Second World War battles. I remember him lounging on the sofa reading and loving her – unrequitedly, because she seemed to be only attracted to bad men.

Our rent was cheap enough, but we had no money, so I spent most of the time in Paris, where usually I had work. Peter came over to see me. I was still shocked by his affair and was leaving him slowly, particularly my body. I was glad to be working so hard, because then I did not have to sleep with him. I suppose I was stupid not to have realised Peter would be unfaithful sooner or later. He loved women. He went after them all. He couldn't say no.

Joan Ogden had another baby and called him Peter, again following the Haden-Guests' names. He had blue eyes, unlike her two older children.

The two Forbes girls told me what had happened to my baby. Mrs Forbes of course feared the worst when Eileen turned up with tiny Anthony. But she soon accepted that he was a sort of political refugee, and then an extraordinary thing happened. Margaret Forbes was in her fifties, a real Bostonian *grande dame*, a tall cold blue-eyed beauty with a no-nonsense manner. She was married to James Grant Forbes, a financier working for Banc-America and a private bank, Blair, based in Paris. He came from an old Boston family, and Margaret was a Winthrop, one of the oldest families in America. Her forebear was the first governor of New England. They had eleven children – James, Jock, Griselda, Angela, Rosemary, Eileen, Monica, Alastair, Ian, Iris and Fiona – but Mrs Forbes found it very hard to show affection. She was able to be warmer towards her animals. She kept many horses and dogs at her country houses – the hunting lodge at Pau, a château at St Briac in Brittany, Squerryes Court in Kent, at one time Bective House in Ireland. She would get up at six to groom her favourite horses, although she had a staff of twenty-two between her establishments.

Anthony, who was a very comical baby, was not afraid of her. He laughed at her and touched her. He crawled into her boudoir and flung his arms around her legs. None of her children had dared. It was what I had wanted to do with my own mother, only to be repulsed. Anthony won her heart, and it was a love that lasted all her life.

I did not meet Mrs Forbes until later, at Raphael Street. She was very reserved. Had she been poor, she would have cut out a splendid career for herself. She was lonely, I think, and her personality, though strong, was undeveloped. Auntie Forbes had everything except the *tendresse* of her children, so she fell in love with a baby boy who did not keep his distance. Anthony called her Auntie Forbes, and I soon did, too. She described herself as his godmother. She decided Eileen was spending too much time on him, and hired a starched Irish nanny to come to Pau.

I got on well with her at the beginning: people with her style often have a taste for eccentricity. She regarded me as a strange sort of animal. I think I was corrupted by her charm and ease – by the instant provision of Marmet prams, air tickets, and everything else money could summon.

In the summer, the Forbes family moved to their Brittany château with Anthony, and Peter and I went to stay there. Auntie Forbes thought Peter was marvellous – so charming – and he liked her and her ambiance – twenty-two servants and everything perfect. The two of them called me 'Mother Earth'. Peter was unfathomable. He had great self-control: in his twenties he tried not to laugh so as to avoid lines on his face, and he trained himself to write with his left hand in case he ever lost the other one.

9

Among the Painters, Paris, 1938-39

In Paris, I rented a little *pavillon* (lodge) in the Parc Montsouris, just south of Montparnasse. My best friend was Giselle, who like me was enrolled at the Sorbonne, though my studying was erratic. I knew a lot of people in Paris, but you never have more than two friends: never more than two you can trust with your pride. I only ever have two people I can go to and say, 'I am tired, I am hungry, I have killed, I have lied' – stark naked. The rest I befriend and I love them.

Giselle and I had coffee every morning at a bar in the rue Tournon. Her lover was very passionate. She would say '*Regards!*' and pull the neck of her blouse for a better view of the bruises and bites. I think she chose thin material so they would show.

There is no harm in being beaten up by a man if he loves you. I have often been beaten, through jealousy or because we were quarrelling. You enjoy it because he is your man and he is attacking you out of love. Peter held a knife to my breast and said, 'You were flirting with him – I will kill you now.' To be beaten by a man when he loves you is all right. It is when he stops loving you and still beats you that it becomes wife-battering.

Giselle and I had many giggles. Monique was another friend, and one day she telephoned to say she was in bed with bronchitis. 'Oh,' said Giselle, 'not another Greek!'

We used to go to the *bal musette*, where a man would come to your table, take your hand and lead you away to dance, body to body, his hands on your bottom, your arms round his neck, and then lead you back, all without a word. Usually he had a cigarette dangling from his mouth, anyway. Oh for the accordeons and the *bals musettes* on the Mont Ste Geneviève and the rue de Lappe in St Denis and the Moulin Rouge in Montmartre.

One Saturday afternoon in the autumn, Giselle and I went to the Moulin Rouge, posing as usual as working girls, and were picked up by two young men doing the same sort of pretending. Yves Rigelot was the one I chose, or who chose me: he was a painter. His friend, Pierre Billetdoux, worked in his father's corset factory. They asked us to have supper with them, and afterwards Yves took us all to his studio. I stayed the night.

Now came several months of great bliss. Yves' studio was at 8 rue du Douanier Rousseau, next door to Braque at number 10 (we used to go to tea with the Braques, known since my Communist days). Yves was very handsome and looked like the young Gary Cooper. We had an idyllic secret love affair, very passionate, very erotic. Every time he walked out of the bathroom his male organ was jutting out of his towel, and he would say, 'You see what you do to me.'

He was rich – his father was a painter of the Fontainebleau school, who sold his pictures by the yard and had made a great deal of money. Yves was ashamed of his father's untroubled facility. His mother was an enchanting old-fashioned French lady. Yves was right-wing: every morning the maid brought the newspapers in with the breakfast – *Action Française*, the Cagoulards' paper, for him, and *L'Huma* (*L'Humanité*) for me. He belonged to a group of Montparnasse painters, just one rung below the Picasso, Braque, Matisse group - they were *les Jeunes*, who still had their reputations to make.

Yves drew and painted me until I achieved utter nonchalance about my looks. I have not spent a second in front of a looking-glass since. '*Que tu es belle*,' Yves and his friends would say. I knew I was not beautiful, but I did come to think I was a *jolie laide*, attractively ugly, and that the eye of an artist had seen something the world could not. I felt close to these painters and I still feel close to artists, because of their feeling for beauty.

Every evening at about half-past six, Yves and I went to the Chope Raspail on the Boulevard Raspail, where our group met. There were André Marchand, Francis Tailleux and his best friend Francis Gruber ('*les deux Francis*'), Roland Berton, Pierre Tal Coat (Blockhead – his real name was Jacob), Jean-Pierre Rhein, and on the edge, Yves Tanguy and Alberto Giacometti. They abused each other's work and paid for each other's meals. Each put whatever money he had on the table, just like the comrades. The wives and mistresses would arrive.

After the meal we set off past the Café Dôme and the Coupole down the Boulevard Montparnasse, having a quick look to see who was in the other cafés, making for the Flore to be with Picasso and his group, *les Vieux*. There we listened to Picasso, Matisse, Tristan Tzara, and Michonze the lovely Russian painter. Picasso always played the great man, like Chaplin, whom I met later in the film studios. Chaplin and Picasso were both small, Picasso the more muscular, and they had the same vanity, the same meanness, the same sexuality and the same kind of ruthlessness. To me they seemed like twins. I believe very much that personality can be read in a person's body.

Our *bande* went to two bistros as well as the Chope Raspail. 'Bistro' was not a category of restaurant – it could be a café or bar; '*notre bistro*' meant simply 'my local'. In Paris, the *bistro du coin* is the meeting place of the landlord and tenant, the Communist and Fascist, the lover and mistress and even the husband and wife. You basically live at the bistro and sleep at home. Regulars are '*tu*' to the *patron*, who tells them whether their *copains* have been in and lets them run up a bill.

La Grenouille was in the rue des Grands Augustins. It was tiny: one rather grubby bar and five tables, run by Roger with his wife and old mother, '*la Vieille*'. At the back was an open range where Roger cooked our *boudins*, singing while he worked. He loved art. On the wall hung paintings by Balthus which had been exchanged for meals. Balthus did some wonderful paintings of the family. When we were really poor, we used to take Roger a piece of meat, or a fowl sent from the country, and he cooked it for a few centimes. During the war, politicians began to go to La Grenouille and Roger became famous and rich.

The other bistro was in the rue Tournefort, near the Panthéon: Chez Solange, who before the war was still not quite young. Rough, ugly, fat, snarling, Solange would let in only people she liked, but behind her ferocity was a big heart, a huge intelligence and a passion for her guitar. She had four daughters, an open fire, wax flowers, innumerable paintings, and everybody ran around serving.

I went back fifteen years later, not daring to hope I would find her. My knees wobbled as I went in. The same dark red walls, even more paintings, the same oilcloths, the same Solange, fatter, older, even rougher, with a flicker of a smile. '*Tiens, te voilà; vas t'asseoir là.*' ('So it's you. Sit there.') The sweet sweet sound of her snarl.'*Qu'est-ce que tu manges?*' I would eat gigot, of course. '*Et Pinot?*' Same old questions. Bottle on the table. And then the two words I was waiting for, '*Ça va?*'

After our group left *les Vieux*, we would often go on to one of the brothels for *un dernier coup*, a last drink. We liked the homely Panier Fleuri in St Germain, but one brothel was very like another: extremely clean, usually tiled, with Madame sitting at her desk beside a pile of fresh towels. Behind her was a board of lights showing which rooms were free. Past the Madame was the big room where the girls waited, talking or playing cards or doing a piece of secret knitting. The room was like a brasserie, with mirrors all round it, and we would order coffee and chat to the girls. As soon as a customer came in, up they all got and each beckoned with her own enticement. Some were naked, some wore a little voile. Tricks earned them extra money. One girl would get a customer to put a pile of coins on the corner of a table for her to pick up with her vagina: as many as she could suck up she kept. She tried to teach me how to do it; I think I could have learned, having been a good gymnast. Another could smoke through her vagina.

I felt sorry for them at first, but they defended their job. They asked why they should sit in an office, or clean out chamber pots, when they could be well looked after in the brothel and in ten years save enough to get a husband and buy a farm or dairy shop. To them a farm, or even more a *crémerie*, was wholesome and clean. In almost any Paris *crémerie* of the time you would have found an ex-'*grue*' – slang for prostitute, *grue* meaning crane.

One night a peasant family brought in their sixteen-year-old boy to be deflowered: grandfather, grandmother, father and mother. They did a bit of drinking and the father and grandfather selected the girl, a wholesome, buxom, motherly type. They asked whether he liked her. He blushed to his ears and said 'Yes'. She grabbed a towel, took the boy by the hand and led him up the stairs to the bedrooms. Other customers came and went, and the little family was drinking and jolly. After quite a wait by brothel activity timing, the girl appeared with the boy, and the father shouted '*Il a bien fait?*' The girl, walking downstairs, holding by the hand the boy who was flushed and grinning, said, '*Mon Dieu! Quel soixante-neuf.*' Everybody applauded, the corks popped, the boy was clapped on the back and we all got a free drink. It was a wonderful social occasion. All the brothel girls hated initiating older virgins. They did not mind young boys, but when it was frustrated men they did not like it.

Our brothel visits showed me the sane and simple attitude towards sex, division of mind and body. I would wish for a brothel in every street, a kind of medical relief station. Brothels were the great savers of marriages. I cursed Madame Robert, who after the war managed to illegalise brothels in France. We were also friendly with the street prostitutes and musicians. I remember walking past Edith Piaf singing outside the Dôme. She wore a leopard-skin coat, which she would throw open occasionally to show that she had nothing on underneath.

By a coincidence, Eileen Forbes joined our group, as Francis Tailleux's girlfriend. She and Flavia Blois had got to know him, and Eileen married him. Francis was the son of the owner of the Métropole Hotel in Dieppe, and his painting career was partly financed by the leader of the Liberal Party in Britain, Sir Archibald Sinclair, who discovered him on a holiday.

Yves Rigelot gave me driving lessons. I was not very apt, but I passed the test, I think partly because the inspector warned me about people crossing the road, *pédestres*, and I asked why I should watch out for *pédérastes*. He burst out laughing. I was able to drive an ambulance during the war, but I am not a natural driver. I get confused by the little mirror on the side showing traffic rushing at you, and I love accelerating and despise braking.

Peter sometimes brought his Oxford contemporaries to Paris, all interested in ballet: James Monahan, Tangye Lean, Donald Hodson. Margot Fonteyn and June Brae, chaperoned by their mothers, came over to dance. Two young men came with them. Margot's admirer was a handsome and very shy Slade student of nineteen called Patrick Furse; his sister, the actress Jill Furse, was a friend of Margot's. I never imagined that Pat and I would end up together.

Time seemed suspended. This was the 'phoney peace' (preceding the more famous 'phoney war') just after Chamberlain conjured up a mirage at Munich on 29 September 1938. There was a lull in film-making, mostly because of the situation.

At Christmas, Yves did something beautiful. One night he asked, 'What would you like from Père Noël?' I said, 'I've got everything I want,' but he insisted: 'What would you like?' Half asleep, I said

'A leopard coat.' On Christmas Eve, Yves said, 'I'm taking you somewhere.' We got to the Boulevard Raspail and he told me to close my eyes. He led me into a shop, and I felt something being put over my shoulders. It was a leopard coat. I had forgotten having asked for it. I have been lucky in my life to have had lovers who showed imagination, poetry and generosity. The next day we had invited all his group to a Slav meal in the studio. I roasted a goose and cooked red cabbage. Christmas to me is sacred. And I felt that this was the last Christmas.

After Munich, W. H. Auden, Christopher Isherwood and other British people left for America. Carmel Haden-Guest was set on Peter going: she was determined not to risk her only remaining son in 'a capitalist war'. Peter asked me to go with him; his mother had offered to support him, and the move suited his career. My divorce from Bertie Coker would soon be final, so we could marry. I said I was not sure I wanted to leave Europe.

In January 1939, Yves and I and our friends (Eileen was not there) went skiing near Chambéry in the Haute Savoie, taking our food with us from Les Halles – a ham, a sack of beans and a huge cheese. We climbed six hours on sealskins and came down in twenty minutes, so we never had accidents because our muscles were warm and loose. We climbed and climbed with our bamboo sticks, took the skins off, waxed the skis, waxed and waxed, and went gliding down with our christianas and telemarks.

I love the silence of the mountains. It is a different silence from the sea silence. But I belong to the sea, not to the mountains.

We had hired a hut with bunks. It was fine sleeping all together, until some of the men started sex with their girlfriends – Francis Gruber was one – and I got very upset. I put on my skis and skied away. Yves came after me.

I can't bear private things in public. To discover the body is a mystery and an adventure. All this 'tits out' is boring. I was always a prude. They used to invite me to daisy chains, but I only went once, and fell asleep. In a daisy chain, you lie on the floor with no clothes on and each does something to somebody while somebody else does something to you. They mounted each other and had somebody at the back. They played around with their bodies. It was quite innocent and primitive. They sweated like hell and there was a lot of noise and dust. I was a bit too private to be there.

At two o'clock one night in January or February in the rue Douanier, Yves, my tender lover, woke me and told me that we were going to Amsterdam to look at the Rembrandts. We collected Pierre Billetdoux and set off in Yves' Simca and by about six had reached the dunes of the Dutch coast. It was still all inky black, but we stopped to listen to the sea. Nothing can ever keep me from the sea. I took off my clothes and in I went, and came out beautifully burning, in an icy wind – it was like rolling naked in the snow. We arrived at Amsterdam at eight and had a huge Dutch breakfast with cheese and sausage, and tiptoed into Rembrandt's house in Jodenbreestraat with great reverence, and then to the Rijksmuseum. There I wept, as I always do, in front of the painting of Saul and David, a picture that hits me in my very depths. Then we dashed back to Paris, and work. But the old Dutchman had had his say in the struggle going on in my mind.

Forty years later, when I read Lisl Bergner's memoirs, I discovered that she loved that picture too and I wrote to her: 'It has been the most important painting in my life – for it made me take the measure of art – and I wept in front of it and go back to it and go back to it and have never forgotten that red velvet drape, the eyes, the harp, the eyes. And that you should mention it in the book – the only painting you mention – is somehow eerie . . . and I felt that my passionate and compassionate love for you – my childish involvement with you and your life – had a sound basis.'

Auntie Forbes was worrying about Anthony. My divorce date was near, and she pressed me to marry Peter and have Anthony adopted by him as soon as possible. She meant very well, and she was right. She said, 'If you don't adopt Anthony, I would like to.' But I became a cavewoman. 'No,' I said. 'Anthony is my child.' Mrs Forbes had to accept that, but she still loved him.

My divorce came through, and I married Peter Haden-Guest on 16 February at Caxton Hall, Westminster. Donald Hodson and Ronnie Emanuel were the witnesses. Then Peter formally adopted Anthony. Auntie Forbes was happier because Anthony was socially secure. Little did she know that he would be barred from inheriting the peerage Attlee gave his grandfather the Doc in 1950, because by law he was an adopted child, not born in wedlock.

The marriage finished my romance with Yves, even though he knew that Peter was leaving for America. He said goodbye. I felt quite broken-hearted. When Yves went into the army in September he was posted to Alsace Lorraine, and I lost track of him.

Again, I sank myself in my work. I had a dubbed film to do, which earned me £8 a week. After it finished I went back to Raphael Street in London. By scrimping and saving I got enough together for what I knew was a crucial journey.

10

The Last Summer and the Phoney War, Sweden, Ile de Ré, Paris, 1939–40

I wanted to go back to the Baltic shore of my childhood, the birch forests and the yellow sea. There I would decide whether to stay and fight in Europe or take Anthony to America with his father.

I got a commission through a friend, Vilgot Hamerling, the Swedish press attaché in London, to write a series of articles about Sweden, Norway and Finland. In May 1939 I packed a rucksack with a dirndl dress and Shaw's *Intelligent Woman's Guide to Socialism*, and carrying my portable typewriter, I took a boat from Harwich to Esbjerg in Denmark. From there I hitchhiked across the mainland and the islands to Malmö in Sweden.

By now I was heavily sunburnt. I was given a lift by a Swedish father and his daughter, who looked astonished when I took out my book. 'Can you read?' asked the girl. 'Yes,' I said, 'and I can write, too.' 'We thought you were a gypsy.'

So I went by stages to Stockholm, a silvery, watery city, where Vilgot had given me several introductions. Barbara Alving, a generous and well-informed journalist, told me that I should not go over the Baltic to Finland because of the danger of a Russian invasion (it came in November 1939). She suggested I follow the coast of Sweden to its northernmost point.

Leaving Stockholm, I looked for a lift to the north. I wanted an open car. Most Swedes drove conventional Ford V8s and little coupés, but I wanted to feel the wind on my face and in my hair. Then I saw an open Opel coming along, canvasses sticking up at the back. The driver was very handsome, with fair hair and blue eyes. He stopped for me, and I learned that he was the painter

Bertil Nordstrom, setting out on a working trip to the very places I wanted to go.

For seven days and seven nights I was with him, and he paid for everything. Every day I ate three meals. While he painted and sketched, I lay face down in forests of white birches and dark green pines. Through the needles and the moss I breathed in the scents of my childhood. He let me run naked and swim in heavy water where the flounders flap across yellow sands. I picked wild pinks from the dunes and combed the water's edge for amber. I smelt, I tasted, I felt, and knew I was home. He let me lie peacefully while he did his drawings, and when he worked he played Sibelius, Schubert and Mendelssohn on his portable gramophone. We stayed in little hotels, and I was expecting him to try his luck, but the door handle never rattled. At the northern end of the Gulf of Bothnia, near the Finnish border, he said we must turn back. In Stockholm he invited me to stay in his house. My bedroom door had no lock; I thought, this is it – but nothing disturbed me. I didn't particularly want to be disturbed, but I thought it funny that I wasn't.

When I got back to London, I went to see Vilgot and recounted my adventures. I told him about the beautiful, blue-eyed Bertil Nordstrom, who was such a gentleman, and he burst out laughing. 'Elisabeth, you have been travelling with the most famous homosexual in Sweden!'

The journey had made my mind up. I was a European, heart and soul. If I had still loved Peter as I had at the beginning, I would have gone to the ends of the earth with him. But I wanted to stay. I wanted to die, if Europe had to die. I could not leave the people I had fought for and fought with – I had to see it through with them. The Nazis had destroyed much of what I loved, and had condemned me to death. I would meet them again and fight them. I couldn't leave my arch-enemies: I was bound to them by hate. I told Peter and Carmel that I was staying, and keeping Anthony (who was still at Pau) with me in Europe.

I went back to France and began training as an ambulance driver with the SAAF, Section Ambulance Alliée Française. I joined the SAAF unit at the British Hertford Hospital, in a suburb south of Paris. I drive dangerously because I do it like riding: before an obstacle I speed up. The old general in charge said the Germans should give me the Iron Cross for damage to France. We waited around to be needed.

Peter Haden-Guest left for America in August. I accepted an invitation to join a group of friends on the Ile de Ré, just off the Atlantic coast at La Rochelle.

Charles and Geneviève Geoffroi-Dechaume were a beautiful couple, very musical, who had ten children, five boys and five girls. Charles had lost a leg in the First World War. They were Anglophiles and often stayed in England, where they were part of the Wiltshire set. They took in British young people as lodgers at their house in Seine-et-Oise. I had met them through Julian Trevelyan, the painter, who also came on this holiday. He arrived with his wife Ursula, born a Darwin, and several other painters: Mary Wickham; Michael Wickham (no relation) and his wife Tanya; Diana Lodge, without her husband, son of the physicist spiritualist, but with her three-year-old child Tom; Bichou Oliveira da Silva, Portuguese, and her Hungarian husband Arpad Szenesch – both painted, but she was famous.

The Ile de Ré was not well-known then and the beaches were empty. The Geoffroi-Dechaumes had taken a house, but Diana Lodge and little Tommy and Mary and I slept on the sand. The others 'camped in a half-built little hotel – tiny whitewashed rooms full of light – nothing but a bed in each,' remembers Ursula. 'We fed in a café – small oysters and local white wine, and bicycled each day to a wide beach, where we all bathed naked.' There was a beach café with a band and we danced at night. Our party contained several children, and one day the boys bicycled round the island swapping the signs for the villages. We felt hedonistic and irresponsible, knowing that this was the last summer of peace. The eldest Geoffroi-Dechaume, Antoine, had a Danish wife and three children. Antoine and his teenage brother Denis fell in love with me. Denis would ride round on his bicycle, nursing his schoolboy crush. Antoine and I flirted in the sun and held hands under the moon, but nothing more. We were merely full of erotic feeling.

Perhaps it seems like boasting when I tell these things, but it would be untruthful to leave them out. People in their twenties who get about do have erotic encounters and many opportunities. When writers leave out all but the serious relationships it gives a false impression. I never got desperate for physical love, so I have probably had fewer incidents than most. When my daughters ask about my sex life I say I have not had a sex life – I have had a love life. I have never been to bed with a man I did not really totally love and whose child I would not have borne. I am glad to say I was never liberated by pills nor hamstrung by birth-control methods of the olden days – that vinaigrette and those balloons! It was all so very lovely and fearless and loveful and forever.

On 23 August 1939, the Russians went over to Hitler: we heard on the wireless that Ribbentrop and Molotov had signed a German-Soviet pact. My former friends were going to fight alongside my enemies. On 1 September we heard that the Germans had invaded Poland, and we knew the last holiday was over. Next day we all drove home, the Geoffroi-Dechaumes and I heading for Paris.

I arrived back in my room on 3 September, the day France and Britain declared war on Germany. When I heard Chamberlain on the wireless from London, I began to weep uncontrollably. I had a map of Europe on my wall, as I always have wherever I live. I banged my head against it in rage and despair.

During these years I rode down to Notre-Dame on my English bicycle at eight most mornings, as I had at seventeen. I did not pray, I just sat there, with perhaps one or two worshippers or a nun arranging flowers. I love the spirit of churches. A church holds the souls of those who have felt intensely in it. I do not believe in an afterlife, but I sensed that Notre-Dame was full of the spirits of people who had bared their heavy or light hearts. It is the same with a concentration camp. When you go to Dachau or Belsen or Buchenwald, the people are still there, in the air. It is the same at Ephesus and Delphi.

I went to Notre-Dame on 4 September, and could hardly find a seat. People filled the church, kneeling, praying, weeping, moaning and holding their heads. I was ashamed of them. In easy times Notre-Dame was empty, in fearful times it overflowed. I couldn't belong where people came only out of fear and never to give thanks. I walked out, and never went back. I always loved Christ, even when I was deepest in Communism. He is my comrade, and if I had lived in His time I would have washed His feet, because I love people who give their lives for others. I love dedication, and I love generous hearts. When I was young I did not accept weakness in other people. Now, perhaps, I do. But in September 1939, tolerance would have been no help in what I felt I had to do.

We had been expecting war, but the violence of my reaction knocked me out. That day I went down with jaundice, all green and yellow, and had to spend four weeks in the Hertford Hospital. My friends in the ambulance unit said I was the first casualty of the battle. When I was well enough to rejoin them, we still seemed to be waiting. This is what the British called the 'phoney war', but the French description, the '*guerre des nerfs*', war of nerves, was better. We drove around the Ile de France delivering blood plasma and medical supplies.

Antoine Geoffroi-Dechaume, my friend from the Ile de Ré, visited me in Paris, and we began an affair. He was a poet and a musician, who played the organ. We would go to concerts at the Salle Pleyel, and at weekends I sometimes went to his parents' home at Valmondois. My being invited seemed natural after our holiday together. Sunday luncheons *chez* Charles and Geneviève Geoffroi-Dechaume were tremendous occasions. Their children and grandchildren, friends and lodgers, all gathered round the big table and were expected to sing before eating. Charles would bang a tuning-fork as the signal to roar out Bach or Schubert.

I moved to a tiny room, a *chambre de bonne*, in the rue Victor Considérant. Antoine was called up and posted to Meaux on the Marne, about 30 kilometres east of Paris. This was an important defence post, and it was difficult to get a pass, but I did. He was allowed to play the organ in the cathedral, and it was a thrill to listen to him playing just for me. I wanted to hear him again and again. But my next visit was disastrous. His family turned up at the same time and saw me there enraptured. It was the end.

Men always came to me for poetry. One of my later lovers said, 'With you I can fly.' It is not very nice for their wives. I am feather-light with men, not weighty: not the *Hausfrau* type. If my man wakes me at one in the morning and says 'Let's go to Timbuktu,' I say 'All right, let's' – no questions about is the climate right, is it practical, and things like that. My love life with Yves and with Antoine was based on the fact that we had no hope of a future because in the future there was war and there was death. My relationships with them were entirely based on catching the last bit of life and poetry and music and Christmas, drinking it in and storing it up for the time to come of coldness and aloneness. I shall never forget or regret the intensity of those loves born out of despair.

The ambulance unit was ready, but there were no casualties. In

January 1940 I left the unit temporarily to do some film work in London. I stayed with William Hayter, the engraver, and his wife, a sculptress, in Chiswick, and met my Ile de Ré friends the Trevelyans and Mary Wickham again. I did some sub-titling in Wardour Street, and went to concerts whenever my soul was wingless and my heart heavy. I rode through London on my shiny, heavy-tyred bicycle and worried about Anthony's safety.

It was a beautiful spring. Primroses unfolded their pale yellow petals and daffodils their dark yellows. Everything bloomed and flowed, but it felt eerie and unreal, like a long intake of breath. Uniforms appeared on the streets, and everyone carried a gas mask.

On 9 April the Germans invaded Norway and Denmark. I managed to get a plane to Paris, and rushed to my little room. I put my mattress on the floor and made it up as a bed for Anthony; I would sleep on the springs. Then I set out for Pau by train to fetch him.

Auntie Forbes was very surprised to see me. Anthony had been with her for two years, looked after by Miss Stark, his sixty-year-old Irish nanny. Mrs Forbes was about to move the household to England. My decision to fight the war in Europe had to her the logical consequence that she would take care of Anthony.

That was how the world saw it. But I had been seized by a cavewoman urge to have my son with me. I truly felt that a mother and child should live and die together. Physically he was better off at Pau, because of his lungs, and because he was well away from the advancing Germans. But I told Auntie Forbes I had come to take him to Paris. She said it was not safe. I said, 'The only real safety for a child is with his mother.' She said she would not allow him to be taken into danger, and ordered Miss Stark not to pack his clothes. I pretended to go to bed beaten, but in the middle of the night I took him from his cot, leaving a note for Auntie Forbes, and fled to catch the Paris train.

The Germans were coming, and I felt I must have Anthony with me, to protect him. There was no logic, it was instinct. I am a very atavistic human being. It could have been said, and it was, that I grabbed Anthony to protect myself. I know that a mother's instinct said 'have him with you', but I do not know whether I sensed subconsciously that a mother and child are safer than a woman alone. Sometimes I thought 'Anthony is my mascot, so I will survive.' Later on, the men who had to decide my life or death took into account that I was a mother. Every man who was supposed to send me into another world behaved like a man first and an executioner second, but I think it was because I behave like a woman first. Maybe I had no right to have the child with me. Maybe those who blamed me were right. But later, when I had four more children, I always had them with me in times of trouble and danger. It is animal stuff. You fling yourself over the child.

I had got hold of Anthony. But it was difficult to look after him and be in the ambulance unit, which was now calling in its members. My friend Véronique, a medical student, took care of him while I was working.

I am not afraid of asking people for help. I feel perfectly free about it, because I help everybody when I can. If I need help or somebody needs it from me, we get closer to each other. I believe people like doing things for others, contrary to what is said. They like being good. Since I have become old, I find it harder to ask for help. But when I am travelling I do, and I receive it; from women mostly, particularly old women.

On 9 May 1940 the news came that the Germans had broken through the Maginot Line. They poured forward. On the 10th, they invaded Holland, Belgium and Luxembourg.

I had a task to carry out. Julian Trevelyan and Bill Hayter wanted me to persuade Picasso to leave Paris. They were convinced that if the Germans got there, they would execute him because he was thought to be a Communist. He was no Communist, but he had signed all my petitions. I went to Picasso with my message, but he said, 'Let them come. Let them torture me, and let them kill me. I'm staying.' When the Germans arrived a month later, they did go to Picasso's house, but not to take him: they brought flowers, and butter and potatoes and flour, because they loved art. Picasso never forgave destiny for having cheated him of the one gesture he was prepared to make. After that, he became callous. For an artist to live five years in a city at war and do not a single painting of the people's suffering condemns him, to my mind: because the basis of an artist is compassion. Picasso was ever afterwards interested only in sex and money, because the Germans had deprived him of his chance to be a martyr.

I received letters, telegrams and telephone calls from Auntie Forbes and the Haden-Guests pleading with me to take Anthony out of France. Mr Miller of the American Embassy in Paris tried personally to make me go. I still refused, saying I had my ambulance duties. Auntie Forbes asked me to at least take Anthony to her Brittany château, and she would send Nanny Stark to look after him.

The Germans had by this time captured Rotterdam and entered Boulogne. As they approached Paris, single women in the ambulance service were being sent to the front, but not mothers with children. I decided to go to Brittany.

11

Occupied Brittany, 1940

I took Anthony by train to Dinard and we got a taxi to St Briac. The Forbes château was called Les Essarts, meaning a forest clearing. It was of medium size, very strongly built, with a lawn running down to the sea. In normal times this lawn was trimmed in the English fashion, but it had been dug up for potatoes as part of the war effort. The potato plants had been attacked by Colorado beetles, *doryphores,* and Vaudin the gardener was devastated. *Doryphores* was also what the French called the Germans.

Nanny Stark had already arrived from Pau. I did not get on with her – for one thing, she disliked the dungarees I put on Anthony – but she was efficient. One breast had been removed because of cancer and she carried nappies and hankies there. She had been thirty years in France, and spoke French with an Irish accent and English with a French accent. She was anti-Church, and taught Anthony this answer to 'What do the church bells say?': 'Hurry up, people, don't be late, put a penny in the plate.' She had white hair and was immensely greedy; she simply could not understand how to do without cream.

Most members of the Forbes family had left France. Eileen and Francis Tailleux were living in the Château Noir at Aix-en-Provence, a rambling château inhabited by several artists – Cézanne had painted there. Because Francis had a withered arm, he was not called up. Monica Forbes was in England, where she married a naval officer, Dunstan Curtis. Auntie Forbes was still at Pau.

The servants at Les Essarts were Antoinette Doucet, the housekeeper, a po-faced Frenchwoman who did not like me; Vaudin, who was a Jersey man, and his French wife Louise, who did the cooking; and a maid. Les Essarts was American property, and the Germans would have no right to occupy it. The château had stables, outhouses, gardens and a private beach. It had been idyllic when the house was full of young people; now we were a quiet few, with a frightening future ahead of us. I had Anthony, though, and after two years' separation, I took such pleasure in playing with him and putting him to bed.

Every day of that May was beautiful – the sun shone, the sky was blue, and the beaches were empty. It was oddly silent. At the end of the month, we heard that the British army was leaving from Dunkirk to the north. The roads around St Malo were crowded: people were fleeing in cars, carts and on bicycles, and the countryside was littered with the débris of the British army. They had abandoned jeeps and lorries, packets of Woodbines and cans of bully beef. Brand-new motorcycles had been thrown aside as the men struggled forward to the coast.

British soldiers were leaving from St Malo in small boats, from St Briac even. A few brave French boys crossed with them. Some soldiers politely asked if they could 'borrow' the Forbes boats. I said 'Take them.' I knew that Peter and the Forbeses would expect me to do the sensible thing and try to cross with the retreating British. But I did not. By the end of the first week in June, the Dunkirk evacuation to the north was finished, but soldiers were still leaving down our coast.

The wireless brought bad news every day. On 10 June 1940, Italy entered the war on the Germans' side. On the 14th, Paris fell. On the 15th, the Germans' allies, the Russians, occupied Estonia, Lithuania and Latvia. On the 16th, Churchill offered dual nationality to every patriotic French person, and a joint War Cabinet, but was rejected. On the 17th, Marshal Pétain formed a new government and asked the Germans for an armistice.

Then, on the 18th, came something for our side: General de Gaulle, who had flown to London from Bordeaux the day before, broadcast on the BBC. 'I, General de Gaulle, at present in London, invite the French officers and men who find themselves on British territory with or without their weapons to contact me . . . the flame of French resistance must not and will not be extinguished.' I cheered and cried.

The way de Gaulle fought for France was like a mother, like a lioness. The next evening he broadcast again: 'I, faced with the liquefication of a government which has passed into the service of the enemy . . . I, General de Gaulle, conscious that I am speaking in the name of France . . . state that every Frenchman still bearing arms has the absolute duty to continue resistance. Soldiers of France, wherever you are, step forward!'

That was me. On 19 June, a hot, perfect day, I felt I had to go to St Malo to help with the evacuation. I have an uncanny sense of timing and I was right once more. As I approached I could hear the crump of explosions and see a black cloud over the port. The British were blowing up the petrol tanks before they went.

Ships were lined up to take British and Canadian boys back to England. The soldiers were being embarked from the jetty by junior officers who guided and shepherded their men. They were all very young. Around them, tanks of petrol were exploding in hot gouts of fire, and they were under a constant bombardment of flying pieces of metal. I ran around trying to be useful and give cheer to the boys.

Amid all the din and the shouting, the heat and horror, was a YMCA tea van, a calm centre in the commotion, and a sergeant in his twenties pouring tea for the soldiers. A lieutenant said to me, 'Are you coming home with us?' as though offering me a lift back after a party. I said, 'No, not this time. I have my baby and staff further along the coast.' He said, 'You'd better go and fetch them. Jerry will be here before you know it.' I think he was in the Norfolk Regiment. I remember his name was Dick. At that moment there was a violent explosion, and I dived under the tea wagon. A hand appeared under the van, holding a cup. Dick's very public school voice said, 'Teatime, Elisabeth. Sorry – no saucer.' I love such insouciance, and the best thing was that he meant it. That was what kept the British army going: they shaved every morning, and had tea in the afternoons.

I clearly remember the expressions on those boys' faces: they were going home, they would be all right in Britain, and could fight another day. Those that had survived could hope – but some had died, and others were badly wounded. I asked what would happen to the tea van. They were leaving it behind, with so many other vehicles. I said, 'Can I have it? It will help me continue to work for the Allies.' They took me to a Captain Disney, who wrote me a release for it in pencil on graph paper: 'YMCA tea car H080 handed over on Quay St Malo to Mrs Elisabeth Haden-Guest, Château Les Essarts, St Briac, Union Femmes Françaises. 19 June 1940.' We both signed it. I still have it.

I said goodbye to everyone, going round as many as I could. I sent a message to my mother-in-law in London. They asked me to keep in touch. That Wednesday I felt like a mascot – I was their sister, their friend, their luck.

The way back to St Briac was through lines of abandoned jeeps and lorries and motorcycles. There they were, a harvest of machines for the Germans. I stopped, took a hammer out of the tool-box, and felt its weight in my hand. Then, with all my energy, I began to attack the engines. In my rage, in my misery, in my passion, I hit out. I brought that hammer down time and again, with every muscle in my body, with every last ounce of strength. I lammed into metal, I smashed connections and wiring and headlights. I don't know how long I swung the hammer, beating at anything within range. I shrieked hysterically, screamed, sobbed and shouted. Salty sweat and tears ran down my face. When my arms were exhausted, I used my feet, kicking motorcycles, crashing them to the ground. I was possessed, a madwoman, blindly striking out to destroy all that could help the enemy.

After about an hour, exhausted and trembling, I drove back to Les Essarts. It was evening, but the sky was still blue, the sun still shone, the crickets chirped, the birds sang, and behind them was that deathly silence. The reality of the situation had come home to me. The French were turning against us, and we were in a hostile landscape.

I telephoned the American Embassy. Mr Miller told me that Auntie Forbes, her youngest daughter Fiona and their old nanny, Nanny Mac, had taken a ship to England from Bordeaux, but that she had given instructions for money to be sent regularly to pay the staff. Next day, I got two French boys in the local garage to paint over the camouflage markings of the tea van so that it looked like an ordinary van. They said they were going to England in a fishing boat.

Rather late, I tried to persuade Nanny Stark and the Vaudins to leave. I told them that as British citizens they could only expect the worst when the Germans arrived. Nanny, being Irish, was technically neutral. She refused to go, saying that France was her home. The Vaudins felt the same. Poor Vaudin – in a few months he was interned. He eventually died of cancer, but Louise is still at St Briac. I went round the rest of the British in Dinard – mostly old governesses and retired army officers. I told them they might have a chance to escape by way of Bordeaux, but they all refused. I was rather moved by the bravery of these tough, elderly people.

Diana, who ran the English library, was the girlfriend of the Grand Duke Vladimir, a Romanov. There was a large colony of White Russians in Dinard, living off the rich British and Americans. I had the idea that I could organise some resistance to the Germans and took a few soundings: I did find one French doctor willing to join me. Nobody suspected my past. To the expatriates of Dinard I was just another young mother with a child – a friend of the Forbes family, one of themselves.

On 22 June 1940, the French agreed Armistice terms. Marshal Pétain's assembly would govern part of France, the '*zone libre*', from the city of Vichy. The demarcation line between Occupied and Unoccupied France was roughly two sides of a square, with the corner at Tours. The Germans took all the Atlantic coast, and the boundary also dipped sharply south at the north-east corner, towards Geneva, to get more of the Swiss border. The Vichy government promised to collaborate with the Germans, and one of their first acts, the next day, was to sack de Gaulle from the French army.

I put up a notice – 'American property'– at the entrance to the drive. Emotionally I felt a rawness as if I lacked a skin. I took some of Vaudin's vegetables to the village and talked to the people and to officials at the Mairie. Their mood was fatalistic – the Germans would soon occupy us. That the Maginot Line had failed was a shock. 'Where are our armies? Where are our planes?' The grocer's shelves were empty – everything had been bought and hoarded. I felt that the *gendarme* looked at me menacingly. Everyone knew the family at Les Essarts and that they were Americans. For the time being, we were untouchable.

Anthony played on the beach, supervised by Nanny, and Louise produced delicious meals of vegetables. The British colony in Dinard stayed completely calm in that short lull. The governesses and nannies, the colonels and their wives, the majors and the Russian countesses went on calling on each other, shopping and going to the library. The pink dawns rose and the red sunsets fell. The honeysuckle and roses were out.

Two days passed. The French were to stop fighting at midnight on 24 June. During that day, five motorcycles roared up the drive and the German soldiers on them dismounted, peeling off their gloves. Antoinette ran to fetch me, and I met them at the front door. In broken German, with a strong English accent, I said, 'This is American property. You have no right to enter here.'

One of the young men, Oberleutnant Junghanns, bowed slightly and introduced himself. He was pleasant and polite. He set out the terms something like this. 'We have an order to occupy this château, madam. It is convenient for our purposes in this area. Of course we will make restitution for any damage caused, and you will oblige me by making a full inventory with the assistance of one of my men. I will sign it, and it will be perfectly legal as regards any claim you may later wish to make. Officers of high rank will be living in this château. Only officers will sleep in the house – the men will be in the outbuildings or under canvas in the grounds. Please appoint the minimum rooms that you require for yourself and your staff, small rooms, and we will regard them as out of bounds.'

They were Reichswehr men, straightforward army, very correct, not SS. They did not ask for any papers – they thought I was American. They asked if the staff would work for them. I said no: they were employed by the Forbes family and paid through the American Embassy. I remember the clean, enthusiastic face of Oberleutnant Junghanns. I made him sign a paper saying that the house was being taken in defiance of the Geneva Convention. He was a nice young man.

I rang the American Embassy, but they said I could do nothing beyond making the inventory offered. I warned the staff not to accept money, coffee or anything else from the Germans, and said I had told the officers that the servants could not work for them because they were employed by Americans, neutrals.

The high-ranking officers arrived shortly afterwards by car, splendid in their scarlet-lined cloaks, elegant uniforms and black boots. They were General von Falkenhausen and Major-General Teichmann and their staff. Two hundred soldiers came with them. They were under the bullying charge of a sergeant major, a martinet with Ulbricht's cruel blue eyes and a pockmarked face. They took over the stables and outhouses and made themselves fairly comfortable.

On that first night, I put Anthony in his cot and kissed him goodnight. I thought I had done everything possible. The Germans believed I was an American. I had burned all my papers and photographs, except the passports. I went to the rocks overlooking the Channel to watch the sunset. I heard steps behind me, and looked up to see Major-General Teichmann.

'May I sit down, madam?' he asked in excellent English. 'Who am I to stop you, General?' I said. 'Please do.' We both sat on the rocks. He was a white-haired man of about fifty. 'I am an officer of the Reichswehr,' he said. I pretended ignorance and said, 'What does that mean?' 'It means that I am a professional soldier, madam.' His frankness surprised me. I suspected he was an *agent provocateur*. 'Over there is England,' he said. 'But we will never get there.' I said, 'What makes you think that? You have not far to go.' He replied, 'I know England well. We will never get there.' I was astonished. I suppose he thought I had no power to denounce him. I said, 'Well, we'll see.' He continued to talk. He told me he had four children, lived in Stuttgart, and was a Roman Catholic. He spoke of the Führer: he had met him at staff conferences. 'He has a powerful magic, you know, like a faith healer.' 'Only he doesn't use it for healing.' 'Being a Catholic, I know how to escape his magic.'

His soldiers were playing football in the field above the rocks. We looked at them, and he said, 'The sergeant major with the scarred face has more power than I have. He's in the Gestapo.' I pretended not to know what he was talking about, but he persisted. 'Everyone in your household must be careful. He is a dangerous man.'

Then he said, in a kindly voice, 'Don't worry. We'll never get there. May I ask you to do something for me? When all this is over, go to my wife and tell her of our conversation today.' I said, 'Surely there will be no need for me to do that?' 'Yes, there will. For me there will be no homecoming.' '*Für mich es wird kein Wiedersehen.*' I felt sorrow for him. I said, 'I will tell her.' But inwardly I knew we were the same: that I would not survive the war. He bade me good evening and walked away.

I had already felt that I should be wary of the sergeant major, but I did what I could when he was not around. Among the soldiers were two who looked plainly Jewish. I asked each what he was doing in the Reichswehr, and both told me that by law he was pure Aryan – clean for two generations and therefore free of taint; they ascribed their looks to being throwbacks.

I wheedled supplies from the army canteen and took them in

the van to help feed the village. A refugee centre had been set up which the German field kitchen supplied with soup. I almost lost the van when the Germans requisitioned all the cars in Britanny, but wangled a permit for it from Oberleutnant Junghanns, saying it was needed to feed the refugees, and also to get in the harvest. I still have that paper too: '*Permis de circulation permanent. Laissez-passer Madame Haden-Guest Elizabeth Louise Ruth titulaire du permis de conduire No: 1.176.354. Circulant dans la région pour les services communaux, avec une voiture Fordson 7 cv. Saint Briac s/mer le: 17 Juillet 1940.*' It was signed by the mayor and by Junghanns, as adjutant.

The sergeant major watched me suspiciously. He was certain I was gathering information to smuggle to England. He was right. While I was driving around, supposedly on community errands, I found out where the anti-aircraft guns were. I passed this news to my contact in Dinard, who gave it to young Frenchmen who were about to cross by boat to join the Free French. I passed more than one message to my mother-in-law that Anthony and I were safe.

The other servants kept out of the way of the Germans, but I saw the housekeeper Antoinette being friendly. She had supervised the rest of the staff for Auntie Forbes: '*Oui, madame. Non, madame.*' But the perfect servant is the perfect turncoat. It is a type I have distrusted since watching my nurse. They do not like me either: I am too unpredictable. If I think about it, I can predict what they will do, because they always follow power. But I do not like to think about them. I am frightened of meanness, and of people who look after Number One: they warp me, they disfigure me. Antoinette had a son in Dinard, and I caught her taking home parcels of food and coffee and sugar, the rewards of her co-operation. I scolded her angrily, and reminded her she was employed by the Forbeses. She gave me an answer of which I remember the exact words: '*Les allemands sont les maîtres maintenant, madame, et je m'incline devant eux*' – 'The Germans are the masters now and I bow to them.'

On 1 July 1940, the Germans occupied the Channel Islands, forty miles off the coast from St Briac. On the 10th, the Battle of Britain began. There was a great deal of activity at and around Les Essarts. Rubber boats were bobbing in the sea – the Germans were practising for their invasion of England. More German troops arrived from Jersey to be stationed at the château. They brought with them British clothes as souvenirs of their conquest, and proudly showed me pure wool longjohns with the price ticket, though I doubt whether they paid for them. They were expecting to be sent east for the winter, so they needed warm clothes. The bully beef, tea and Woodbines the British army had left behind in France lasted the Germans for months: it was funny but shocking to see German soldiers smoking Woodies.

Going about among the soldiers, I discovered that they were not all Nazis: some were trade unionists, Social Democrats or Liberals, one was a Quaker, one a Jehovah's Witness. I made friends with several and met them discreetly. I walked about like a *somnambule* to feel my way to who I could trust. If I had been awake and realistic I would not have done all the things I did. I could do it only because I was in between being and not being.

I am a sea person, born and bred by the sea, and when I am in the sea, I swim but do not swim, I move about it and am in it. In life, I swim in a sea of humans, swim and float along, sometimes strike out and sometimes embrace (as I might do to the waves), go under, or come out on top. But Me is not. I am a reactor, only alive when another person is there and in need.

My anti-Nazi soldier friends and I listened to the BBC's German Service on the wireless in the servants' hall. It came on at midnight, after the strokes of Big Ben. We had our ears practically on the set, it was turned down so low. One night I took them out in a rowing boat and we sang German freedom songs. We sang '*Die Gedanken sind frei*' that I had learnt from Willy: 'Thoughts are free. Who can guess them?' Later on, in the camps, we used to sing it under our breaths.

I put my head on the block time and again, but there was one act of subversion I rejoiced in. In July or August, an anti-aircraft battery arrived at Les Essarts and took up position in a wood. It was commanded by a young officer in the SS (politically created troops, unlike General Teichmann's) called Fritz Reinlein: tall, blue eyes, flaxen hair, more than handsome.

Fritz was the perfect Nordic-god type. He seemed always to have a book of poetry in his hand, by Heine or Rilke; Heine, a Jew, was forbidden, but Fritz's love of poetry was greater than his orthodoxy. I noticed that he found excuses to be near me. One night there was a little bunch of flowers on the floor of my room, thrown through the window, and then a bunch appeared with a note wrapped round it: '*Ich glaube, ich liebe dich*.' Two nights later, I actually saw Fritz below and caught his flowers in my hand. This was all quite dangerous, with Nanny and Anthony in the next room.

We began to meet in the countryside. He told me that he loved me, he could not get me out of his mind, and that he hated being in the army; when the war was over, and it would be over soon, he was one of those élite young men who were to father pure Aryan children, *Reinekinder*, for the SS centres that would administer Germany's empire. We used to walk and talk in the woods, and he recited poetry. He came from Würzburg in Bavaria, and I remember the exact address: 8 Josefplatz. By this time I was in love with him. We became lovers: it was his first time. We made love often, with urgency and passion. His comrades were ready to warn us if anyone was coming.

I felt that those moments were a victory over evil. Fritz Reinlein was not evil, but he was fated to serve evil not simply as an SS officer but by siring bullies to rule the world. Here was I, Jewish, in the arms of Hitler's shiny hope, polluting the Nazi ideals, showing Hitler and his brethren that love and dreams and poetry and tenderness were more powerful than their murderous laws. I felt the pride flood my body – I, the racial outcast, I, the politically condemned, am defeating your ridiculous cruelty and nonsensical vanity. As we lay there, he in his black uniform and I in the disguise of the underground fighter, we two alone by our love proved the Nazi laws false.

If we were discovered, I knew it might have meant death for him, and certainly for me, because the SS would have found out who I was. I lay down almost on the gallows. I remember so well how death seemed worth it. This was a colder, more profound victory than getting Willy Koska out of the torture house. My time with Fritz was my time of subtle poetic justice – I regard it as my most defiant act. And defiant acts are my life. '*Le défi!*' says my daughter Katya sadly.

The German officers in the house were courteous to me. They clicked their heels and kissed my hand and called me '*gnädige Frau*', gracious lady. I felt it was perfectly normal. I was not always thinking 'if only they knew'.

One day, Oberleutnant Junghanns came to invite me to dinner with General von Falkenhausen and General Teichmann and their officers. This, for me, was a moral dilemma. My presence at the dinner might look as though I had sold out to the enemy. But I was not French, and could not be a collaborator in the sense that a Frenchwoman would be judged to be: I was British, though they did not know it, and the British were at war with the Germans. But I was pretending to be American, and the Americans were still neutral. For myself, I was Jewish and an ex-Communist, and as myself I had to prove to them that they were wrong in their theories and their ambitions and their actions. I had 'soiled' one representative Aryan with my blood, and now I could take another triumph.

I put on a dress of Eileen's I found, and sat down with them to dinner. They were very polite – they didn't talk about the war at all; the '*gnädige Frau*' approach never stopped. But I like to go to the heart of things. I heard myself saying: 'Gentlemen, in this room and at this table, Mr Churchill and his family have very often sat down to dine. They are close friends of this family.' There was a moment's silence, then the talk went on as though nothing had happened.

What I had said was true. The Forbeses rented a house in England, Squerryes Court, near the Churchills at Westerham, and young Mary Churchill was a contemporary and friend of Fiona Forbes's and came to Les Essarts every summer. From that night on, Les Essarts was known to the Germans as 'Villa Churchill', and they burned it to the ground when they left. The Forbeses were compensated by the French government, and built a new house. Forty years later, I wrote to Ian, Auntie Forbes's son who was living at Les Essarts, and confessed that I thought it was my fault it had been destroyed.

September arrived, and the skies we watched so anxiously began to be skimmed by cold. On the 15th, the Battle of Britain ended: the British had won in the air. Fritz left for the east with his unit, after a tearful farewell. I immediately informed my contact.

At four o'clock one morning in September, there was a knock on my bedroom door. There stood Teichmann's batman, who said that the General would be arriving immediately. I received him in my dressing-gown. Teichmann too was in a dressing-gown. He was perturbed. 'We have discovered that you are not an

American citizen, as you claimed, but British. I warned you, madam, to be careful. The Gestapo is coming for you this morning. But you will not be here: I am sending you to an internment camp at Dinan. Get your child and his nanny ready. You will be leaving at 5.30.'

12

The Camps, 1940-41

Dinan was 20 kilometres inland: I was in the camp with Anthony and Nanny Stark before it was properly light. The Germans had not expected to overrun France so fast, and the internment camp, a former convent, was like one of those big muddled Victorian paintings. I greeted my old tough friends who had refused to leave Dinard. Diana the librarian had been brought in, too, but Grand Duke Vladimir soon got her released. The White Russians were not interned, because the Germans considered them to be on their side despite the pact with the Bolsheviks. Nanny admitted at last that she might have been wiser to leave France. Anthony played placidly with his teddy bear.

Then we were moved by train to a camp on an airfield near Le Mans. It was enormous – practically every British person in Northern France seemed to be there, and also a group of gypsies. There was little food, the weather was cold and conditions were primitive. This was our home until the beginning of December. Then Anthony and Nanny and I were directed with others into a train and trundled right across France to a camp called Frontstalag 142, outside Besançon at the foot of the Jura mountains, near Switzerland. During the journey I heard voices speaking English, and I called out, 'Are you English?' But instead of delighted recognition came 'We're bloody well *not* English! We're South Africans and Irish.' For the first time as a British citizen, I realised all was not solidarity in the English-speaking world.

At Besançon, we were shown into an old army barracks, the Caserne Vauban of the Napoleonic Wars. There were over four thousand in the camp. One of the youngest children was Anthony, so he was pleased when a playmate of five, Two Two Craig, arrived with her parents, Edward Gordon Craig, remembered from my signature-collecting in Paris, and his secretary and mistress Daphne Woodward. Gordon Craig was sixty-eight, one of the youngest men there. Males of under seventy or over seven were not supposed to be in our camp. Most of the inmates were elderly women – British, Polish and others.

Though we were technically internees, Besançon was like a prison. We slept on straw bags in four- or five-decker bunks, and water had to be drawn from a pump some distance away. The lavatories were open latrines. The food was abominable, and strictly rationed.

The camp had almost every female British passport-holder in the country. The Germans had rounded them up in response to the British mass internment of Germans in the Isle of Man, and we all arrived at Besançon in the first or second week of December 1940. There were Irish clairvoyants; all the British dancing girls from Paris – the Bluebells, the Tiller girls, dancers from the Folies Bergères; a few students; retired army officers with wives and teenage daughters; nuns, some of whom had been cloistered for thirty years; Palestinians; the South African Boers, who hated the rest of us; English prostitutes from the Place de l'Opéra, who were allowed to earn money by plying their trade, if they chose, with the German soldiers.

There was one huge Negro, who in peacetime had made the coffee at Maxim's in Paris; he was soon liberated, because the German officers complained about the decline in the coffee.

The Germans had found a store of 1914-18 French army uniforms which they made us wear. Our hair was cropped because of the lice, and I heard an Irish nun ask one woman 'Are you a boy or a girl, dearie?' The old barracks were infested with lice, which came out of the walls: some internees they ate completely up and some they wouldn't touch. That's why I don't believe in not kissing people with flu: some people catch it, some don't.

Since the British were the largest group, they soon established the traditional British order: they divided promptly, neatly, and quite naturally into class divisions. The governesses and nannies formed a separate caste, keeping up their pecking order and the gulf between those from titled families and the rest. About seventeen religious sects set up their own services and meetings, and Anthony, the camp's darling, was taken from one church to another – indoctrinated at the age of three. He was loved by all and everybody called him Tony. He never complained.

I was the outsider. I felt very lonely. People could not make me out: because I spoke German, some may have thought I had been planted as a spy. I did make one or two friends. A sweet girl of eighteen called Joan Hilton had the bunk opposite mine. (Anthony slept below me.) I used to pick lice out of Anthony's hair and put them in a mug. At night, the German guards came in to take roll-call, and the nicer boys would talk to us, sometimes with their helmets off. One evening I caught Joan Hilton's eye and dribbled lice into the thick Aryan hair.

We were given forms to fill in, showing family descent, blood group, and so on. I put down 'J' for Jew for Anthony and me. A few hours later I heard over the loudspeaker a summons to report to the Commandant. I found him with our forms on his desk. He was a grey-haired general of about fifty-five. '*Was ist das*?' he asked. '*Mein Fragebogen*.' ('My questionnaire.') He eyed me sternly, '*Ich meine Jot für Jude*.' ('I mean J for Jew.') He obviously thought I was falsifying my race on principle. 'Yes,' I said, 'that is the classification we have under your law.' '*Nein, nein*.' '*Ja, ja*,' I replied. But he overruled me. 'You cannot be a Jew. *Sie haben doch keine Angst vor uns*.' ('You're not afraid of us.') 'Besides, Tony is blond and blue-eyed.' With that he tore up the forms. 'Go back to the barracks,' he said, '*wir sprechen davon nicht mehr*.' ('We'll say no more about it.') For the second time in three months I felt that my life was saved by a German because I was a woman, and he was a decent man.

The German guards told us constantly that the British would soon sue for peace because they were starving, and because Britons and Germans were the same Aryan race. But one day Red Cross lorries drove in through the gates, and the news flew round – 'Food parcels from Britain'. An attempt was made to form orderly queues, but they broke up when people rushed forward to snatch a parcel. Hovering at the back were those who had been taught manners by their parents or nannies. But there were enough for all, enough for the Germans, too, who ordered that parcels should be distributed to the German nurses and guards. We protested at this dishonesty, but could not stop it. I said to one nurse, 'Well, *Schwester*, how can England be starving when you are eating English food?' 'It is not English,' she said, 'it comes from Geneva.

It is Swiss food paid for by the rich English.' But the tins said 'Made in Canada', 'Made in Australia', 'Made in Britain'. What riches were in those parcels – twenty-six items, down to salt and soap. There was bully beef, dried milk, blackcurrant purée, chocolate, steak and kidney pudding, Lyons tea, Irish stew, powdered milk and Woodbine cigarettes.

We each had the same parcel and the same daily ration, and I saw what happens after the 'equal distribution' the Communists idealise. One person would barter and bargain until she became 'rich', exchanging, say, two tins of dried milk for a packet of cigarettes. A few revelled in their own hardness: the power that I saw a woman with three fags wield over a nicotine addict was dreadful. Another gave almost everything away, smiling into the cup. Another would eat all the ration straight off and then starve, unless someone took pity on her. But if you saved up your bits of bread, they could be stolen as you slept.

We managed to have a lovely Christmas. I bribed a guard with cigarettes to get a scrawny little Christmas tree for our bunkhouse. The nuns found candles, and we held a camp concert in which the Bluebell and Tiller and Folies girls pranced and kicked and did comic routines, taking the mickey out of the Germans and some of the internees who had given themselves authority. We laughed at our masters.

At the beginning of January 1941, Edward Gordon Craig and his family were released, at the instigation of a German who visited him at Besançon. This man was building up a theatrical archive for postwar Germany – Gordon Craig's stage sets were better known in Germany and France than in Britain. The Craigs went to live in Paris.

At the end of January, I was told I was to be taken under guard to Paris with Anthony to a *résidence forcée*, house of detention. The Germans knew I was the daughter-in-law of a British Member of Parliament, therefore a *Prominente*, a prominent person, who could be used as a hostage. From the *résidence forcée* we would be sent to a hostage camp in Germany.

I cannot remember exactly how I managed to escape from our guards. We had been speaking German on the train to Paris, which had perhaps relaxed them. When we got to the Gare de Lyon, I said Anthony needed to go to the lavatory.

They did not know the station as well as I did. Somehow, I gave them the slip, and escaped into the street via the buffet, which was being cleaned, tugging Anthony behind me by his little harness. Outside, I hurried for dear life along the pavement, hiding myself in the crowd. As soon as I could, I forced myself to walk normally, still attaching myself to other walkers. In the eight months since I had been in Paris, the rules had changed. The Nazis would execute not only me if they caught me, but anyone who knew who I was and helped me. My mind darted about in search of a bolt-hole, and I chose the Hôtel Henri Quatre in the Place Dauphine, where I knew the manager, Monsieur Balitrand. Like the staunch friend he was, he gave me a room without registering. I left the hotel, still with Anthony, and made my way to the apartment of a friend, Hélène Bergerot, whose husband Pierre was a pilot in the French Air Force; I knew that their concierge could be trusted.

By incredible good fortune, I found Hélène in, with Pierre staying just that one night. He had decided to join the Free French in London, and was crossing into Vichy (Unoccupied) France the next day. He promised to make arrangements for Anthony and me, including false papers. Of all my pieces of luck, this was perhaps the greatest. No wonder some people don't believe my stories. Charmed lives are suspect lives.

While I waited for the papers, I did something audacious. I made things safer for us and for Monsieur Balitrand by reporting my presence to the Kommandantur, pretending I was still living in the *chambre de bonne* in the Porte d'Orléans area. I was right, because they didn't bother to check. I was just a little British girl to them, with a charming small son and the politeness of having learnt German.

Eventually Pierre Bergerot sent me false papers with a courier, who instructed me how to get into the Vichy zone. I was to dress as a widow, in black, and take a day train to a town near the demarcation line. From there, I should take a bus to a village beside the line, where I would be met by a guide. He gave me the passwords. The guide would help me cross the border with Anthony. Once in the free zone, most people wanting to leave France made for Marseille, the biggest port, where the American consulate was looking after British citizens.

I got some sleeping pills from Hélène, and gave Anthony half of one so he would sleep on the train. He was asleep when two

German soldiers got into our compartment. Some time later he began to wake, and muttered something in English. The Germans paid no attention, but a woman opposite asked what the language was. I said it was Dutch, learnt from his grandmother, and slipped him another half pill.

At the village, I saw the guide, and gave the password: '*Bonjour, Charles.*' He said, '*Bonjour, Charlotte*,' and took us into a room to wait for nightfall. The demarcation line was just outside the village, and ran through a field and a bed of reeds. It was regularly patrolled by German guards with bloodhounds. There was a no-man's-land of about 500 metres. The guide explained that we could go through by the reeds. We would have to stealthily walk, wait, crawl, and then wade through mud and cold water. He gave me some powder to throw to put the dogs off the scent.

I was afraid of Anthony making a noise or even crying. He was not quite four. I taught him what to do, making a game of it. We rehearsed a code of signals based on his harness and reins – a pull on his right-hand rein meant turn right, left meant turn left, and a sharp pull meant stop. When the reins were held loosely, he should carry on ahead. I told him he must be absolutely quiet and say nothing, and that nobody would say anything to him. In the little haversack he carried on his back, he had his teddy bear and his Dopey the Dwarf doll.

The night was cold and cloudy, which was better than bright and clear. We set off behind our guide in silence. We could hear the German sentries and the dogs, and see the glow of cigarettes. On we went. Minutes seemed like hours, and hours like days. Then, at last, we saw a French sentry-box occupied by a French soldier. With the scent of the mud still in our nostrils, we edged forward, still cautious, until the guide stood up and waved his hand. He said, 'We are there.' I snatched Anthony in my arms and hugged him and wept. We straightened up and walked forward. There were shots behind us. The French soldier said, 'They got that one all right.'

Another contact over the border had been alerted to expect us. He took us to the station so that we could go on to Marseille. In the train, Anthony again began to talk in English. The other person in the compartment was a young man, not tall, dressed rather flamboyantly in French clothes. He looked French, and spoke French, but he asked me in a broad Scottish accent, 'Are you English?' He was Lewis MacDonald, a wireless operator in the Royal Corps of Signals who had killed a German guard with a brick to escape from Loos prison near Lille, so he was, like me, on the Nazi death list. He was on his way to the Pyrenees and home. He had no papers, so when the German guards began going down the train he jumped off as it slowed.

13

Marseille and MI9, 1941

In Marseille, I went immediately to the American consulate with Anthony. Two British consuls, Dodds and Dean, had been allowed to stay on under Hugh Fullerton the US Consul General, and I found myself in front of Major Dodds, who seemed the model for Pierre Daninos' wonderful stuffy Englishman Major Thompson.

We had not changed our mud-stained clothes since crawling through the reeds, and we looked and smelt disgusting. I suppose I expected to be welcomed and congratulated; instead I found myself back in pre-war Society. Both Hugh Dodds (formerly of Nice) and Arthur Dean (Monte Carlo) had been in the smart set on the Riviera. They had shepherded the Duke and Duchess of Windsor out of France in June 1940.

Major Dodds obviously did not find Anthony and me at all charming. He looked glassily at us. No papers to speak of? No money? Well, he could do very little. Marseille was full of people trying to get out of France. We would have to find somewhere to live and take our places in the queue. He said, 'Your name, please, madam?' I gave it. He got a copy of *Who's Who* and looked up the name Haden-Guest. 'And you are?' 'I am Mrs Peter Haden-Guest and this is Anthony Haden-Guest.' He did not bother to conceal how utterly this changed things. He gave me money and said he would get in touch with the family in London. He said he would ask a lieutenant in the Coldstream Guards, James Langley, to lend us his flat. Jimmy Langley had escaped to Marseille and had a place in the town. When I told Major Dodds's sons Quentin and

Colin Crewe this story after the war, they laughed and said 'Just like Dad.'

Jimmy Langley was one of many British servicemen interned at Fort St Jean on the Vieux Port. The officer internees were given quite a lot of freedom: they had only to report each Monday, when there was a roll-call and an issue of rations. Most sold their rations on the black market and used the money to live out, as Langley did. He had lost an arm after being wounded at Dunkirk, and had escaped from the German military hospital by climbing through a window. He was brave and self-contained, but I don't think he ever forgave me for having ousted him from his home.

He took us to the flat, and I was soon out again exploring Marseille. It was a noisy, dirty, almost Middle Eastern city. Cafés and restaurants were crowded, but I could not buy vegetables or milk for Anthony. Then I learned about the rationing and food tickets, and discovered the black market. Green vegetables were always scarce. I used to cook the tops of radishes.

A few days later, I was sitting with Anthony in a café when in walked a tall man in his twenties with the gait of a British officer. That manner of walking with the toes pointing downwards, hands in pockets fiddling with keys, was a give-away to me, and not only to me: it betrayed many British officers to the Germans and collaborators. A man on the run had to try to lose that walk.

To my surprise, this officer was looking for me. He came over and introduced himself as Captain Ian Garrow of the Seaforth Highlanders. Captain Garrow had been stranded in June 1940 at St Valéry in Normandy, where the Highland Division had made a stand after Dunkirk, and he and some of his men had walked across France, hiding and living rough, to the Vichy zone. They had been captured and interned at Fort St Jean.

He told me that he had organised a secret escape route for British servicemen, with Tom Kenny, a Canadian businessman. The men got across the Pyrenees into Barcelona and home by way of Gibraltar or Lisbon. Some were taken off the French coast by Royal Navy submarine or Q ship. There was a constant stream into Marseille of escapers, who had got out of French or German prisons, and evaders, who had not been caught. Many thousand British soldiers were still free after the evacuation, although 34,000 were taken prisoner around Dunkirk, and later, airmen from shot-down bombers were also making their way south.

He did not tell me all this. He said, 'Tom and I can cope with the guides and the organisation, but we need a woman to look after the boys while they are waiting to be sent out, and to hide them and feed them.' He said he spoke only school French, and had heard from Jimmy Langley that I was bilingual. He suggested that I might help them, doing as little or as much as I wanted.

My heart leapt. I said I wanted to be involved to the hilt. He stressed that the work was dangerous, with the possibility of the death penalty if I were caught, since I was a civilian. I didn't tell him I was already under sentence of death in Germany. Garrow struck me as worthy of my loyalty. I felt utter confidence in him, and recognised him as a man in control, an intelligent man, dedicated to the job he had undertaken. I began to work for him with this trust – and I never had cause to waver.

This escape line that Garrow and Kenny had organised had been taken over by a new division of Military Intelligence in London, MI9, attached to MI6. MI6 had a monopoly of British undercover work behind enemy lines until July 1940, when the Special Operations Executive, SOE, was founded by Cabinet decision. MI6 suddenly had a rival, and hurried to set up the southern escape route for MI9 the same month, linking up with Garrow and his brave helpers.

MI9 sent a man called Donald Darling to Lisbon to organise the last leg of the route. His cover was vice-consul in charge of refugees, which meant he could meet people coming through from Marseille and send money and messages to Garrow with American acquaintances. It had been intended that he run MI9 from Spain, but the Spanish government made difficulties and he had to stay in Lisbon.

The Seamen's Mission in Marseille was of help to Ian Garrow. It was run by another Scot, the Rev Donald Caskie, who had been minister of the Scottish Church in Paris, where he had preached against the Nazis. He wisely left for Marseille before the Germans arrived. His residents at the Mission were mostly escapers and evaders, whom he hid and cared for until Garrow and Kenny could arrange an escape for them. The local police knew this, but they tolerated the Mission as a devil they knew and could deal with if they had to.

I met Tom Kenny, an attractive blond Canadian who spoke perfect French and was in love with the seventeen-year-old daughter of the owner of the Hôtel Martinez in Cannes. Garrow and Kenny often used that hotel, and the escape network owes a lot to the Martinez family.

I also met another very interesting member, Louis Nouveau. Nouveau and his wife Renée, a Protestant, had a large apartment on the Vieux Port. He had had an export-import business with Britain, and was mortified by the hasty armistice. His father had been one of the brave ones who stood up for Dreyfus in the Dreyfus Case of 1894, when a Jewish army officer was convicted on insufficient evidence. Louis took the unpopular side in 1940. He had met Garrow, Kenny and Langley and started to entertain British officers from Fort St Jean every Monday. He found out that Garrow and Kenny were running an escape organisation when they helped to get his son Jean-Pierre to Spain on his way to join the Free French.

Louis was well known in Marseille for his bow-ties and elegant clothes, and he became better known for his outspoken opposition to Nazis and collaborators. His style was dangerous, perhaps, but it was disarming: nobody suspected that the Nouveaus' flat was teeming with escapers and evaders. He made notes on at least 156 British and Polish servicemen who stayed there, writing in the margin of one book of his seventy-volume edition of Voltaire. His record number for one night was sixteen people.

Two others of our band were Nancy Fiocca and her husband Henri. Nancy, whose maiden name was Wake, was an Australian who openly befriended British officers in Marseille. She was a big girl in every way – she wore huge hats, flamboyant clothes, and she was open-handed and open-hearted. She was the headmistress of the black market, and there was no shortage of anything at the Fioccas': Nancy gave us drinks, cigarettes and soap. She did all the talking; Henri, a nice man, squat and square and blue-eyed, smiled but said little. He ran a scrap yard and acted as Garrow's banker and treasurer. (Louis Nouveau also raised and gave money.)

Auntie Forbes and the Haden-Guests had been busy. Peter had arranged for papers and Clipper tickets so that Anthony and I could fly from Portugal to New York and live in America. I was summoned to the consulate by Major Dodds. 'Mrs Haden-Guest, your husband wants you in America, so there is no question of repatriation to England.' I said, 'I will go soon, Major, but Anthony needs for a while to stay in one place. He does not seem quite well.'

This was true. The people at the consulate advised me to take him to Dr Rodocanachi, an English-born Greek who drank Earl Grey tea. He diagnosed rickets, caused by lack of vitamin D. Dr Georges Rodocanachi was sixty-four when I met him. He had qualified as a doctor in Paris and set up practice in Marseille, specialising in children. During the First World War, he had renounced his British citizenship and become French so as to join the Chasseurs Alpins as a doctor. Like the Nouveaus, he had been disgusted by Pétain's capitulation. He tore off his ribbon of the Légion d'Honneur, which he had been awarded on the battlefield at Verdun by Pétain himself.

Georges Rodocanachi had been enrolled by the American consul as an examining medical officer for Jewish immigrants who wanted to be accepted by the United States. As well as hospital work and his practice, Dr Rodo examined more than a thousand Jews in two years. Hugh Fullerton also appointed him to represent British interests on the Medical Repatriation Board, which was a legal way for Allied soldiers and airmen to be allowed to go home. Dr Rodo coached several candidates to seem iller or worse wounded than they were. In February or March, he arranged for Jimmy Langley to be repatriated because of his arm, and Jimmy gave up his flat.

Ian Garrow told me to say to Major Dodds that I was moving to the country for Anthony's sake and that I would send him my address. I looked for a place where I would be inconspicuous, and found a brothel, 5 rue Belloi, which let rooms to clients by the hour. The *patron* was sympathetic to the British: he let Anthony and me have a room without registering. Garrow was rather shocked, I think, that I was living in a brothel, and that I knew so much about them. At 5 rue Belloi, each room had a huge double bed, mirrors, a wardrobe, and a bidet and basin behind a curtain. The sheets were changed regularly. Though no bedroom door had a lock, the police never went upstairs, they just inspected the register. I felt comfortable and safe. I was in sympathy with the girls and the maids and they looked after Anthony when needed.

In March 1941, the Vichy authorities moved the British prisoners from Fort St Jean to St Hippolyte du Fort, about 160 kilometres to the north-west. When Ian Garrow heard they were leaving Marseille, he failed to turn up for roll-call, and went underground. Vichy, under pressure from the Germans, asked Mr Dean to leave France, and he went in April, followed by Major Dodds.

Visiting Dr Rodocanachi with Anthony, I recognised the spirit of this dedicated man. When I was sure I could trust him, I told him what Garrow and Kenny were doing and asked him to join us. He said he would discuss it with his wife, Fanny.

Fanny was a great and brave lady. The Rodocanachis came in with us, and offered Ian Garrow a room, which would be safer than living in a stranger's house. Their maid Séraphine was equally staunch. Their apartment on an upper floor in the rue Roux de Brignoles was a 'safe house' for nearly 200 men between June 1941 and February 1943. They had ten rooms, including three for the doctor's practice, arranged around three small courtyards, or wells as they are called in England.

Dr Rodocanachi introduced me to Fanny's nephew Georges Zarifi, and I recruited him into our line. He made the proviso that his parents should not know. His mother, Fanny's sister, was head of the Marseille Red Cross, and she never did know about her son and brother-in-law being in the Resistance until things went wrong. Another Greek, Mario Prassinos, also came in with us that summer of 1941, so it was not surprising that the Germans' code name for us was Acropolis, as we later found out. I also recruited the Lobbes, a French Jewish couple from the North who were waiting for their American papers. He became a big noise in the United Nations after the war. They hid soldiers, and sometimes looked after Anthony for me.

Eileen Tailleux, in Aix, was helping the Resistance, and always willing to have Anthony. The wife of another of Yves Rigelot's group, Hildegarde Berton who married Roland Berton, was in Collioure with a child, which was another place for Anthony and a bed for me on my journeys.

Finally Ian Garrow found a permanent guardian for Anthony. A gentle, dreamy young schoolteacher, Jean Fourcade, had asked his help to get to England to join the Free French. Ian recognised that Jean was brave and reliable but perhaps not suited to active service. Sensitively, Ian persuaded him that looking after the child would be the equivalent of military service. So Jean took Anthony to live with him in the rocks above Marseille, where he kept a pet fox. Anthony called it '*le loup*', the wolf.

There were helpers in the North who fed our line. Garrow went up and came back very enthusiastic about an Englishman, 'Captain' Harold Cole, an evader from the British Expeditionary Force who used the name Paul Cole. He had admitted to Ian that he was in fact a sergeant. He had had some daring successes getting men through to Vichy. Shortly afterwards he arrived in Marseille. I met him and

Garrow at room 530 at the Hôtel de Noailles, which we rented for our meetings, and where we kept money and some papers. The hotel concierge was a friend of the Fioccas and we thought we could trust him. Paul Cole was tall, lanky, red-haired, shifty-eyed and ingratiating. He shook hands in a vulgar way, and his hand felt like a fish.

To me, human beings are like materials. You touch them and you feel the silk or cashmere or cotton or Terylene. When Cole had left, I said to Garrow, 'I don't want to work with him – I don't trust him.' Garrow argued, on the grounds that he was already arranging escapes and doing it extremely well. He said, 'You've worked with Greeks, Jews, Belgians, Canadians, Australians, Poles, French and now you object to one of your own, one of us.' I went on defending my instinct. In the end, Garrow produced his last word – 'George'. 'George' was his shorthand for our work, for patriotism, for duty. We all knew that George was not to be argued with. I said I would do what I had to for George, but that I did not trust Paul Cole. Cole began to work with us, travelling back and forth across France from his base at Lille, near the Belgian border, to Marseille, shepherding little groups of British servicemen.

I was made the contact between the Seamen's Mission and St Hippolyte du Fort. I would go to St Hippolyte by train and wait in the café to meet the officers and men, who were allowed out because they had given their *parole d'honneur*. I got on well with the camp's guards: I spoke French, I was one of them – not a blonde blue-eyed foreigner. The rest of the world always disliked the British for their effortless superiority. The upper classes have it for obvious reasons, the working classes have it because of their strong sense of humour: they made the Nazis furious in the prison camps by joking at terrible treatment. The British do not know hatred, for their emotional life is pretty repressed, if not feeble. I chatted to the prisoners. I was their family life. One or two of the officers were a bit in love with me. Garrow did not approve. In war the relationship between man and woman is so desperate and so intense and so needed.

There was a strict hierarchy for escaping. Of the men waiting at St Hippolyte or the Seamen's Mission, Ian Garrow chose first the airmen, and the best-trained of those, because the War Office needed RAF men and paid for their escape on a scale related to training. Group captains were worth £20,000, wing commanders £8,000, a pilot £800, and an ordinary airman or soldier only £200 – we didn't see many ordinary soldiers passing through our hands. This hierarchy shocked me at first, but Ian explained that it was purely practical. It broke my heart to have to tell prisoners that the War Office did not yet need them back in Britain.

Pilots were the most difficult to handle. They were literally air men, hopelessly lost on the ground. One day they had been up in their element delivering bombs, the next they were skulking in a foreign country, dressed in other people's clothes and being told by strangers not to pull the lavatory plug. We made our charges wear bedroom slippers, to muffle the sound and prevent them going out; we allowed them out only when we took them to be photographed for their false papers. The pilots were timid even when they were carrying phoney papers and wearing the disguise we found for them. Their fright perhaps contributed towards their arrogance – they seemed to think that we, who were trying to hide them, should be grateful to them. The Polish pilots were even worse than the British. They were longing to die: they were good at dying. They ignored safety precautions and cared very little what happened to them. That was their temperament, and we had to convince them that they had to live, to get back to fight again. Soldiers were in comparison marvellously safe on the ground and to conduct about, and a holiday after the boys of the air.

I once had a row with Louis Nouveau for taking a risk that might have drawn attention to himself and blown an escaper, Sergeant Herbert, but he thought me the indiscreet one. He described in the book he wrote after the war, *Des Capitaines par Milliers*, how I walked about with my '*petit garçon dont l'immense chapeau de paille de forme mexicaine l'empêchait de passer inaperçu*' (little boy whose huge Mexican straw hat prevented him from going unnoticed).

The difference between me and the others was that I was a professional, trained in undercover work, and knew what was safe and what was not. They were fearful of everything, and as they did not know my background thought me a liability. When I went out strikingly dressed, with Anthony in his big Mexican hat (he also had a Glengarry one of the soldiers had given him), I was doing it on purpose to establish an extrovert character. The local security men, the Secrète, would never believe that so obvious a young mother and child could be doing partisan work. This allowed me to be invisible at other times, when I would dress dowdily and quieten my voice and actions and move about unseen. Louis had to admit that I was '*une enthousiaste, se dévouant corps et âme à Garrow et à l'organisation.*' I did indeed love Ian, and had begun an affair with him. He called me Eskimo Nell.

I was given the responsibility for hiding four young airmen from St Hippolyte waiting to leave France. Trusting my experience of brothels, I went to the red light district in the Vieux Port and into the first one I saw. The *patron* was a fat Italian, sweaty, with his sleeves rolled up. I told him I wanted a room and he said it would be expensive; he assumed I was a tart. 'It's not for me – it's for four boys,' I said, and he looked even more suspicious. 'Do you know what this place is for?' 'That's why I'm here,' I said, and I took all our lives in my hands. 'They're four British airmen. I need to hide them for a few days before they can make a run for England. They have no papers, and it will be a risk. Will you help?' For a frightening moment he looked at me, then he said, 'I'm Italian, but I'm here because I'm anti-Fascist. I can't get a job – all I can do is keep a brothel. Bring your boys.' I was so relieved I flung my arms around him. Then I rushed out into the street. It was a miserable grey day, but to me the sun shone and the sky was blue.

I took my boys to the brothel and left them with some bread, smoked fish, oranges and a bottle of wine. I tried to make them draw up a rota for sleeping in the bed, and paid off the *patron*. They were very young and very trusting, and as green as little apples. While I was there, we heard noises from next door. There was a cry from the woman. The boys looked worried. 'Is someone hurting her?' 'No, no,' I said, 'it's just the French – they're noisy people.' There were groans and whimpers. One said, 'Are you sure you shouldn't get somebody to go and help her?' I had to tell them some facts about a brothel. Four young faces looked completely unconvinced. They thought a brothel was somewhere you got soup.

Anthony was happy in the hills with his friend Jean Fourcade and the fox. Jean often brought him down to see me. He was wonderful with him. Some male nannies are better than females; when a man is good with children, he is usually better than a woman.

The passing of messages to and from Donald Darling in Lisbon was risky. We hit on a method by accident. An American journalist we were in contact with was arrested in Clermont-Ferrand, but Tom Kenny picked up his suitcase before the Vichy police went to collect it, and brought it to my room in the rue Belloi. Among the clothes and papers was a box of little balloons. 'These will be fun for Anthony,' I said. 'He can't have them,' said Tom Kenny, 'I need them. I am getting married.' He had become engaged to Sue Martinez. Ian Garrow said, 'Sorry, you'll have to do without them. George.' Garrow used the French letters to hold messages to be inserted into toothpaste or face cream. I was put in charge of the French letter post office. One day Ian came to my room and found Anthony amusing himself by holding the balloons under the tap one by one. He was not pleased.

The cinemas in Marseille were full, because of the swollen population, and a film shortage forced cinema-owners to dig out old British and American movies: *Fury* (1936), *Green Pastures* (1936), *The Private Life of Henry VIII* (1933, made by Korda), all the Laurel and Hardys (no Chaplin – he was banned, as were Russian films, by German order to Vichy). The German-approved studios had been busy, and I remember seeing the new version of *Jew Süss* (1940), a remake of Michael Balcon's 1934 film of Lion Feuchtwanger's novel satirising anti-semitism. The Nazi film followed the story well enough, but the anti-semites were the heroes. Another difference in the Goebbels *Jew Süss* was the pornography. I was with Ian Garrow and two other hard-boiled fighting men, and I sensed them sitting rigid in their seats as the Jew raped Aryan women in one amazing scene after another. Technically the film was excellent, with faultless cutting, photography and rhythm, but it left us with a very nasty taste in our mouths. One man with us was rather anti-Semitic when he went in but came out converted. A few French youngsters said something about '*sales Juifs*', but the general French reaction was the same as ours. As a contrast to this was the showing of *The Private Lives of Elizabeth and Essex* (1939). Of course we were prejudiced for it, but so were ninety per cent of the French audience, who clapped wildly in the most inappropriate places, starting with the title.

The Haden-Guests and Auntie Forbes kept up their pressure on the American consul, and I was told I should take Anthony to the United States as soon as possible. I stalled. I said Anthony was too ill to travel yet. The consular officials were ignorant of the escape route, at least officially.

Garrow kept the strands of his activities separate, letting each of us know only as much as we needed to. This was the basic rule of intelligence work, and he was cautious and discreet by nature. He recruited another young man to our band, Pierre d'Harcourt, the son of Robert d'Harcourt, a leading French Catholic active in the Resistance. I loved Pierre, but I knew very little of what he did.

Pierre was in love with Nadia de Pastré, daughter of the Countess Lily de Pastré, an American who lived at the château de Montredon near Marseille with a butler, footmen and an English nanny. The count was dead. Nadia was in love with someone else, but she and Nanny were always willing to hide men if we needed. The countess was not supposed to know, but she did.

One day Garrow and Pierre and I were asked to lunch at the Pastrés' château. The table was laid with much silver and glittering glass, and presided over by the Countess. The dishes were offered by a footman wearing white gloves. At the other end of the table sat Nanny, acting as the second hostess as a quiet challenge to Vichy. The meal was a welcome change from how we lived in Marseille, and the last ritual was the most elegant: the butler went round the table with a silver salver upon which each guest gracefully placed a food ticket.

A British nanny was always a signal to me. I met a rich young couple from Alsace with two babies, and when I heard they had a Scottish nanny I knew they would help the line. Those nannies were an Allied network on their own. They brought up their children to be against any bully like Hitler. It dawned on me that the nanny was the person responsible for British civilisation. Her main lessons were modesty and self-discipline – old-fashioned words maybe, but what wonderful results. It was the nanny who produced those British who were so admired in the rest of the world for their fairness, their politeness, their patience.

Germany declared war on Russia in June 1941, so Britain gained an ally. In June or the beginning of July, a new member joined us from St Hippolyte du Fort, Pat O'Leary, a naval officer of thirty who had come literally out of the blue. On 25 April 1941, he and three companions were captured when their motorboat was chased by a Vichy coastguard cutter near the Spanish border. He told the police that he was Patrick Albert O'Leary, a French Canadian serving in the Royal Navy, and they sent him to St Hippolyte. Garrow met him when he was out on parole, recognised that he had character and ability and told him where to come if he escaped. He did get out and made his way to Marseille.

Pat was good-looking, fair and blue-eyed, and he spoke perfect French with a northern accent. I suspected that he was a doctor, because once he tapped Anthony all over very professionally and confirmed that he had rickets. None of us knew his true background until after the war, but I turned out to be right. He was a Belgian, Albert-Marie Guérisse, who had served as a doctor with a Belgian cavalry regiment until Belgium capitulated, and in May 1940 escaped from Dunkirk. In September, under the name O'Leary, he became a lieutenant-commander in the Royal Navy and first officer of HMS *Fidelity*, a ship which had been the French *Rhin* until her captain, Langlais, took her over to the British, who used her for SOE work. Guérisse/O'Leary told only Langlais that he was a doctor, because he wanted to continue the fight more actively.

Pat became one of the great heroes of the war, but perhaps the people who became heroes needed the war. He told me that he did not mind dying, because his first wife had committed suicide and his second marriage broke up around 1939. He was not a bad husband – it was just that he was attracted to neurotic women, as I am to over-refined men.

What he had done before dawn the morning he was captured was to drop two SOE agents on a beach near the Étang de Canet and take the *Fidelity*'s lifeboat on to Collioure to pick up fourteen Polish airmen. They were not there, and the SOE men were taken prisoner. After he escaped, Pat O'Leary moved into the Rodocanachis' flat with Garrow, and MI9 gave us a coded signal on the BBC that he was to stay with our line.

One day, Ian Garrow, Pat and I went to Nîmes for a meeting with the captain who acted as escape organiser in St Hippolyte, and we were joined by a soldier who had escaped from there for the second time. Who should it be but Lewis MacDonald, my friend from the train. We four spent two or three days together in one room, and Little Mac, as we called him, put me in a bag at bedtime and tied it round my neck because he did not trust Pat and Ian, sleeping either side of me. Mac was quite a danger to most girls himself. This was the beginning of a lifelong friendship. Little Mac's father was a forestry worker in Murthly, whose wife ran away leaving Mac, six, and three younger children. They were taken from his father by the authorities, which broke his heart, and he died in a mental home. Mac and his brother were sent to an approved school for delinquents. Mac joined the army at fifteen and a half, followed by his brother David (killed at sixteen in the Far East) and sister Isabel.

I persuaded Garrow that Mac should be sent home down the line – the War Office was bound to benefit from a man like him. Mac was to cross into Spain with two Argyll and Sutherland soldiers and three airmen, but only Mac got through. The airmen were not fit enough to complete the Pyrenean crossing, and the Argylls got picked up on the train to Barcelona. Mac saw the Guardia Civil boarding the train twice, but slipped off at the other end and got back on behind them.

Pat met Paul Cole on one of the man's trips south, and did not like him any more than I did. Cole was a boaster and tried to charm women, but Nancy Fiocca disliked him too. However, he seemed to be doing well for 'George'. He was very fond of Anthony, and brought him cherries. People who are not straight usually try to make friends with children, to regain their innocence.

My work was often routine. There was constant tension, of course, people coming and going, Ian Garrow's contacts showing up and disappearing again. I went regularly to St Hippolyte, helped to find food and clothing for the boys hidden in safe houses, and kept constantly in touch with the Fioccas, the Rodocanachis, the Nouveaus and the rest of the group, passing messages, arranging for couriers between France and Spain and Lisbon, keeping my head down and taking every possible precaution – because I always felt we were being watched.

We were safe so far, I thought, not because we were clever but because the police and Vichy did not want to catch us. So long as we operated extremely carefully, we were in very little danger: except, as it turned out, from the traitor in our ranks.

14

Women's Prison, Marseille, 1941

One day in July I went to the rendezvous at the Hotel de Noailles. There I was to meet several contacts, including Tom Kenny and Pat O'Leary. I had also arranged for Jean Fourcade to bring Anthony. Pat arrived first, and I thought nothing of it when the concierge called me on the telephone in room 530 to come down: two men were asking for me.

I left Pat and went to the lobby, expecting to see two contacts, but the men were strangers. They said they were from the BMA (which had taken over from the Deuxieme Bureau – in other words, secret police) and asked me to go with them. I said I was waiting for my little son, and the policemen said, 'We won't keep you long. We just want to ask you a few questions and then you can go.'

I remember walking to their car and being driven to Fort St Nicolas, which faced Fort St Jean at the mouth of the port, all the while feeling my heart thump as I worked out lines of defence. I had no idea what they wanted, or what would happen to Pat, and the others who turned up at the hotel. One of the concierges, I believed, had betrayed us, but I put my faith in the other, the Fioccas' friend, to let them know I had been arrested.

When we reached the fort, the two policemen disappeared for an hour or so. When they returned they said, 'We must find Captain Garrow. It is vital that we warn him of his imminent arrest.' Ian Garrow was at the Rodocanachis', but I was not going to tell them that. 'Captain Garrow has left France,' I said. 'He's back in England.' They said, 'You worked with him, didn't you?' I said, 'I know him very well. We're both British, and naturally we know one another here.' They began to get angry. They shook me by the shoulders and pushed me about. They brought their faces close to mine and jeered, 'Do you know why you're here? You were betrayed by your own countryman. No Frenchman betrayed you, no Greek, nobody but one of your own.' I remembered Ian saying of Cole: 'He's one of our own.' I was charged with organising the escape of British personnel. My great fear was that I would be extradited to Germany to face the Nazis.

The police brought in Francis Blanchain, a new man in the network, a Mauritian who had come to us because he wanted to join the Free French. I had been due to meet him that afternoon at the hotel. In came Tom Kenny, Mario Prassinos, and Pat O'Leary too. The police had obviously waited to catch whoever came to the room.

Pat was tremendous. He came in swinging a suitcase, pretending to be a commercial traveller. He had papers to confirm this cover, and the case was the perfect finishing touch. When I had not come back to room 530, he had picked up an empty suitcase and walked downstairs. He had been arrested there, probably identified by the treacherous concierge. At the fort, he waited to be questioned, calmly ignoring the rest of us. We were all interrogated separately, but none of us admitted to knowing where Garrow was.

Jean Fourcade and Anthony were brought in. Anthony was pleased to see me, and did not question the surroundings. Jean looked crestfallen and then nervous as Anthony began talking about life in the hills with him and '*le loup*'. When Jean was questioned, he told the truth – that he had been looking after Anthony most of the time outside Marseille. Though the police pressed, there was nothing to be got out of him, and he was released, to the relief of his friends more used to inventing.

Mario said he had only come to congratulate Tom Kenny, who had married Sue Martinez three days earlier, and he was released. He went to the Nouveaus with the news. At first they would not listen to him, as they had not met him before and feared he was an *agent provocateur*. But when they did, they realised the seriousness of the situation: four members of the organisation being interrogated. Pat talked away to the police in his perfect French, and eventually he was allowed to go.

Anthony was shut up with me. He slept on a table, with telephone books for a pillow, but when he was awake I kept him close to me, often in my arms. I was interrogated for several days, constantly shouted at, and occasionally struck with a fist or the palm of a hand – nothing too dreadful, except that the repetition of the same questions was psychologically wearing. Finally, they gave up on Blanchain, Kenny and me, and we were held for eventual trial. Not that they told us that. They said that they had nothing against me as I had told them nothing, and that I was to be freed. Anthony and I were driven back into the city. But not to the Hotel de Noailles. The car drew up outside a large old fortress with barred windows. We got out. 'Is this freedom?' I asked. 'No, this is a prison. If you do not tell us where to find Garrow, you will never see your child again.'

I knelt on the pavement and hugged Anthony, knocking off his Glengarry cap. I remember saying, 'Darling, be sure to brush your teeth every day and go on your potty.' At the end, there was none of that film nonsense such as 'Your mother has gone, in the fight for liberty': there was the child's physical well-being. That is motherhood. Anthony said 'Yes, Mama,' and he was put back in the car.

One of my escorts rang the bell. The gates opened and I went in. The prison was called Les Presentines and the building dated from the Middle Ages. I was shown into an office, where guards took away all my papers, money and belongings. I signed a receipt, and was handed over to other male guards, who stripped and examined me. Then they wavered. One said to the other: '*On lui fouille dans la nature?*' (search her vagina). The other said: '*Elle est parentée de Churchill . . . Que'est-qu'on fait?*' Rumour must have reached them that the Haden-Guests were related to Churchill. The decision was: '*Bon. On la fera ecarter les jambes et tousser*' (make her spread her legs and cough). I realised that this gave me a future hiding-place. Having been a good gymnast, I could cough without anything dropping out. The girls in the Paris brothel would have been proud of me. I was allowed to dress, and was put in a cell on my own.

My cell was hot, although the stone walls were thick, and there was no light except what came through a tiny barred opening in one corner of the ceiling. On the floor were a straw mattress, a bucket of water for washing and a lavatory bucket. Twice a day a cup of water, grey bread, soup and a plate of maggoty rice were pushed through the door. I decided to treat the maggots as protein, and ate them. I soon lost track of the days, and often the hour of day. I remember shouting through the *espion*, the spyhole in the door, 'What time is it?' and the female guard, who was a Corsican like all prison screws in France, answering, 'Are you catching a train?' She knew I might be executed. They were mostly lesbians and they got young criminal prisoners to be their girlfriends; for that those prisoners were allowed to serve the soup. I thought of my comrades, Garrow and all, and trembled for their safety. I knew somehow that Anthony would be all right. I menstruated for the first time in three months, very heavily. When I saw the clots of blood in the lavatory bucket I thought I had lost Garrow's baby. Women soon stopped menstruating in the prisons and camps.

People think time must go slowly in prison, but it goes fast: probably because you think a lot. You are woken at six and wait for the *gamelle*, a metal pot with what's supposed to be tea. If you have a window, you watch for a cloud or for the sun to reach you. You savour children's voices in the street and clocks striking. If you are in a cell with others, it goes even faster.

I was taken out of solitary and put in with six to eight other women. My cellmates were Gaullists. There was a little elderly woman called Margaret Peyret, who had worked in a small bar and had helped Gaullists escape. She had TB and coughed incessantly, bringing up blood. Every day she pushed her little bit of bread over to me, saying, 'You are young, take it. Please eat it so that you can carry on the fight. I'm useless now.' And she did die in that foul prison, a heroine and a saint to her last breath. These things are not forgotten by the survivors.

The Gaullists were considered the lowest of the low, traitors - they were called '*les politiques*', the politicals. It was a terrible loneliness. We could not be put with the ordinary criminals because they beat us up. We saw them only in the exercise yard, which we were allowed into once a week. The criminals and Communist prisoners went out every day. I remember a quarrel between a Gaullist girl and an Arab prostitute in the yard. The Gaullist called the tart a murderess, and the Arab shouted, 'I only killed my *mec* (pimp). You betrayed your country.'

When a new prisoner came to Les Presentines, each political group tried to make contact with her in the hope she was one of theirs. I heard about a woman called Colette, who with her man, René Sanson, was a leader of the local Resistance. René was in Fort St Nicolas. I saw Colette through the spyhole and talked to her on the water pipes, but I did not meet her until after the war. She and René both survived, and married.

Our cell was full of fear and dirt. There was one slop bucket for six women, one mug of water apiece, and the unvarying grey bread and maggoty rice. We would lie on our straw mattresses and take it in turns to describe what we would be doing with the day if we were free.

A girl would tell how she would get up and see her husband off to work. She went shopping, buying cheese, vegetables, meat and fruit. We heard what shops she went to and what she and the shopkeeper said to each other. She went home and made lunch, her husband came home for lunch, and they made love. He went back to work, and she made an elaborate dinner, describing exactly how she prepared and cooked each dish. In the evening he came home again, they had a *vin blanc* and ate the dinner. He praised and criticised it minutely. Then they went to bed. The most important was the description of their love life, and what they liked doing: from the back, from the front, with their fingers, with their mouths. Each woman described everything he did to her and she asked for, and everything she did to him and he asked for, with no inhibitions, in fact with exaggerations. By the time she had finished, she was exhausted. Everyone told their own story, elaborating more and more, vying to fantasise about the wonderful food and the terrific love-making. It helped to make up for the fact that we were starving. We were forced to watch our cruel Corsican guards eating their long *baguette* sandwiches in front of us very slowly with lip-smacks. I found I did not long for delicacies like oysters or steak, but clean fresh simple food. I fantasised about a jug of milk, a lettuce with plenty of heart, two new-laid brown eggs, a loaf of warm new bread.

Some of the girls had been through their interrogation and trial in Fort St Nicolas and were waiting to be sentenced. When a woman was told she was going back to court, her cellmates helped to make her proud and beautiful. We scraped chalk from the walls to powder her face, and used the pink tooth stone – we had no toothpaste – as rouge and lipstick. Paint from the door could be scraped off and softened in the sun for kohl. Her hair was cut with sharpened corset bones. Whenever a woman came in wearing a corset, we pulled the bones out and rubbed them on the flagstones until they were sharp enough for cutting. We made curl papers, *bigoudis*, from the letters we got from our lawyers. If anybody came in wearing a good dress, it was carefully folded and kept pressed under the straw to be used for a court appearance. Girls walked into their military tribunals, which meant perhaps death or twenty-five years, like the prettiest dolls ever. And when a woman came back and it was the death sentence, we sent it round the prison on the water pipes: tap tap tap.

Sometimes the women in the cell experienced a rare mood of oneness. The sky was usually blankly blue in our small window, but on this particular day a little cloud appeared and began to travel across it. The journey of the cloud enthralled us. What had it floated over before it reached Les Presentines? Where would it go next? We gazed at it and imagined it slowly sailing over fields and farms and woods. It would cross Provence, looking down on red roofs and lavender bushes. Its shadow would pass over unbroken forests. It would reach peaks with snow in the crevices and mountain goats on the patches of grass. When it slipped from sight on the other side of the window, we were meditative and stronger.

We tried to keep our self-respect, but the conditions were horrible. Once when I was carrying out the foul-smelling slop-bucket I slipped and splashed the mess on myself. I wept and felt degraded for the first time.

One day a fair, blue-eyed German girl, very haughty, was shown into the cell. We got out of her that she was a countess, had come from North Africa, and could not understand why she was shut up in Les Presentines with spies, prostitutes and Gaullists. She was too grand to talk much to anybody.

That week I was called out of the cell. Guards took me across Marseille in handcuffs to Fort St Nicolas. '*Enlevez les menottes!*' My handcuffs were taken off and I was shown into the office of Captain Dutour, the judge of the Tribune Militaire, and left alone with him. In Vichy France, not everyone was pro-German. Dutour said something like: 'I wish to ask you a favour, madame. In your cell is a German countess we suspect of having collected military intelligence in North Africa and to be working for Admiral Canaris (head of the Abwehr, the Intelligence section of the German War Office). We believe she is communicating somehow with him, and we must see anything she writes before she hands it to her lawyer. Does she write in the cell?' I said she did, and that she kept her notes under her mattress. Dutour suggested that before the next of our weekly exercise periods, I should say I was ill, and try to copy what the countess had written. I managed to copy and translate what I found and get it to Dutour, who was pleased with his little coup and grateful to me. He admitted that if the German girl had suspected me and told the German authorities, they would have demanded I be handed over to them. I said, 'I am here to live and die in the fight against Hitler.'

The military police who took me to and from Captain Dutour's office called me '*Elisabeth l'anglaise*', or '*Elisabeth d'Angleterre*'. I have not a drop of English blood, but they wanted me to be English so I became English. For our work I had always become what I needed to be. Playing a part liberated me. It never wiped anything out of me because I never was.

After about a month, I was put back in a cell of my own. I hoped this meant I was soon to be released, but first I had to be interrogated by the Tribune Militaire.

On 1 September, as I found out later, the British government authorised payment by the American consulate in Marseille for defence counsel for Tom Kenny and me. Louis Nouveau knew a young lawyer, Gaston Defferre, and my friends commissioned him to represent me. He wrote to make an appointment.

We were each allowed to see our lawyer alone, cooped up with him in a little cell we called the '*cage aux poules*', the hencoop. The guard stood outside. Gaston Defferre came in, good-looking, elegantly dressed in the British style, and unsmiling. I had been worried about meeting him. He could have been a Vichyite, or even an agent for the Germans, and what news would he bring? I had built up such hopes and fears of this contact with the outer world that I burst into tears. But Defferre did not comfort me. He was all business. Coldly and precisely, he said, 'Madame, your friends have sent me to take care of your case and conduct your defence.' He explained the technicalities. He did not bother to reassure me or promise the improbable, but said only, 'We shall do our best to get you out of here.' I somehow knew that Defferre's best, and Garrow's best, would be very good. I decided I could trust him, and I said I wanted to send notes to Ian Garrow. I asked him to bring a small pencil and some paper on his next visit. He nodded, but looked rather surprised when I also asked for condoms so that I could hide the messages inside myself. I already knew the danger of hiding anything under the straw mattress, and we were stripped and searched thoroughly before and after any contact with the outside world. But I trusted I could avoid a vaginal examination.

My first message warned that Cole was a traitor; although I hoped they had already acted on that. It was amusing to deliver these messages to the cool, elegant Defferre. He had to take the moist rubber with the note in it and surreptitiously transfer it to his briefcase. He told me there was a chance of my being handed over to the Gestapo, and brought money so that I could bribe the guards if necessary. This went into the vagina. I had to spread my legs and cough, and all stayed in – one million francs.

Always Gaston Defferre remained aloof, professional and uninterested in his own safety. He left my heart lonely but my mind securely at peace. I found out that he was Colette's lawyer, too. I admired him particularly when one day he could not come, so sent a young woman from his office instead. Her name was Ginette Kahn, and she was Jewish. In Vichy France at that time, in late 1941, it was not just imprudent for a professional man to employ a Jew: it was an open expression of defiance.

After the war, I read what had been going on behind the scenes in the American External Affairs papers which are now in Washington.

FILE July 28, 1941

IMMEDIATE AND STRICTLY CONFIDENTIAL

RB1-2622

The American Ambassador presents his compliments to His Majesty's Principal Secretary of State for Foreign Affairs and, with reference to Mr Loudon's letter of May 22, 1941 to Mr Achilles regarding Mrs Peter Haden Guest and previous correspondence, has the honor to cite below for the strictly confidential information of Mr Eden the substance of a message dated July 25, 1941 from the American Consul General at Marseille, through the American Embassy at Vichy: 'Despite repeated warnings from me to obey instructions and repeated promises from her, Mrs Haden Guest refused to leave France where, for some time, her position has been known to be dangerous. She has been placed under arrest now, along with Thomas Ken—, and it is understood that Captain Garrow, who is known to Ambassador Hoare, is being sought actively but has disappeared. The French police state that the charges are serious and that the case is in the hands of the military authorities, although I have been unable as yet to see the prisoners. My suspicions are that the charges include assistance rendered in the escape of

British soldiers and De Gaullist recruits and possibly espionage ...

LONDON, July 28, 1941 JDB:MJR

FILE

IMMEDIATE AND STRICTLY CONFIDENTIAL

RBI-2644

The American Ambassador presents his compliments to His Majesty's Principal Secretary of State for Foreign Affairs and, with reference to Mr Winant's note RBI-2622 of July 28, 1941, regarding Mrs Peter Haden Guest, has the honor to state that according to a correction received the words underlined in Mr Winant's note under reference should read as follows:-

Page 1: Thomas Kenney

LONDON, July 29, 1941 JDB:MVG

MMG DUMMY Rec'd August 10, 1941

INCOMING TELEGRAM

FROM VICHY

AMERICAN EMBASSY

LONDON

222 August 9, 1pm

A strictly confidential message referring to the embassy's (Vichy) 214 July 25, 1pm regarding British Interests and concerning Lonsdale, Guest and Kenney.

LEAHY

MR JOHNSON

MR BEAM

FILE

RBI-2803

The American Ambassador presents his compliments to His Majesty's Principal Secretary of State for Foreign Affairs and, with reference to Mr Winant's notes Nos RBI-2622 of July 28 and RBI-2644 of July 29, 1941, regarding Mrs Peter Haden Guest and Thomas Kenney, has the honor to set forth below the substance of a telegram dated August 9, 1941, received from the American Embassy at Vichy:-

The Consul General at Marseille ... has been so far unsuccessful in his efforts to see Haden Guest and Kenney. It would be appreciated if you would ascertain whether the British Government is willing to authorize for these two the payment of expenses of defense counsel.

LONDON, August 11, 1941 JDB:ADF

Tel to Vichy. Sept 1, 1941. JDB/

No KW15

Immediate

His Majesty's Principal Secretary of State for Foreign Affairs presents his compliments to the United States Ambassador and with further reference to His Excellency's note No RBI-2803 of the 11th August transcribing the text of a telegram from the United States Embassy at Vichy regarding ... Mrs Peter Haden Guest and Mr Thomas Kenny, has the honour to request that the United States Embassy at Vichy may be informed by telegraph that authority is given for payment from British official funds of any reasonable expenses which may be necessary for defence counsel for Mrs Haden Guest, and for Mr Kenny provided he holds a British passport, or the Embassy are reasonably satisfied that he is a British subject.

FOREIGN OFFICE, SW1

30th August 1941

MMG DUMMY Sent Sept 1, 1941

OUTGOING TELEGRAM

AMERICAN EMBASSY

VICHY

223 September 1, 11pm

A strictly confidential message concerning British Interests and referring to Vichy's 222, August 9, 1pm re Mrs Haden Guest and Kenny.

WINANT

AMERICAN AMBASSADOR

MR BEAM

Charge Foreign Office

KW15

Original not found in file 820,02 – possibly is with other British Interests correspondence.

AEA

No KW15

His Majesty's Principal Secretary of State for Foreign Affairs presents his compliments to the United States Ambassador and with further reference to His Excellency's note RBI-2803 of the 11th August on the subject of the arrest of Mrs Peter Haden-Guest, has the honour to state that according to a communication from Messrs Silverman and Livermore, Solicitors, of Cliffords Inn, Fleet Street, London, EC4, Mr Peter Haden-Guest, who is the husband of Mrs Lisa Haden-Guest now under arrest, and the father of Anthony Haden-Guest, the child aged four understood to be in the care of friends in Marseilles, is desirous that arrangements should be made for the child to be sent to the United States of America.

2. It will be recalled that prior to Mrs Haden-Guest's arrest she and her son were expected to leave for New York via Lisbon (see Mr Achilles' letter of 31st March last).

3. Mr Eden is unable to suggest what steps could now be taken to meet Mr Peter Haden-Guest's wishes in regard to his son, but he would be grateful if Mr Winant would be good enough to communicate the foregoing to the United States Consul-General at Marseilles by telegraph

at Messrs Silverman and Livermore's expense, with a view to any steps which he may be able to take to arrange for Anthony Haden-Guest to travel to New York. The address to which he is to be sent is 15, Christopher Street, Greenwich Village, New York City, which is presumably his father's residence.

FOREIGN OFFICE, SW1

5th September, 1941

Decoded by AGR & CVF

Copied MVG GRAY Rec'd September 19, 1941

INCOMING TELEGRAM

Transcribed in note RBI-3571

Sept 20, 1941. JDB:IMS

TO MR BEAM FOR ACTION

AMEMBASSY

LONDON

Following telegram has been sent to the Department:

1201 September 18, 9pm

British Interests

Department's 676, 4th from Fullerton

French authorities consider request for extradition Mrs Haden-Guest highly improbable. Adopted son 4 years old in good health and staying with Mrs Francis Tailleux old friend of family in Château near Aix who is unwilling as is his mother that he should leave France until she does. As Mrs Haden-Guest apparently exercises custody of child arbitrary action our part leading to his departure for the United States would seem improper. While Consulate Marseille has as yet no authorization to interview Mrs Haden-Guest in prison her lawyer is now in contact with her and is hopeful case may eventually be dropped.

Repeated to London

LEAHY

FILE

IMMEDIATE AND STRICTLY CONFIDENTIAL

London, October 7, 1941

Dear Sir Harold:

I desire to refer to our note RBI-2622 of July 28, 1941, and our note RBI-3571 of September 20, 1941, and other correspondence regarding Mrs Haden-Guest and Kenney. In this connection I transcribe below the text of a telegram dated October 3 received through the American Embassy at Vichy from Consul General Fullerton at Marseille:-

'Following receipt of long delayed authorization by Vichy Government to visit Mrs Haden-Guest and Charles (?Thomas) Kenny (?Kenney) I visited them yesterday in Marseille prisons in which they are confined. I was accompanied by a French army colonel, the military judge charged with the prosecution and by an interpreter.

Mrs Haden-Guest who is in civilian women's prison is in good spirits and fair physical condition.

Kenny who is in military prison is also in good spirits, complains of slight stomach trouble, which is alleged by prison authorities not to be serious. Both are adequately represented by counsel who express confidence charges against them will shortly be dropped.'

Mr Fullerton adds that the military judge, Captain Dutour, who informally received him a few days ago and was exceedingly cordial, said that confidentially he could confirm the impression of the defense counsel that the charges against the prisoners might be dropped owing to the inability of the authorities to ascertain the whereabouts of, and to arrest, certain witnesses who to the prosecution were essential. Captain Dutour, however, could not name any even approximate date for the release of Kenney and Mrs Haden-Guest.

I might mention that Mr Charles Ritchie, of the Canadian High Commissioner's Office, has inquired of me concerning Kenney, who appears to be a Canadian citizen. I told him briefly about Kenney's detention in prison, as described above, but I think Mr Ritchie would like to have a fuller account of the background of the case. I have not considered it appropriate to transmit this without your authority, but I know that he would be most grateful for a further statement, and I would appreciate it very much if you could see your way clear to transmitting this provided no objection is perceived.

Sincerely yours,
Jacob D Beam

JDB:MVG

Mr Harold Satow, KCMG, OBE
Foreign Office
London SW1

The Americans visited me and called me 'you naughty girl' for the trouble I had caused. Nancy Fiocca brought food. I was very grateful, knowing the risk she was taking.

Auntie Forbes meanwhile was furious that I had for a second time failed to get Anthony to safety. Why had I not left Marseille? She became convinced that I was a German agent. She sent a telegram to the American ambassador in Vichy, Admiral Leahy, a family friend, saying I should hang in the Tower. Dutour obviously knew about this, and at one of our meetings said, 'The people you think are your best friends are really your enemies, madame. But their allegations against you help you.' I thought he was trying to undermine my loyalty to the Haden-Guest family and paid no attention. He also told me, 'They think you are a German agent, but we know who you are.'

He treated me as well as he could, and I also got on well with the military police who took me on foot, in handcuffs, between Les Presentines and Fort St Nicolas. Dutour authorised them to let me buy some essentials on the way. I saw they were just ordinary policemen, without links with Vichy Intelligence, and I horrified Louis Nouveau by getting them to wait at the entrance to his apartment building while I climbed to his fifth-floor flat (I did not of course use the lift) to borrow 200 francs. He was terrified that this would bring the secret police to his door. I spent all the money on food and chemist's supplies for our cell on the way to the interrogation, and with great cheek called on Louis for another 100 francs on the way back. I knew, with my experience, that there was no danger to the Nouveaus, but they thought I was wildly rash, which Louis put down to my being half Slav. He says in his memoirs: '*Son hérédité mi-slave explique probablement ce comportement inattendu, incohérent et imprudent.*'

The hatred felt by most of the Presentines guards and Fort St Nicolas staff for the political prisoners was balanced by a few who were secret Gaullists. Once when the policemen had escorted me to the fort and unlocked my handcuffs, and I was alone with the officer who would take me to the *instruction*, the interrogation, he bowed, kissed my hand and murmured, '*Vous avez grande mérite pour la France et l'Angleterre. Maintenant à l'instruction.*' I have never forgotten his praise and encouragement. It lifted me through the long days when everybody was against me. It reminded me I was not alone, and that I was fighting in a great fight.

In spite of Captain Dutour's goodwill, the possibility hovered that I would be handed over to the Gestapo and executed. In October, Ian Garrow decided to gamble on the prosecutor's honour. He contacted Dutour, and arranged that he himself would appear at his office in the fort to sign a document clearing me of working in the escape network and saying that I acted merely as a 'housekeeper' for British servicemen on the run in Marseille. Dutour, *parole d'officier*, would give Garrow two hours to get away.

I knew nothing of this plan before I was brought again into Dutour's waiting-room. I was terrified when all of a sudden Ian appeared, bounding up the stairs. I looked at him, trying to tell him to get out, but he said, 'It's all right, it's been arranged.' He disappeared into Dutour's office, and I was taken in within two minutes. Dutour was sitting at his desk holding some papers Ian had just signed. He said, 'Captain Garrow is here to save your life, Madame Guest,' and Ian kissed me before going back down the stairs.

Dutour himself was probably true to his word, but one of his clerks was in the pay of the Germans and had betrayed the agreement. When Ian left Fort St Nicolas, he was immediately arrested by the German faction in the police and put in the military prison. He was sentenced to ten years' detention, and sent to Mauzac, a concentration camp on the Dordogne river east of Bergerac. Pat O'Leary took over command of the line, which was afterwards known by the workers as 'the Pat line' and officially as PAO, after his initials.

Decoded by DM BROWN Rec'd Nov 6, 1941
Copied by PB

INCOMING TELEGRAM
TO MR COE FOR ACTION
From Vichy

Substance to FO with RBI-4386 Nov 6, 1941. RDC:MJR
AMERICAN EMBASSY
LONDON
250, November 5, 4pm
British Interests
My 214, July 25, 1pm
Following from Marseille:
Now confirmed that Captain John Garrow, known to Hoare, arrested recently and detained military prison, Marseille. Am I authorized defray legal counsel as authorized for Mrs Haden-Guest? Latter and Thomas Kenny still in prison but attorneys hopeful will be released shortly.

LEAHY

Thinking Ian was still free, I was taken back to Les Presentines. In a few days the guards came for me, and my clothes and bag were returned. The secret police officers who had originally arrested me arrived: I was sure I was for the chop. But I was told I was to be taken to Aix-en-Provence to collect Anthony from the Tailleux.

When we arrived at Château Noir, Francis Tailleux was not pleased to see me. He shouted to my escort that I was a Red, and got his gun, saying I should be shot. At first he refused to give Anthony up. But the police insisted and he was obliged to let him go. Anthony took it all with his usual placidity. He was nearly five.

The police took us to a small hotel, where I waited with Anthony until they gave me a travel permit and tickets and put us on the train to Spain. In Barcelona, we were taken in charge by the British consul, who drove us to Madrid and handed us over to the Second Secretary, a man called George Young. He debriefed me at great length. Finally we were driven to Lisbon, where we stayed for two months. I gave a full report to Donald Darling.

Lisbon was neutral territory, and British people and Germans lived side by side. On 7 December 1941 the Japanese attacked Pearl Harbor and went on to invade Malaya. On 11 December Hitler declared war on the United States – he did not want them to get in first with their declaration. But the Russians had stopped the Germans in Moscow.

I was taken by Donald Darling and some others from the Embassy to a New Year's party, and near us, at another table, was a group of Germans. One of them was photographing his friends and suddenly turned his camera on us. At the same moment Darling pushed my head under the table. He apologised to me and explained it was to protect my identity. I was still a profound puzzle to the Germans.

Auntie Forbes's telegram to Vichy accusing me of being a German agent may have done me a good turn by confusing the Abwehr and its two rivals the Sicherheitsdienst (the Intelligence branch of the SS) and the Gestapo. They must have wondered if I was working for one of the others. I did not find out about what happened to the Pat line and my friends in Marseille until after the war.

My experiences in France I remember in all their detail. I can see them and relive the fear and excitement. But Eileen Tailleux has a different version. She says I wrote to her at Château Noir from Besançon camp, saying we were freezing and that Anthony had bronchitis and there was not enough to eat. She went up to Paris and pulled strings to have us released. The head of the Pasteur Institute, Monsieur Couteau, a family friend, gave her an introduction to Fernand de Brinon, the *délégué général du gouvernement francais dans les territoires occupés*, who was dealing with the Germans on behalf of the Vichy government. She went to see him at his office in the Palais Matignon. He promised to have Anthony and me released, which Eileen says was quite in order as 70 per cent of the women were released; the Besançon records are in the Archives de France in Paris.

Eileen did not tell me this story of hers when we met again in Provence. Her Resistance work sometimes overlapped with our line, and Donald Caskie sent her some British soldiers to hide. According to her, she often looked after Anthony, sometimes with Jean Fourcade, a rich young man whose family had a house and large garden at St Loup. She says Jean told her I was in Les Presentines, so she fetched Anthony from St Loup and took him to Château Noir – whereas I remember kneeling to say goodbye to him at the entrance to Les Presentines and not knowing what would become of him. When I was let out, and arrived at the Tailleux' to fetch him, she says they did not want to give him up because Eileen was sure I was on some adventure and she feared for him if I was arrested. She says I said that if they didn't release him, I would tell the police about hiding the British soldiers. Francis flew into a rage and fetched his gun, giving me Anthony and shouting that they never wanted to see me again. According to Eileen, I was alone, and did not have two policemen with me.

Eileen says that just before the war she and Francis were living in a *pavillon* in the Parc Montsouris; they had one side and Flavia the other, and during the war, Braque, who lived round the corner, took over Flavia's half for his sculptures. She says I had a room in the flat of two doctors in the neighbourhood. I remember clearly living in the *pavillon*.

Monica Forbes says that Antoinette, the housekeeper at Les Essarts, is very unlikely to have collaborated with the Germans, and that the parcels she was taking out of the house were the silver and linen, which she brought back to the Forbes family after the war.

It is a mystery why I was released from Les Presentines. Some of the younger Forbeses are convinced I gave away names. People always think I must have been a spy, because I can arrange to get out of tight corners. But I don't give information – I just talk my way out. Peter Haden-Guest thinks that the US State Department, prodded by him and Auntie Forbes, pushed Vichy to drop my case, and that the prosecution had also failed to find essential witnesses. I remember what Ian Garrow signed about me, and I believe that his statement allowed Dutour to release me, as Dutour wanted.

15

Mixed Welcome in London, 1942–44

Early in 1942, Anthony and I flew from Lisbon to Shannon and on to London. I arrived with about £10 in cash. In the two and a half years since I had been there, London had suffered the Blitz and food was rationed. I went to my mother-in-law's flat at Bray House in Duke of York Street in St James's.

Carmel was astonished to see Anthony and me and not pleased with me. She said we could sleep there, but first she gave me a long passionate lecture: I had to go to America straight away because Peter had registered for the draft, and if his dependants were with him she said he would not be called up. I told her I was determined to stay in Europe and do war work. Carmel's concern was Peter: she brushed aside my time in prison. If Peter died fighting in this capitalist war, I would be his murderer.

I had to have somewhere to live. Carmel found me a room in Pimlico, but I was looking on my own. I noticed a flat in Bray House was empty, so I went to the estate agent and asked for it. The name 'Haden-Guest' helped, and I got the two-and-a-half-room flat for £2 10s a week. I collected a trunk of clothes and belongings that I had left with a friend, and furnished the flat with a second-hand stove, a cot, two beds, a table, chairs, some second-hand sheets and two mattresses, all from a junk shop in Chelsea.

I got the money for these and the first week's rent by selling one of my two stop-watches to Patrick Furse, the art student who had followed Margot Fonteyn to Paris. He was stationed at the War Office in London, and I think Margot told him I was back; he turned up on my doorstep. He generously gave me £10 for the watch. Those stop-watches, the tools of the continuity girl's trade, were like currency to me: I had often pawned and redeemed them in Europe. I took a lodger into the little room, who paid 30s.

I was resourceful enough to get us a home, but it was strange to be out of prison. Everything was easy behind bars. You did not have to decide about survival, only how to behave when they came to take you away for ever – and that was easy. Now I had to make up my mind what to do, what to wear, when to eat, drink and sleep. At first I did not know whether to do such a simple thing as shutting a door; it was an effort to walk along the street. I was bewildered by having to make my own life after submerging myself in the needs of others. Freedom, to me, was a loss of focus. I felt very alone. I felt guilty to be free when others were imprisoned, and homesick for comradeship.

In March 1942 I was invited by a young man in the BBC, Henry Swanzy, to record talks for *Radio News Reel*. These talks brought me a real friend in Henry, who shared my love of poetry. He had the scholarly habit of writing everything down, so of things we did together there is a record since the day we met.

> I first set eyes on Elisabeth at 5.30 in the afternoon of the 5th April, 1942, at Broadcasting House. The script was the 298th in the series of very short talks, three or four a day, that I would get down in some way on paper for the censor and, after recording the speaker on disco, put on a programme which was heard all over the world, except in the UK. Before me stood a small, attractive figure, clad in a leopard-skin overcoat above a black and white suit. She had a gamine look, the sort of person who is whirled over the shoulders of apache dancers at a nightclub. The script was about the way she led Anthony by a nursery harness through the reeds into Vichy freedom, and she delivered it in an eager voice, very faintly foreign ('I will explain you'). In the note-book I kept of programmes recorded, I find the single word 'ectoplasm'.
>
> But the thing most intriguing about Elisabeth was the mystery she evoked. Hardly had the talk been recorded for Radio News Reel than we were informed that it was not to go out. It was understood that Dr Haden-Guest, MP, supported by high authorities in the Foreign Office, regarded her as unreliable, even dangerous. At that time, the Empire News Talk unit was working in Broadcasting House. Almost the

only other programme people in the building were the new Director-General, Professor Ogilvie from Belfast, and A. P. Ryan, his adviser, an *éminence grise*, who had worked on the *Manchester Guardian* and *The Times*. When Ryan was appealed to by my boss, Peter Pooley, he said unhesitatingly that the talk could go out, for he had a great dislike of Dr Haden-Guest, not the most popular of men.

Elisabeth delivered three more talks that month, and Carmel Haden-Guest told the world of the collection for a saddle to be presented to the Russian C-in-C, Marshal Timoshenko. I was presented to Anthony, a charming, gap-toothed child, wearing a little black Glengarry cap. I was bowled over by Elisabeth's extraordinary mixture of toughness and softness, childishness and maturity – she had a favourite phrase I remember, 'wet behind the ears'. Above all, I admired her readiness to plunge into intimacies. I was an intellectual, too strong to follow, too weak to lead, one of Elisabeth's *bêtes noires*, as I subsequently learned. But there were also many affinities. We were both pyknic types, short necks and rapid reflexes, good at synthesis, bad at analysis, with visual minds. We were both paradoxes, Elizabeth an amoral moralist, I a careerist in the world of the spirit.

I knew de Gaulle's right-hand man, Maurice Schumann, through Maurice's friend Cécile Macworth (Cécile de Doncelle). I was introduced to de Gaulle, and all he said was a quick '*Merci beaucoup pour la France, et au revoir.*' He was a man who brought everybody to their natural size. The Free French arranged for me to give a press conference, which was on 22 April 1942. Anthony was the star; he crawled under the table and pinched a girl reporter's ankle. I got him out, and demonstrated for the photographers how we had crept through the mud, me guiding him by tugs on his harness.

The journalists were excited, because no one else had got out who had such tales to tell. The *New York Times* ran the story the next day on the front page, with the headline 'Fleeing France, Mother Drugs Son To Prevent His Speaking English'.

London, April 22. How an English woman and her five-year-old son, who had been drugged for four days and nights to prevent

> him from betraying them by speaking English, escaped from a German prison camp in France was told in London today. The boy, Anthony Haden-Guest, who is the grandson of Islington's Labour Member of Parliament, and his mother, Mrs Peter Haden-Guest, were caught in Brittany when the Nazis entered France. They were taken to the prison camp at Besançon. Following an outbreak of tuberculosis, they were transferred to Paris, where they managed to slip away when they got into a crowd. Aided by French people, who Mrs Guest said were wonderfully kind in hiding, feeding and clothing them, they managed to reach unoccupied France. 'I had to drug Anthony but once in the train he awoke and said something in English,' Mrs Guest related. 'The Gestapo, who are very overrated, noticed nothing, but to one woman who said something, I replied that he was talking in Dutch . . . I then gave him another sleeping draught.'
>
> Mrs Guest said when they got near the border line of unoccupied France she had to awaken Anthony as they had lots of walking ahead of them. 'We spent six hours crawling over the frontier on our stomachs, Anthony in front of me attached by a lead,' she said. 'All the time in the dark we could hear sentries pacing between the fifteen yards of distance of the border. As they crossed each other and walked the fifteen yards on we crawled a few more paces until we crossed the line. Ten minutes later other people trying to escape were killed.' Twenty-four hours later they arrived in Marseille . . .

There was a little note at the end, headed 'Father teaches ballet here'. It said: 'Peter Haden-Guest, the father of Anthony is employed as a teacher of ballet and callisthenics at the Repertory Dance Theatre, 54 East Thirteenth Street . . . The father came to this country in 1939 shortly before the war broke out and has been trying to make arrangements to have his family brought here since then, he said.'

The Americans were avid for war stories, as they had only been fighting for four months. Also on the front page with unimportant Anthony and me was news of 'Order Freezing All Prices at March Level Expected; Gasoline Rationing May 15', 'Rationing of Sugar Set to Begin May 5', 'British Commandos Raid Boulogne', '5 Vichy Aides Quit Washington Staff: Two Embassy Veterans Join de Gaulle – Denounce Laval as "a German Agent"' and '100

Hostages Slain in Week To Protect Nazis in France'. The British press were more blasé. *The Times* didn't report our adventures, the *Daily Telegraph* had a short piece about Mrs Haden-Guest, 'daughter-in-law of the Socialist MP for North Islington'.

> On being transferred from the camp at Besançon to Paris, they got away from their guards. 'I was helped and hidden by French people,' she said. 'Later, disguised as a peasant woman in deep mourning, I took Anthony by train to the dividing line, after having given him sleeping tablets so that he should not speak English. A Frenchman agreed to guide us into Unoccupied France. On approaching the frontier we began to crawl on our stomachs. And we crawled for six hours, with long periods during which we were motionless, waiting for an opportunity to slip through the gap between two sentries. I told Anthony that there would be no more birthday parties or Christmas presents or nice food if he said a single word, but that if he kept quiet he would never see a German soldier again. He was duly impressed . . . My last recollection of France was that of a porter who refused a tip. 'We owe England a debt of honour and we are waiting for you,' he said to me.

The newspaper reports did bring me a friend, the American journalist Ed Murrow, who was working for CBS in London. He telephoned to ask me to broadcast to America on conditions in France, and I went to meet him.

With his first words, Murrow earned my love and respect. As a compassionate and dedicated American among us, he knew that conditions in Britain were tough, but not as tough as living under an occupying power. He seemed to understand the loneliness of all homecoming soldiers who find civilians hard and absorbed in their own lives. He said how awful it must be for me to be cut off from my friends. His directness, his frank recognition of my feelings, was simply human. He asked, too, whether I was managing to eat, and how I was adjusting. I loved him for his straightforward compassion. Then he interviewed me and allowed my heart to speak. He did not pressure me to deliver propaganda, he did not urge me to embellish the facts – he allowed me to be heartbroken and honest. He was direct, and he allowed me to be simply direct – that was his gift to me. Ed Murrow gave me the courage to carry on in that strange thing we call freedom by making me feel that he, too, had a mission and needed help to accomplish it. We were shoulder to shoulder in the work; we were, for a while, comrades in arms – our arms were our words.

Auntie Forbes had taken a flat in Swan Court in Chelsea and had her house in Kent. When she read about me being back, she asked to see me and offered her help. I said No. She would have done anything to have Anthony with her, and after a few months I let him go for the weekend: I felt I could not deprive him of so much love. She sent a car and chauffeur, and she had his room ready with the *Blue Fairy Book* and other books and toys. Anthony always enjoyed being with her because she read to him. She was very intelligent. I remember her bicycling off to see Mrs Churchill at 10 Downing Street, saying she was going to tea with 'that chicken-brained woman'.

Anthony and I saw Walt Disney's *Bambi*, which made him cry, but as he never cried he could not understand what the tears on his cheeks were. He asked me, 'Mother, is it raining?' The CBS broadcasts gave me enough money for rent and to feed Anthony and myself: I was paid a guinea a minute, and I think I did four talks. The £20 I earned kept me going while I looked for work.

I heard that two girls who had escaped from Besançon after me, Freda Stewart and Rosemary Say, had reached London in March 1942. They had crawled under the barbed wire of the camp in November 1941 and made their way to Marseille, which was so crowded that the American consul took a room in a brothel for them. Freda got a job working for de Gaulle and the Free French at Carlton House Terrace, Rosemary joined SOE.

I applied to the War Office. There, to my surprise, I found my one-armed landlord Jimmy Langley from Marseille now in charge of training the MI9 agents and setting up routes from France to Spain. As far as I know he had not worked with the escape route in Marseille. He was not one of our group.

When I offered to return to Europe, Langley was discouraging. He was not pleased about the press conference, for which neither I nor the Free French had asked the War Office's permission: he thought it was dangerous, adding that the publicity had made me so conspicuous that I could be of no more use to the network. What I did not know was that he always deeply distrusted anyone who was released from a Vichy or German prison for no apparent reason.

Again I tried to get into the fight. I contacted old colleagues in the film industry in the hope of a job on propaganda films, but was astonished to find I was not given security clearance by the War Office. I discussed this with Pat Furse, and he persuaded his father, Sir Ralph Furse, the director of recruitment for the Colonial Service, to arrange for me to meet his great friend Sir Hanns Vischer, who was then in charge of Political Intelligence.

This very elegant gentleman in his fifties, Sir Hanns, took me to the Berkeley Buttery and asked me kindly what my problem was. I told him I couldn't get security clearance. He had clearly briefed himself, because he was able to quote from my file at MI6: he said that on my file there was a little word, not important but bad enough to damn me. The word was 'indiscreet'.

I was shocked. I speak my mind and I like conversation, but I do not give away secrets. There are things I talk about and things I don't: I never mix the two up – and I do not drink. I knew I had been valued and trusted by my colleagues in Europe, so I felt the 'indiscreet' must have come from an enemy in Britain – I have never discovered who. I decided it was not my mother-in-law: she was open about her poor opinion of me, but she would not have gone behind my back. Her bitterness came from unhappiness. She had been badly hurt by her husband and was frantic about the safety of her son. All doors seemed closed to me by the influence of the Forbeses, Dr Haden-Guest, the War Office or the Communists.

I would have been ashamed to go to safety in America. There was nothing there for me – I was finished with Peter, and I could not abandon my friends in Europe. And the Intelligence services had dropped me as a burnt-out case. I had to try to put a life together for myself and Anthony. I went to my film union the ACT and they were overwhelmingly nice and got me continuity work. This brought me £5 a week. I also began to receive a naval wife's allowance, because Peter had gone to Canada when he realised that Anthony and I were not coming, and enlisted in the Royal Canadian Navy Voluntary Reserve: he worked in Ottawa (apparently he was in Intelligence).

Soon after I got back to England, I noticed Anthony could not throw a ball. I took him to the doctor, who diagnosed wasting of the spine. Dr Haden-Guest confirmed the diagnosis. It was incurable. Anthony would die before he was fourteen. I could not, would not believe it. I heard of a Mr Wyllie, a doctor who specialised in the nervous systems of children, and took Anthony to him. Wyllie was tremendous: he thought Anthony had probably been wrongly diagnosed and offered to treat him. If he was wrong, and Anthony's spine trouble was physical, the treatment might make things worse. If he was right, and the paralysis came from the shocks Anthony had been through in Europe, he would get better. It was kill or cure. I decided to trust Wyllie, and Anthony survived. He was treated at Great Ormond Street Hospital as an out-patient for two years.

To get him away from the bombing I took him to a Montessori nursery school, Elmtrees, which had been evacuated to Paccombe House in Devon. It was run by a salt-of-the-earth Miss Wilson, whom the children called Willo. The day child's fee was £2 10s a week, or £3 for boarders, but as I earned so little she let Anthony board for £1 10s. The other Paccombe mothers were fascinated to hear about Occupied Europe. David and Lorna Lea, who were at the school, remember me telling their mother about drugging Anthony and pulling him under the wire fence of Besançon camp.

I saw a lot of Henry Swanzy. I had been taken on by Humphrey Jennings to do the continuity for a documentary on bombed towns. One of the towns was Bristol, and Henry came down for the weekend and I made him hide a lily I had nicked. I remember the train running past Bath and a little boy murmuring 'poor Bath' as he looked at all the unroofed houses. Henry's memories are more exact than mine.

> That spring and summer we went round together. I found her completely anarchic, a kind of female Puck. She loved *épater les bourgeois*. At Chiswick, she picked a rhododendron flower and insisted I bring it out of the garden under my mackintosh. On the other hand, I earned respect for taking her on the roof to watch the bombing, or walking from her flat, in the black-out, to my flat on Primrose Hill, listening to the tinkle of anti-aircraft shell fragments on the tarmac. And always she had the strange power of coming on experience like recollection.
>
> We would exchange poetry. Elisabeth had a passion for 'If', and Kipling generally. One of her friends was the formidable Monica Felton, a novelist with a noble head on a crippled body, a Chief Clerk in the House of Commons, companion of Lewis Silkin, MP. Later she was embroiled with the Americans over the Korean War, accusing them of using germ warfare. My mother came over from Bedford to meet Elisabeth, but the meeting was not a success. Anyone less

like the 'nice' girl she so earnestly wanted for me cannot be imagined.

Henry Swanzy and George Weidenfeld were both at the BBC – George, who came from a rich Viennese Jewish background, was in the Monitoring Service. They decided to share a flat, and I found them one in Iverna Court in Kensington. I used to go to Sunday breakfast with them, and afterwards George would leave for the Cumberland Hotel (which was the lively place in 1942) and order a cup of coffee and watch the people walking through to spend £10 on lunch. 'One day I will be one of them,' he said. He was twenty-two. He certainly made it, in every way.

With Pat Furse, I was seeing Margot Fonteyn and his friend Peter Frankenburg, whose mother turned the whole of their large house near Manchester over to the care of evacuated children. Margot had become interested in the composer Constant Lambert. I sometimes say that Pat came to me on the rebound. And I was befriended by Carmel's sister Gladys, the Dowager Lady Swaythling.

Aunt Gladys did not have much soul, but she was the essence of Edwardian kindness and worldliness. She was a sort of mother to me, and I loved her. We sometimes stayed with her for weeks. She was immensely practical, but did not mind that I was not. Her name for me was 'Crazy Jane', and she used to say 'Darling, darling, you should have been born in woad.' She lived in a large house in Kensington Court, and the family had a country seat at Swaythling near Southampton. She was served by Ward the butler, Nancy the housekeeper, Hunt her personal maid, Hilda the housemaid, Becky (Miss Becker) the secretary, who did not live in, and a cook. Queen Mary often visited her, and would extract a good table or chair or even a well-trained maid. Queen Mary loved being given things; she did not directly ask for anything but made it clear she wanted it.

Aunt Gladys was on the committee of the National Society for the Prevention of Cruelty to Children, and once a week she visited the office in Leicester Square. As it was wartime, she had given up her car and chauffeur and used the bus for the first time in her life. She got the number 9, carrying a bag of sweets to offer the conductor and anyone else she thought deserving. She was so used to inquiring after the welfare of her servants and tenants that she treated the conductor and the driver the same way, and took a genuine, gracious interest in them and their families. They thought her a terrific old girl, and stopped the bus wherever she wanted. The number 9 became her car and chauffeur. During the bombing, she went to the air-raid shelter exactly like everyone else, except that she had got Hunt to pack her most precious belongings in a large pram, and when the sirens sounded, Ward pushed the pram to the shelter, followed by Aunt Gladys, Hunt, Hilda, the secretary, housekeeper and cook. It was a sight worth seeing.

She had a fancy to pretend that I was well off, and took trouble to tell me that in such and such a country I should always go to such and such a grand hotel, because they had bidets. She gave me her secret treasure, a white metal bowl, for when there was no bidet. 'Huntie, fetch our little secret for Mrs Elisabeth.'

Aunt Gladys loved Pat Furse, and realising that he and I might become lovers, she gave me some advice. 'My husband worshipped the ground I trod on, and that is because he never saw me naked. Always in the dark, darling, always in the dark. You go to bed first, and cover yourself well. The man can always slip the sheets off when he comes to you – but don't make it too easy for him. And before you go to bed together, make sure that all your clothes are properly laid out, should you not have a maid. You might wake up ill or dead, and you would not want the doctor to be embarrassed by the state of your bedroom.' This was said to a woman who had lived with three men, been through a war, borne a child, and married twice. I thought it was enchanting.

She knew the Empress of Japan, and used to supply her with English corsets. I heard her once at dinner tell her son Ewen Montagu and his fellow naval officers how worried she was about 'the poor Empress in Japan' with no new stays, and to ask them whether she could send them through the Red Cross. This was in 1942; the Japanese had taken Singapore and Java in the spring.

Aunt Gladys had several children. Stuart, Lord Swaythling, had joined the family bank Samuel Montagu, and was serving in the Grenadiers. He was divorced, and he married the head of the women's army, the ATS, Jean Knox, in 1945. Ewen was a lawyer in Naval Intelligence. After the war he wrote the book *The Man Who Never Was* about a hoax Intelligence played on the Germans in 1943: a corpse was equipped with fake plans for an Allied invasion of Greece and washed ashore in Spain. Ivor Montagu was a Communist, famous in the film world. Their sister Joyce, who was nice to me, married a rich man called Oliver Frost.

Through the union, I got a job doing continuity at Gainsborough

Pictures in Islington. The bus fare from Piccadilly was a penny. My first film was a musical, *Miss London Ltd* (which came out in 1943), with the comedian Arthur Askey and Anne Shelton, directed by Val Guest.

At the studios, the director had four assistants, the cameraman had four assistants, the sound man had three assistants, the make-up man had three assistants – everyone had assistants except the continuity girl. She was either brilliantly efficient, neat, did shorthand and typing and could take photographs, knew everything and was a terrific technician – or she was me, couldn't do shorthand, could barely type, was not interested in continuity, but was endlessly fascinated by the actors and their rapport and laboured to keep everyone happy and working together as a team.

My shortcomings sometimes got me into trouble. For one scene, we actually hired Waterloo station. There was a train with 2000 extras milling around, and Arthur Askey was filmed in long shot walking up to a kiosk with a newspaper under his arm. He was wearing a white shirt and a striped tie. Six weeks later, the kiosk was built in the studio to do the close-ups of him, and thanks to my lack of continuity, he was wearing a striped shirt and plain tie. When the location and studio shots were cut together for the film, we noticed. That was a clanger. It could have cost the studio a lot of money. But the producer Fred Gunn decided to show the film to his friends and family to test whether they saw anything wrong. And they did not.

My salvation was men, who knew how inefficient I was and how much I loved the job. They took me in their stride, because they liked me and because I was always in a happy fuss that they loved to deal with in their masculine way. They looked after me. But I was not a parasite. A person who gives heart to a team and is a sort of mascot does help the work, even if she makes a few mistakes.

On 8 November 1942 the Allies invaded North Africa, and three days later the Germans took over the Vichy zone in France, so as to control the Mediterranean coast. I feared for my friends in Marseille.

Carmel died in 1943. The housekeeper at Bray House came to fetch me in the morning. Although Aunt Gladys arranged the funeral, I had to sort out Carmel's things. Her diamonds and tiara were hidden in her Court shoes, wrapped in newspaper at the back of her wardrobe.

Because Pat and I wanted to get married, I filed for divorce from Peter. I asked my future father-in-law, Sir Ralph, to use his contacts in the Foreign Office and Intelligence to get Auntie Forbes to officially withdraw her accusation that I had been a German agent. I do not really blame her for thinking I was an agent. I was born for Intelligence work, where loyalty and knowing who to trust is the key. But I could never do it professionally, only where the heart is involved. I never want to be in command of anybody. I like to be beside the man or behind the man; or if it means shooting, in front of him.

Pat was due to be sent away by the army. We realised the Allies were getting ready to invade France. He asked me to take Anthony down to a cottage on his parents' estate in Devon to get away from the bombing, but I put off deciding.

Henry Swanzy and Pat and I went down to Ightham in Kent one weekend. Henry described it:

> Elisabeth had gone to meet two literary Louises, friends of Carmel Haden-Guest, and there was a village fete and bowling for a pig. Another person came with us, a young Captain in the Rifle Brigade, with a blue wing on his tunic. His name was Patrick Furse and he was the son of the man who, four years before, had regretted to inform me that I had not passed my probation in His Majesty's Home Civil Service in the Colonial and Dominions Office. What I did not also know was that he had been living with Elisabeth for the last 18 months and had even seen the death of two little boys, thanks to miscarriages. I liked him very well, and felt no rivalry at all.

I later asked Sir Ralph why he had turned down Henry Swanzy for the Civil Service. He said he was too clever. I said, 'But surely you need clever men?' 'Clever men are cads.' 'Who do you take, then?' 'Scotsmen, and parsons' and soldiers' sons; you can't go wrong.'

After Pat left London, I wrote to him every night. I had two places I liked to sit: St James's Church in Piccadilly or the Palm Court at the Ritz, where I ordered a cup of coffee and wrote my letter. I was the only one there in the evening. I saw other people come in and go downstairs to the bar, I supposed because they wanted a drink. I sat in splendour by myself in the lovely room, until one day the maître d'hôtel politely asked me why I always sat there, and drew my attention to the roof, all glass. He said it was probably the most dangerous place in London. So I went down to the bar. But it is hard being a non-drinker among drinkers. I ended up writing at home.

I don't write letters, I talk on paper. I let loose to people. I never read a letter over: I take it out to the letter box and let it go, full of passion, full of fervour. I have lost friends with my letters. Sometimes I think again and take one back. Sometimes when I think I should take it back, I see my hand reaching out and putting it in. It is what I call destiny, when you say No, and against the No your fingers open and the letter drops. Then you just shrug your shoulders and say 'what the hell'.

The Allies went into France on 6 June 1944. But the Germans had a weapon up their sleeve: on 13 June the first of the flying bombs, the V1s, landed on England. They began to come over London and the Home Counties nightly – which meant over Anthony, who was now in Great Missenden, because Willo had had to move her Elmtrees school back to Buckinghamshire. If Anthony was killed I wanted to go with him, so I took a room in Great Missenden opposite the school, in the house of a retired bank manager, for 10s a week. I dozed through some nights literally on the doorstep, like an animal protecting her cub. Those flying bombs – what a strain they put on the spirit. You could see one coming, breathing fire like a great dragon, and you heard it cut out and you heard it drop and you felt a guilty relief because it did not drop on you. I have never forgotten that sense of fear, relief and guilt.

I used to take Anthony to and from Great Ormond Street on the little train from Marylebone. My life was divided between the studio, Great Missenden, the hospital and the flat in St James's. Then Great Ormond Street Hospital was bombed and partly destroyed. The doctors told me to take Anthony right away into the country if possible and give him good food, good air and exercise: that would complete his cure. I asked the Furses if I could rent a house on their land, and they arranged for me to take Newcombe Cottage from a tenant farmer called Black for 3s 6d a week.

16

Marrying into the Furses, Devon, 1944–45

Newcombe Cottage in North Devon was heavenly, but no evacuees would have considered it, since it was two miles from the village of Dolton and had no telephone, no running water and no electricity. It was thatched and whitewashed, dripping with the dampness of the stream, surrounded by the wildest orchards and populated by one white owl, a roaming fox, Anthony and me. The nearest farm was quite a walk away, and the farmer said, 'The gypsies will murder you one day, Mrs Pat.'

I got oil lamps and candles, and some furniture from a second-hand shop in Great Torrington, and collected wood for the fires. I enrolled Anthony in a dame school in the village to be taught by the Misses Waddington, who adored him, as everybody did. We lived on apples, eggs, mushrooms and sorrel, and I sent eggs to Aunt Gladys in London.

Furses had owned the land at Halsdon on the Torridge for centuries. They were completely English, profoundly bound up in the old ways, which may partly explain their attitudes – their Anglican church allowed them to get away with anything. The boys have for ever gone to Eton and Balliol. They staffed the army, the church and the navy. They populated Kenya with their black sheep. The Furses went up with the Empire and in with the Empire and down with the Empire and out with the Empire. There are no Furses in *Who's Who* today. When I got engaged to Pat there were five: a bishop, a general, two knights and a dame – Dame Katharine Furse, who founded the women's navy, the WRNS and who was the widow of the painter Charles Wellington Furse.

Other members of the family were almost as important: Roger the stage and film designer and his sister Judith Furse the actress, and Pat's elder sister Jill, also an actress. The Furses were artistic – they wrote or painted, apart from their public service. 'We are servants of the King,' my father-in-law told me. They were related to the Mauds, the Lubbocks, the Johnstons, the Abrahams, the Duckworths, the Vidals, the Stones, the Cunliffes and the Wedderburns. Oh those beautiful Liberal faces: you don't see many like them any more.

Sir Ralph's father, the animal sculptor John Henry Monsell Furse, despised Winston Churchill for escaping from prison camp during the Boer War after giving his word of honour not to (he was a journalist captured with a troop train). Mr Furse had lost his mind, and he would sit outside the manor shouting 'Shoot him! That traitor, that cad Churchill – shoot him!' while the villagers listened nervously to the Prime Minister being attacked.

Sir Ralph had been knighted in 1941 (the Furses despised peerages – such common people were given them) for his work at the Colonial Office. Before that, as a civil servant, he had been Assistant Private Secretary or Private Secretary to among others Lord Milner, Winston Churchill, the Duke of Devonshire and Leo Amery and in between won a DSO and bar in the First World War. He had worn a hearing aid from about the age of twelve. His children called him 'Didda'. He was a master to servants and a servant to masters. He was a romantic, very distinguished-looking – tall, craggy-faced and foxish, oozing charm. After he was knighted, he asked his uncle Michael Furse, the immensely tall Bishop of St Albans, to allow him and his old schoolfriend Hanns Vischer, who had also been knighted, to keep a night-long vigil in the cathedral. I understood that gesture.

His wife Celia was the daughter of the poet Sir Henry Newbolt, remembered for 'Drake's Drum' and 'Vitaï Lampada' ('Play up, play up and play the game'). Celia wrote a novel, *The Visiting Moon*, about her childhood in the West Country. It was a warm-hearted picture of manor-house life that was kinder than I found her. She was just and fair, but heartless. Pat was her eldest son, and she said to me before he went to France, 'If his right hand is shot off he won't be able to paint.'

Pat took after his mother, so he was not really a Furse but a Newbolt. He was intelligent and gifted, very good with his hands. His sister Jill took after the Furses. She was kind and welcoming to me, and very beautiful and talented as an actress. She had married the poet and glass engraver Laurence Whistler. There were two younger Furse children, Nicholas and Theresa.

As a future Furse, I was told by my parents-in-law I must never go into the pub and must not call on the farmers at mealtimes, which would force them to offer me something. I did occasionally visit the people on the estate and sit in their kitchens eating buns. Their attitude to the Furses was not as awed as the Furses probably thought. There was a church set, led by the Furses, and a chapel set, led by the local grocer. Some of them had never been out of Devon. I love people who never leave their roots – there is so much steadiness there. I wrote to Henry Swanzy:

> Do jump on a train and spend a weekend by a big log-fire, picking nuts and blackberries . . . There was a wild moonlight sky last night and my very own beloved wind howled round the cottage . . . I am reading, not much, just enough to keep my mind and thoughts on the go when collecting wood, carrying coal, pumping water, doing the lav bucket and crossing over many fields and hills to fetch milk, mail and provisions. Life is simple and leaves one space to become civilised and not too hard. The beauty of the land here almost chokes me sometimes – and gives me pangs in the heart. Anthony is radiantly happy with his home, his nursery, a nice day-school, and people who like him around.

On 15 August 1944, Allied troops landed in the south of France and on the 23rd took Marseille. Paris was liberated on the same day. On 29th, Allied bombers destroyed half of Königsberg, which had been Hitler's chief naval base on the Baltic.

I did not know it at the time, but five weeks before the Allies arrived on the Riviera, my cousin Yuri (George) Makowski from Tallinn, who as a young man had wanted to marry me, and who was second-in-command (codename 'Gin') of the Resistance network 'Anne' which covered the coast as far as Perpignan, killed himself when the Gestapo came for him rather than risk breaking down under torture. He had always been terrified of physical pain. He lived with his mother in an apartment on the sixth floor of the Promenade in Nice. She was very beautiful and had had many admirers; we called her 'Musinka' ('little mother'). When the Gestapo arrived on 6 July, Yuri said '*Au revoir, Maman*' and jumped out of the window. Musinka tried to live on with her daughter, but she could not. Ten years later, on the anniversary of Yuri's death, she had herself killed on the same spot by lying in the road in the dark until a car ran over her. So I was told.

In September I wrote to Henry:

> For weeks I have been unable to put a word on a piece of paper, but have been, and still am, living in the past and the future. Do you know what that means? Reliving the thirties, 1940, 1941, 1942, Pause, 1944. And the future? I am arguing it out – with the Russians, the Communist Party, the Maquis, the Gaullistes, the Vichyistes! The City and Wall Street people and the people who sit back smugly and say '*Aren't* we doing well?' and the blood flows in streams all over Europe, and I have dreadful visions of new wars and civil wars. Beware of Stalin afterwards and the Americans.
>
> Oh, Henry – will our children have to die too? Victory only belongs to those who have gone, never to return – victory is something very doubtful and dreamlike – maybe, to be modest, let us call it bread and wireless sets and newspapers. The only real victory is the victory of the spirit against physical power. Victory belongs to the prisoners who went to their death singing and smiling for they had vision. When, oh when, will their victories come true? It is all very simple and clear, but so terribly hard to bear – it is so easy to suffer oneself, but to sit back and watch and feel the sufferings of so many many others, innocent people – *that is hell*. I am waiting for my new time to come, for the new fights and the new, or renewed, dark days, which were light and heavenly compared to these. Those boys, all over the world, dying and fighting, Lord, why not let us alone do it – those who were born to fight and die for others – *they* were not meant for it – *we were*.

On 3 October 1944 the Warsaw rising was crushed by the Germans. On the 4th I wrote to Henry: 'I am sitting at night in front of my fire, and travel back to where I came from – the incredibly long road – and then I travel forward and see the bloody fights ahead . . . I am glad I am not in the bustle of London. One forgets too easily there.'

Pat's sister Jill was expecting her second child. She was living in another cottage on the estate; Laurence was in the East Midlands with his regiment, the Rifle Brigade – the same regiment as Pat. Jill was delicate, and some nights I went over to be with her, leaving Anthony asleep in Newcombe Cottage. He did not like being alone, and he has not forgotten that I left him.

I think the Furses could only love one child, though they had four. Jill was the one they loved, and she was taken from them. In November, Jill had her baby, a daughter, at the Cottage Hospital in Torrington. Laurence did not have leave. Two weeks later, Jill died of a rare blood disease that inflamed her joints. She was twenty-nine. It was all the more terrible for Laurence because his brother Rex Whistler, the stage designer and painter, had just been killed in France. Jill had been a very lovely human being, and I was brokenhearted.

Pat was at an advanced airfield on the German border. At one time he liaised between the Canadian and Polish Air Forces, and by Christmas 1944 he was liaison officer for the the Canadian Air Force. I put up a tree, and on Christmas Eve I was sitting by the fire writing to Captain P. J. D. Furse, 137064, Rifle Brigade, 468 Air Liaison Section, 123 Wing, Royal Air Force, British Liberation Army, France, when somebody rapped on the window. I thought: The farmer was right – the gypsies have come to murder us. I went to the window, and there stood Pat. He had come over to make a report and been given forty-eight hours' leave. He had flown to the nearest RAF station and walked ten miles to the cottage.

We spent a happy and thankful night together, and on Christmas Day we took Anthony over to the Big House. The Furses were overjoyed to see Pat, until they heard he had arrived the night before. This shocked them. They reminded him about the daughter of one of their tenants who had had an affair with a married man on the estate and been forbidden to cross Furse land again. What was a sin for a working girl could not be condoned in the squire's family. We were ordered to leave the cottage immediately.

I was numb. I thought: What is worse, being haunted and hunted by the Nazis or being haunted and hunted, in a free country, by the family of the man you love? Pat accepted it. He did not say 'You stay in the cottage.' We ordered the village taxi and Pat and Anthony and I took the train to London. Pat went back to his unit and Anthony and I went to my little flat, in which I had a Yugoslav scientist lodger in what had been Anthony's room. Anthony and I shared my room.

We listened for the improved flying bombs that night – the V2s had started coming over in September. Then I became angry. I wrote to Mr Black the farmer and to the Furse family. I said they could go to law if they liked, but I was keeping my cottage and would live there until it was safe to go back to London. I never saw the Furses, but the farmers were wonderful. Mr Black was told to give me notice, which he did, and I rejected. I stayed on the estate until the spring of 1946. I loved my fairy-tale cottage.

One day in Bideford, I met a soldier, a bricklayer in civvy street, who was sullen and unhappy because he had no one to talk to and no one to understand what it was like 'out there'. He had a squint and a stutter, but when we parted after five hours there was a shine on him, and he was happy because he had met someone to talk to about the world after the war and international trade unionism. I felt this was a small piece of war work.

The Furses had not taken a single evacuee child into their big house. They had no values, only loyalties. I had four extra children in my cottage for a short time, sent to me by Willo from Elmtrees in Buckinghamshire to get them away from the bombing. (There had been more than a thousand V2 rockets over London, which had killed two thousand people.) Unfortunately, my evacuees were in for a surprise. I upset a frying pan of burning lard over my hands and had to be treated by doctors at the RAF camp at Winkleigh. The same evening, one of the children came down with measles, Anthony came down with flu and I was handless and helpless. So I sent a frantic message to the Misses Waddington at the school, and they sent a young woman (expecting a baby by God knows who), and some parents turned up plus another child, and suddenly the cottage was filled with twelve people and I slept on the floor. But I love people just as much as I love complete solitude. My hands acquired a brand new skin like a baby's bottom, and I could use them again.

In March 1945 the Russian army besieged Königsberg, which surrendered on 9 April. A quarter of the population were killed – Hitler had not allowed them to be evacuated. On 26 April I wrote to Henry Swanzy:

> I do not want to talk about Germany and the war, for my whole inside rises, and I feel physically sick when I read *now*, after twelve years, those indignant articles about the camps, etc. For how long were we persecuted, laughed at and called all kinds of names, for how long did our poor comrades have to suffer and

die, just to keep asleep the smugness of the world! I remember as if it were today the day in May 1933, in the Luetzow Platz, when I handed over to poor old Norman Ebbutt, the *Times* correspondent, eye-witness accounts of what was going on in Dachau, Oranienburg and Buchenwald, and he said, 'My people in London chuck them into a drawer, and they will never be published.' And Freddy Voigt of the *Guardian* said the same thing. And now they are staging this scene of 'horror', for their own aims.

They do not so much as mention that most of the killed and tortured were German anti-Fascists, Socialists and Communists, and many from other countries . . . My instincts are bound up with fears of what may come, indeed I am desperate, for I know the evil power of hatred and revenge.

On 8 May the war against Germany officially ended.

Three days later, 11 May 1945, was the date set for my divorce. I went up to London and in twenty minutes was divorced from Peter Haden-Guest on the grounds of desertion. It was undefended, very straight and clean, but I felt rather guilty. The Conservative press made a lot of it, because of the connection with Dr Haden-Guest the well-known Labour politician. Henry Swanzy sort of held my hand, as in all my bad times. I wrote to thank him: 'God bless you, dearest, and keep you as are, except for knocking over things and wearing untidy clothes.' Pat and I were free to marry when we could.

Churchill called a general election for 26 July, and I wrote to Henry Swanzy: 'Labour is getting very strong in the strongholds of the feudal Furses – I fear I make no secret of the way I intend to vote.' Labour's decisive win was a shock for the officer class; Attlee became Prime Minister. I wrote to Henry: 'I feel that there is hope, and the people have not suffered in vain these last six years. I am a stupid sentimentalist, but I am full of joy that those villains the Brendan Brackens, the James Griggs, the Amerys, are out.'

On 6 August 1945 the Allies dropped an atomic bomb on Hiroshima. I wrote to Henry:

Again I have to sit down and just let my hair down on you, my dear. The Atomic Bomb has shaken me to the very core. I walked and talked to the farm people and, first and foremost, and perhaps my *only* reaction was this: *thank God* the Germans

> did not have it. But all the same it brings us nearer to the dissolution of the world. Why should we be sad at this? Maybe because it is sweet to carry a baby in one's belly, maybe because of the few moments of peace and happiness.
>
> I wish you were here to put me right on facts and figures. I just toddle about in a labyrinth of thoughts and emotions and quarter-knowledge. If only one could believe in the greatness and strength of the human being, but people do not seem to be able to take happiness – they simply seem to be chasing pain.

I invited Henry Swanzy to stay for two weeks in September. He arrived on the 3rd, the day after the war finally ended. He kept a diary, so I can be precise about what happened. I met him at Great Torrington station in a taxi; he noted my bad habit of telephoning for two or three taxis and taking the one that comes first. He said:

> although ostracised by the family at Halsdon, E seems on Christian name terms with many people, tenant farmers, village schoolmasters, all of whom voted Labour. One can imagine the embarrassment she represents to the Furses – and almost sympathise with them. The entire countryside had been warned that Pat and E were living in sin. When someone pointed out that Jill and Laurence Whistler had once been in the same state, the reply was 'not under our roof' . . . We had visits from a Norwegian boy, Heironymus Heyerdahl, and his Cockney friend Charlie, from RAF Winkleigh, and a handsome German POW, a railwayman from Siegen, who wants to know whose zone the town is in now, and whether he can get news of his family from Pat, who is in a school for air support in Paderborn.

I always listen to Henry's criticisms, as he chides with reason and love. Dreamers need the reasoning mind to test their wilder flights on.

An expedition to Torrington was arranged: I hitched a lift and Henry bicycled, with Anthony sitting behind him. Little Mac, my friend from Marseille, arrived in a small car to stay. Anthony threw some tantrums. We were all trying to prepare him for going to boarding school that month, Spyway in Langton

Matravers, Dorset. Pat had been to the Old Malt House school in the same village.

I had made friends with Jack Heard, the gravedigger. He said to me one day, leaning on his spade, 'Getting mighty close in; us just coom upon a gennelman us knew.' Henry met him during his stay, and wrote:

> Jill Whistler's grave is still fresh, a mound of earth, no stone as yet, two apples lying on it. E introduces Jack Heard, the gravedigger, a character out of Thomas Hardy, huge head, wide blue eyes. When he started work sixty years ago, he earned 1s 3d a week, which later rose to 1s 9d. In the late war he and his wife took in five evacuee children for the duration – and from that effort she died three months ago.

Charlie from RAF Winkleigh visited us again with a friend from the camp, and Henry was not pleased with what was said.

> The conversation was exclusively on the best way to bilk the railway. None of the four, Elisabeth, Mac, the two RAF boys, ever pays the full fare. Either they do not buy a ticket, or they buy a local one and travel with it to London, or they take a ticket beyond their destination, keep it, and then use it again (this is the most sophisticated method) or finally they alter the date with a razor. I was half serious when I said that this kind of fiddling and breaking the law goes a little bit of the way to the chaos produced by the Germans in the last war, from which it stems. No respect for tradition and authority.

Pat and I were married on 3 December 1945 at the Chelsea Register Office. I was given away by Lewis Silkin, then Minister of Town and Country Planning, and Pat's best man was his commanding officer. We had lunch at the House of Commons. Aunt Gladys lent me her sables to wear: Ward was sent to get them from the bank, and as soon as the ceremony was over he respectfully took them from my back to the vaults. Aunt Gladys gave a reception for us at her house in the afternoon. She had a last piece of advice for the bride. She took me to her wardrobe and showed me a pink satin nightdress with a lace yoke, and said, 'Satin and lace, Elizabeth, satin and lace always does it. Keep your undies dainty, and never, never let him see you in the altogether.'

Sir Ralph and Lady Furse came to the wedding, and were in the group photograph, but you cannot see their faces in any of the prints. They never pushed themselves forward. We had a blessing later in the church at Dowland. My parents-in-law came, but none of the rest of the family.

17

Fates of My Family and the Escape Route After 1941

No one at home knew the fates of individuals in Europe, cut off by war and secrecy and censorship for seven years. Posters had warned 'She knows what you want – she wants what you know.' I gradually learned what had happened to the Marseille escape route since I had tried to warn them about the treacherous Sergeant Cole.

Cole had had a lot of luck not to be suspected sooner. Donald Darling in Lisbon tried to check up on him. In 1941, he looked up Captain Harold Cole in the Army List and did not find him. Darling told MI9 in London, who asked Scotland Yard. Scotland Yard did know a Harold Cole: he was a convicted conman and thief with a prison record. Sergeant Harold Cole was found in army records: he had stolen the sergeants' mess fund in France in March 1940, but escaped from military prison in Lille at the beginning of June as the Germans approached. Cole had stayed in Lille, where he began to help other evaders and escapers. He was probably not a traitor when Ian Garrow met him around February 1941, but he had found out how to make money from the work. The people who helped us were glad to do it unpaid, but Cole invented expenses and begged money from sympathisers. Garrow gave him large sums that he thought were going to the escape route's northern banker. Cole also took bribes from civilians to smuggle them out of France with the servicemen.

This was all pieced together after the war by Brendan Murphy, who wrote about Cole in *Turncoat*. Murphy thinks Cole might even have been working for two branches of British Intelligence:

the main MI6 as well as our small MI9. Perhaps for this reason, or because he was a success in getting men to Marseille, or just through inefficiency, MI6 did not tell Garrow and Donald Darling about Cole's criminal past.

But Garrow was forced to hear more and more tales of Cole's opportunism, until in September 1941 he saw it with his own eyes. Cole, with one of his mistresses and a woman friend of hers, had brought down a batch of airmen, been paid, and departed again for the North. The next day in Marseille, Pat O'Leary happened to see the woman friend. He drew her into conversation, and she said that Cole and his girlfriend were still there and that they were all going dancing that evening. Pat and Garrow turned up at the dance hall. Cole was spending money on the women, drinking and enjoying himself when he suddenly saw Garrow. He made excuses for being there and said he was leaving the next day.

Garrow sent Pat secretly to the North to investigate. In his own mind, Garrow had already decided that Cole's deceit and greed were too dangerous. While Pat was away, Garrow asked Dr Rodocanachi about killing Cole, and Dr Rodo gave him a syringe of insulin which would put Cole into a coma. In that state, he could be tipped into the harbour at night. But Garrow did not get the chance to tell Pat this, because at that point he himself was arrested.

In the North, Pat discovered from the route's northern banker, François Duprez, that Cole had not paid him any of the money Garrow had sent. He asked Duprez to follow him to Marseille so that they could confront Cole. Pat got back a day after Garrow's arrest, and took over the escape route.

They had to wait until Cole returned to Marseille. The confrontation was in Dr Rodocanachi's flat on 1 November 1941. The timing was bad for Pat: there were three escaping airmen in another room and Fanny Rodocanachi was giving a tea party in the salon for several ladies, including her sister Mrs Zarifi of the Red Cross.

Duprez hid in the bedroom next door to the one in which Pat, Mario Prassinos, an Australian called Bruce Dowding and another member of the route met Cole. Pat accused him of keeping the money intended for Duprez. He denied it and said that he had handed it over. Duprez was brought in. Pat hit Cole so hard his hand never recovered (he would not ask Dr Rodocanachi to set it because he did not want to admit to so much medical knowledge).

Cole grovelled on the floor, apologising and pleading. Bruce said he should be killed. They locked Cole in the bathroom looking on to the well while they discussed it. Suddenly they heard a noise. Cole had got out of the window and climbed across the well into the little window of a lavatory. He ran down the corridor on the other side of the flat and out of the front door as Bruce approached it by the nearside corridor.

Pat O'Leary, Bruce Dowding and François Duprez went north to warn other members of the line. On the morning of 6 December, Cole was arrested near Lille by the Abwehr and apparently 'turned' to work against the Allies. But it is possible that he was already working for the Germans, either for the Abwehr – which would mean his arrest was staged – or the Abwehr's rival the Sicherheitsdienst of the SS. It certainly did not take long to turn him. On the same day he wrote a thirty-page denunciation of members of the line.

The route's northern banker Duprez was arrested that afternoon. The abbé who had forged the identity papers, Pierre Carpentier, a French army chaplain who had continued the fight as a parish priest, was arrested in Abbeville on 8 December, and so was Bruce Dowding, and the arrests continued. Cole was said to sometimes accompany the Germans going to get his fellow escape workers. His treachery was still not fully believed by MI9 and MI6 in London. Abbé Carpentier managed to smuggle a denunciation of Cole out of prison to Pat in January 1942, but when I was in Lisbon it had not yet reached Darling.

Still continuing to pose as an Allied Intelligence agent, in June 1942 Cole visited Lyon in the Vichy zone and went to two former contacts for money, thinking that they would not know he had turned. Both did. The first telephoned Pat in Marseille, who set off with a gun to finish him. The second told Gaullist sympathisers in the Vichy secret police that Cole, a German agent, was there. When Pat arrived in Lyon next morning, Cole had already been arrested.

He was sentenced to death, but was saved again when the Germans took over the whole of mainland France on 11 November 1942. They released their friend Cole, who went back to work for the Abwehr. Hitler dissolved the Abwehr in February 1944 and gave its work to its rival the SS, so Cole got a new boss, Hans Kieffer of the Sicherheitsdienst.

As the Allies moved up France, Cole and Kieffer escaped to

Germany together. In May 1945 they approached an American cavalry unit in the Black Forest, saying that Cole, renamed Mason, was a British agent captured by the Germans and that Kieffer was a decent civil policeman who was bringing his prisoner to the Allies. By Cole's usual luck, one of the American cavalry officers had been in the Resistance and met him in Marseille when he had been thought loyal. The Corps' head of Counter Intelligence invited Cole to join Allied Intelligence and Kieffer was given a permit to go home.

Cole pretended he was rooting out SS officers and war criminals. He was actually extorting money from his former colleagues, often by torture. After torturing a Gestapo officer called Hanft, he and two young French officers and an American captain killed him. The murder was nothing new for Cole, who had caused the imprisonment of at least seventy-five helpers of the escape route, and the death of probably fifty.

British Intelligence at last found out where Cole was and a major in MI5 went to Bavaria to arrest him. Cole was taken to an American military prison in Paris, but once again the cornered rat escaped, and lodged with a woman who owned a bar in the rue de Grenelle, spinning her a yarn about being an English soldier waiting to be demobilised. Her neighbours suspected she was sheltering a German, and told the police. Two French policemen called. One went upstairs with the woman. When they opened Cole's door, he fired twice, but only grazed the policeman, who shot him through the heart. Pat O'Leary was on holiday in Skye with Garrow. He came to Paris and identified the body in the morgue.

Cole's first victims after he turned, François Duprez, Bruce Dowding and the Abbé Pierre Carpentier, all died. They were sent to Germany, and while in Bochum they were condemned to death by a Berlin court. Duprez died of exhaustion in a concentration camp at Sonnenburg in April 1944, Carpentier and Dowding were beheaded at Dortmund on 30 June 1943, with three other members of the escape route.

Ian Garrow had been shut up in Mauzac through trying to save me. After the Germans took over the Vichy zone in November 1942, they decided to move him from Mauzac to Dachau, where he would probably have met his end. When Pat heard about it, he arranged a daring escape. Garrow walked out of Mauzac in December 1942 with the night shift of guards in a uniform Pat had smuggled in, and was spirited across the Pyrenees to Lisbon. Pat said goodbye to him in a Pyrenean shepherd's hut.

When Garrow got back to London, he worked for the HQ of MI9. He was to have been sent to France in the Overlord landings but broke his foot while training. He was stationed in Berlin from 1945 to 1947 and was demobilised as a lieutenant-colonel, with a DSO and Croix de Guerre. Before the war, he had been the black sheep of his family. His father was an eye specialist in Glasgow. Ian lived in Half Moon Street in Mayfair and spent his time fornicating and drinking. The war brought him a *raison d'être* and turned him into a hero. He hardly touched alcohol for the duration. What strange chemistries go into the making of heroes: they are mostly misfits – outsiders, loners, desperados, neurotics, or people who have failed in love, like Pat O'Leary. There are a few lucid and clear activists, but most heroes and heroines are not rounded members of society.

After Ian's demob, he went back to Scotland, and to drinking. When Dr Garrow died, Ian asked the housekeeper who had looked after his father to come to him, but she said they must be married. Ian agreed – he didn't care. I went to visit them in Glencoe. Ian wrote no book about his experiences and used to say, 'It was just a job.' But I was proud that when he knew about my death sentence, and the American papers and tickets waiting for me, he said, 'You were the bravest of us all.' These words from him, and the Vichy officer's '*Vous avez grande mérite pour la France et l'Angleterre*' are what I treasure. In the book *MI9*, which James Langley and M. R. D. Foot wrote after the war, I am not mentioned. But my recognition was given to me by men who were there.

A French traitor working for the Gestapo, Roger Le Neveu, called '*Le Légionnaire*' because he had been in the Foreign Legion, infiltrated and finished the destruction of the line in the South. Through Roger, Louis Nouveau was arrested in January 1943 and Pat O'Leary in March. Dr Rodocanachi was taken in February, probably having been denounced by enemies in the Marseille medical establishment.

Louis Nouveau was imprisoned in Fresnes for a year, then in Buchenwald for sixteen months. Renée Nouveau got out down the escape route to England in the spring of 1943. After the war the Nouveaus went back to Marseille and Louis built up his business again. He died in the 1970s. Renée went to live in Aix-en-Provence. Both were decorated by Britain.

Louis managed to spend three-quarters of an hour with Dr Rodocanachi in Buchenwald in January 1944. Dr Rodocanachi had just arrived, after imprisonment in St Pierre in Marseille and then Compiègne. He was a month away from his sixty-eighth birthday. The Germans had not linked him with the escape route, merely with his Gaullist bias on the medical board, and he could have been released if he had signed a paper promising not to work against them. But he proudly refused. In Buchenwald, he would not follow the order to take off his cap to every member of the SS, and his fellow prisoners saw the SS men hit him on the head each time to knock the cap off. It was 30 degrees below zero. Dr Rodocanachi had angina, and he died on 10 February 1944, fighting to the end. As another inmate, Jean Blanc, wrote to Fanny Rodocanachi later (quoted in her niece Helen Long's book *Safe Houses are Dangerous*):

> He asked me to gather around him as many French prisoners as I could. And he asked us to sing the Marseillaise for him. I admit to you, madame, that our national song came very painfully from our tightened throats. Nevertheless, we managed somehow to sing the hymn that is so dear to all French patriots, and Dr Rodocanachi passed away in this fashion, whispering with his last breath '*Vive la France. A bas les Boches.*'

Fanny moved to London after the war to be near her brother. She died of cancer in April 1959. Their maid, Séraphine, went to an old people's home near Marseille. Her proudest possession was her citation from the British government.

The wonderful Pat O'Leary, the Gestapo's prize catch, was imprisoned in Fresnes, Saarbrücken, Mauthausen, Natzweiler and finally Dachau, tortured half to death, including being shut in a refrigerator, but betrayed no one. In Dachau, typhus broke out, and he at last dropped his secrecy about being a doctor to tend the prisoners. He was the British representative on the body the prisoners set up, the International Prisoners Committee. He had been condemned to execution, but was saved by the Americans liberating Dachau on 29 April 1945.

Pat went to England, but was soon in Paris, after the war in Europe ended in May, arranging for helpers of the line to be compensated. This was administered by Donald Darling, Pat and Sylvia Cooper Smith, a girl on the staff of MI9. In 1947, Pat and Sylvia married. Pat went back to the Belgian Army, and to Korea, where he was head of the Belgian medical service. By yet another act of heroism he rescued a wounded man under fire. He became director general of the Belgian Forces' Medical Service, and was heaped with honours, including a British knighthood, the French Croix de Guerre, Polish Croix de Guerre and the hereditary title of Count Guérisse given him by King Baudouin in 1986. The Guérisses lived at Waterloo. Sylvia died in 1985 and Pat died of cancer in March 1989. Their son is a doctor, named Patrick.

Nancy Fiocca was warned she must escape down the route to England in June 1943. Henri Fiocca was tortured by the Gestapo to find out where she was, then executed in Marseille in October 1943. Nancy trained with SOE and was parachuted back to the Auvergne on 30 April 1944 to work with the Maquis before D-Day. By a coincidence, her Maquis band caught Roger Le Neveu, scourge of the Pat line, and executed him. Nancy was much decorated after the war.

Little Mac, Lewis MacDonald, was sent to North Africa as a wireless operator. He joined SOE in Cairo, got a commission, and was parachuted back into France. After France was liberated he joined the Black Watch, ending the war with many medals. He spent most of his leaves with me in London, sleeping on the floor in the passage. In 1946, Didda, Sir Ralph Furse, helped him get a job in the colonial police, and he went to Nigeria. He retired as a colonel.

Tom Kenny was released from prison in Marseille, went to England and joined the RAF. After the war he, his wife Sue Martinez and their three sons lived in Paris. He died there in 1971.

Gaston Defferre, my lawyer, had with another man been running the 'Froment' Resistance network since 1940. He was made joint Minister of Urban Affairs in the government De Gaulle set up in the autumn of 1944, composed of Resistance workers and Frenchmen from Algeria. Defferre was a Socialist deputy in 1946-58, and Mayor of Marseille from 1953. He died in 1986.

Admiral Canaris, head of the Abwehr and thus the boss of Cole and my German countess cellmate in Marseille, turned out to have been an anti-Nazi who had been wanting to get rid of Hitler since 1938. He was arrested after the failure of the Stauffenberg bomb plot in July 1944 and hanged on April 9 1945 at Flössenburg concentration camp in Bavaria, as the Allies advanced from the south. He was taken to the same gallows on the same morning as Pastor Dietrich Bonhoeffer, the friend and colleague of Pastor Niemöller whose belltower had sheltered Willy Koska.

I was a fighter, not a victim, so I never told my friends in the escape route that I was Jewish and an ex-Communist. They would not have given a job to a woman double branded for torture and death.

I found out after the war what the Nazis had done to my family. My father's textile business was confiscated, and my parents went to Palestine with Gerda and Nurse in July 1934; my brothers Max and Arno were already there. My mother, with Nurse, returned to Berlin to clear up some business, and the SS put her in prison in Alexanderplatz. She sold her properties to pay all the Jewish taxes and got a document saying she owed nothing to the German state (imprisonment was often used by the Nazis to extort money). She rejoined the family in Tel Aviv in 1936. My father could not make a business success in Palestine. He went to England in 1937, but was turned out in 1938 when the Germans declared the Jews to be stateless. He moved to Prague, the Nazis took Prague and he was sent to a concentration camp. My mother got him out by showing her paid-up certificate. They went home to Berlin in 1956. Gerda had married a London Irishman, but decided she must go and look after them. My mother died in 1958, my father in 1965. Max is dead, too. Gerda lives in Berlin and Arno in Tel Aviv.

My feared grandmother Lena Bloch was gassed in Auschwitz with five of her family: Uncle Hermann and his wife, Aunt Anna and her husband and their daughter. My beloved Aunt Sonya and her brother Heinrich were gassed in Majdanek in Poland.

18

Pat and I in London, 1946–52

So there was peace and there were we; poised like racehorses to catch up, to work, to love, to have babies and to reconstruct. Though for me, in one sense, the war had not ended – I could never give up fighting and providing.

After Pat came out of the army in 1946, he and I had no money except his gratuity and what I could earn as a continuity girl. He wanted to be a painter. He could either have a grant of £3 10s a week for two years to study painting and then try to live by his pictures, or £7 10s a week for a three-year art teacher training course. He chose the first, and enrolled at Chelsea Art School.

We had to find somewhere to live. Pat was intrigued by déclassé areas and suggested Tooting. I said Never. I could only ever live right in the country or in the very centre of a city. I have a horror of any edge or suburb, and to me the suburbs start at Hyde Park. Neither can I stand views – I want to be inside the view. All my life I have lived in the dark and watched the people in the light.

I went to the estate agent's department of that heathen place Harrods. I do not like the rest of Harrods – it is *too much*, and an insult to the senses, however much all classes love it. The bus conductors call out the name as though it were a cathedral, and I joke with them 'Surely you mean *Saint* Harrods?' I only buy bacon ends there, the bits that drop off the bacon slicer, and fish scraps, 'for the cats'. But the estate agency is good. They produced a house in Trevor Square, Knightsbridge, with a large studio for Pat. It cost £350 a year – almost twice Pat's income, but we took it. It had been occupied by the army, and was quite bare. We spent

£10 on furniture, and moved in. We were considered respectable – we were Furses – and neighbours like Violet Wyndham and Lady Lewisham came to call and left cards. They did not mind that we had no chairs. With the name Furse we could afford to be poor.

I am lucky in always arriving at a place when something is about to happen. I might have really been a journalist, instead of just writing a few articles and using my press card when I need it (I joined the National Union of Journalists as well as the ACT after I did some articles in the *Scotsman*). Belgravia was going back to private tenancies when we moved in. Interesting young people lived around us, and wasteful older people lived around us. We could not have existed on as little as we did except for the waste of smart Belgravia.

To pay the rent, I took in lodgers. Many have been my friends ever since. Michael Crosfield was a Quaker and had a rich father. Maurits Sillem was a Dutch boy who wanted to be a conductor – later he worked at Glyndebourne and later still at Covent Garden. There was Alexei Poklewski-Koziell, one of two Russian-Polish brothers whose family had had enormous estates and a house the size of Versailles. Alexei said, 'Your great-grandmother used to kiss the hem of my great-grandmother's skirt.' I said, 'Well, things have changed. Now you kiss the hem of my skirt.' Alexei got a job on *Picture Post*. Their friend Jash (John) Pomian was a Polish economist who later ran the Heim Gallery in Jermyn Street. Kazimir Stamirski was another Pole who lived with us. James Wells was an American literary librarian. Anthony Elliott had been at Eton with Pat; he had just been demobbed, and went into the Foreign Office.

We shared everything. We lived on lentils, beans and pasta, with minced meat once a week. Chicken was too expensive, and anyway I only eat animals I like, not animals like hens that I do not like.

It was easier to scavenge in Knightsbridge than in Tooting – I could find the leftovers because I was the only one who knew about them. The street stalls in Soho were good; those across the river were even cheaper. From the Distressed Gentlefolks Association I bought second-hand clothes for ourselves and our friends. I have never bought a new dress: I always had a dressmaker who made my clothes from material I found in the sales. Until the fifties, women in Belgravia who could not afford couture made do with a clever dressmaker – to say you dressed 'off the peg' was quite audacious. This was before there were good copies and shops like Mary Quant.

Pat and I liked the same music, poetry, literature and people. We both loved our kind of living, our kind of poorness. He allowed me to keep an open house and an open heart and be what Americans call 'warm' – rather a horrible expression, like water. But he was not as energetic as me.

By the autumn of 1946 I was pregnant. I had had two miscarriages and one stillbirth since being with Pat so this was another chance. But I was offered a job on location. I wrote to Henry Swanzy on 18 October:

> On the 20th September I was asked to go to Switzerland to make a film. On the 25th the rabbits or mice or whatever they use for the test said I was definitely expecting a baby. I decided to go, as I was rather homesick for Europe, and it was a pleasant way of earning Anthony's school fees quickly before the baby came. So off I went in a violent hurry.
>
> We have been racing across Switzerland, up and down the Jungfrau, etc, and finally on the Matterhorn, where I got an inflammation of the kidneys and almost lost the baby. I remember the blood on the snow and how beautiful it looked.

I was writing from a nursing home in Interlaken, where I had been sent by the Swiss doctors.

> As soon as I can travel safely . . . I shall be on my way home, stopping for a day and night in Paris, so as not to hunger for any part of Europe for the next year to come, when I shall be chained to bearing a little child.
>
> But although I have been seeing incredible and pure beauty, it did not *quite* go to my heart – because I was alone without the ones I love, and because there were always crowds of unbearably banal, stupid and noisy film people around.
>
> Once I escaped them for two hours, high up, and was left alone with God and wild chamois and black ravens and the silence of the snow which knows no equal. I am glad I took my baby up there. It is not pleasant to be in great pain and fear high up in the mountains, but I feel very much stronger and cleaner since having battled through it – like the time I left prison.

On 19 May 1947, I had the baby at St George's Hospital in London. I wrote to Henry: 'He weighed 10½ pounds, and it was HELL. He is a big boy and a tough one and he is called John Henry. It covers us all well because it is *the* family name, and I always wanted him to have something of you.' Pat and I asked Henry to be a godfather. Johnny was the prettiest baby ever, in his little bonnet. When he was three months old, he earned the huge sum of £14 a week for a while, by playing the role of the baby Queen Victoria on stage in *The First Gentleman*, a play about the Prince Regent which starred Robert Morley and Wendy Hiller. He was ferried to and from the theatre in a big car every night.

This year was good not only for me. Henry wrote in his diary for 13 September:

> The Furses are in Paris, having come from Brussels, where Pat went to see the cineaste and visionary Dekeukelaere, on whom he has written an article for his film magazine. They are in a car lent by Mike Crosfield, their Quaker lodger. They bring Anthony, retrieved from St Briac, and the new baby, John Henry, who is shrouded in a vast layette. We get lunch in an expensive house near the Bois, belonging to one René Sanson, a friend in the Resistance, who 'liberated' it in 1944, when the original owner, said to be a German spy, vanished without trace.
>
> Sanson is away at the moment. A photograph shows him as long-nosed and narrow-eyed, standing beside a very beautiful, dark-haired woman, his wife Colette. In the wardrobe ten suits are hanging, all very expensive. Elisabeth explained that she had 'met' Madame Sanson at the prison in Marseille, by means of messages tapped on the pipes. They were almost the only Gaullists there at the time. Later she (Colette) was sent to Auschwitz, but survived. Her husband had been held in Fort St Nicolas. Just after the war, he went as a French delegate to San Francisco, and found Elisabeth in London through the War Office.

Next year I was pregnant again. On 26 September 1948 our daughter Katharine, named after the Dame but called Katya, was born in Westminster Hospital. I wrote to Henry:

> What a whopper . . . Inches of black curls, very nice long figure, well-shaped head and ears, *cavewoman* face! But thank God, she

> is a woman, and she was born on Sunday (something I dreamed of). Now, come what may, I am ready to face life, with two sons and a daughter! Having a baby is just as bad as having an atomic bomb, although of course it does produce something constructive. We are getting £12 from the Ministry of Health, on which we hope to hop over to Paris soon. I swear I shall never again cheat the railways and buses, and will live a clean, civilised life.

But I didn't. When I was pregnant I had got lifts quickly, so when I wasn't I stuffed a cushion inside my coat. I was well looked after by the crews, because most of them are kind to pregnant women and I was always pregnant. Katina Paxinou, that wonderful Greek actress who was in *Uncle Silas*, used to slap my belly when I was carrying Johnny and say, 'Boys, can't you see she's pregnant? Get her a chair.' They nearly fainted at such frankness, being squeamish British men.

Anthony Elliott supported the Labour Party and was a friend of Roy Jenkins's, a man I never took to. I dislike that kind of Welsh pretending to be English suburban climber very much indeed. I joined the Party in 1949, and within a month I found myself Treasurer of the local branch – there were not an awful lot of Labourites in Knightsbridge. I was put up for more and more jobs and could have been elected to the London County Council. They wanted to put me up for Soho, because I knew about prostitutes.

But I did not like what I saw going on. The Communists had infiltrated the Labour Party, as we had been trained to do in Berlin. When I talked about this to Anthony Elliott, he gave me a jolly answer: 'A few Trots and a few Commies will do the Party good, bring some life into it.' I said, 'They are there to bring you death.' He said, 'Your past has played you up.' I said, 'My past has taught me to understand.' He ridiculed me: 'Elisabeth sees a Red under every bed.' But I said, 'No – *in* every bed . . .' I resigned.

I loved Anthony Elliott because he respected me and we feasted together off our political and moral and emotional attitudes and activities. He knew more, but I was more experienced. He could do in three words what I did in twenty, but he seemed to like my words, and he laughed, and he made me laugh, and everyone loves people who make them laugh. Politically, Ant was Party-bound and Roy-bound and so-and-so-bound. I was free and belonged to the 'ordinary people' – people who travel on buses – and I told him about them. He could explain to me the attitudes of the big shots, the ones who do not travel on buses. They never have time to go to markets or even to Hyde Park Corner and listen to the speakers – neither have their wives, too busy being wives *par excellence*. And if politicians think that the occasional visit to the pub in the constituency and talking to the odd labourer gives them enough insight into 'the people', they are wrong. The people usually *are not* – they like quietly to exist. It is only when they get angry that they become something, or when they sing together – but that is rare. When they are angry, there is no holding them back – but then it is too late for the politicians.

There was an amusing incident in 1948, when the cine technicians' union, the ACT, marched to the Houses of Parliament to complain about unemployment and conditions in the studios. Pat and I went with Johnny in the pram, which bore a slogan that was certainly true: 'DAD WANTS BETTER WAGES'. As we walked through Hyde Park, who should we meet but my son Anthony, mounted on one of Auntie Forbes's hired horses. She thought that riding might help to form his character. At least he didn't try to ride us down.

I still went on location in Europe with film crews. I left the babies with Pat and the au pair girl – au pairs were a new idea then in Britain. In 1948 I worked on a documentary which Ray Anzarut, a producer at Shepperton, was making for Marshall Aid in Sweden, near the Norwegian border. The writer was Humphrey Jennings. One railway station was right on the border. On the Norwegian side, the food kiosk had three green apples and some very hard plums; the Swedes had bananas, oranges, huge rosy apples, chocolates galore.

When I was working in England, I set off for the studio at six o'clock in the morning. Pat came with me to the corner of the square, wheeling the pram, then he went back to bed.

Pat was interested in the cinema, and he and Michael Crosfield discussed setting up a company to make educational films, but Pat's main occupation was painting.

In 1948, Michael took Pat down to Devon in his MG and noticed that two cottages were for sale, one in a hamlet and the other just outside the boundary of the Furse estate. Michael said, 'I'll buy the cottage in the hamlet'; it was £400. The other, called Locks Hill, was £700 and Michael said, 'I'll give you £400 if you can manage the rest – the Furses will see their grandchildren whether they want to or not.' So we had a cottage again.

In January 1949, Johnny and Katya were christened at Dowland church where we had had our marriage blessed. Henry Swanzy has come to the rescue of accuracy with his diary, so I know that we took the 5.30 afternoon train from Paddington: Pat and I and Françoise Esparbes, the au pair girl, with the two babies; Michael Crosfield, Anthony Elliott, and Henry and his wife Tirzah. We had a cabin trunk, a bicycle, a haversack and 'five large brown paper parcels, contents undisclosed'.

For the christening, our party sat on the right of the aisle, the rest of the Furses on the left: Sir Ralph, Lady Furse, Theresa, and Laurence Whistler. The godparents were Theresa Furse, Henry, and Katina Paxinou, my Greek actress friend, who wasn't there, but Françoise stood in for her. At the lunch afterwards at Locks Hill, as Henry described it, 'the two groups did not find it easy to make conversation over the claret and crumbly iced sponge cake . . . But John Henry smiled and Katharine looked enchanting, in a cradle covered by blue cloth, and adorned with pussy-catkins and early snowdrops.'

Next day, 'Elisabeth, Pat, Anthony Elliott and I walked in the water meadows by the Torridge, and watched a heron. We make an odd picture. E has a belt slung over her shoulder, for a basket to pile with snowdrops and anything else she can pick up, Pat is like a seaman, A.E. lopes along, like a beetle in his green Loden overcoat.'

Sir Ralph and Lady Furse became fairly friendly towards our children, but they were never treated like the other two sets of grandchildren: the Whistlers and Pat's brother Nicholas's children. The year after our christening, Laurence Whistler married Theresa Furse and they had another son and daughter. I forgave my father- and mother-in-law, and in a strange way I liked them. Their hardness was sometimes petty. Roger Banks, the artist, was living with us at Trevor Square and we lent him Locks Hill to paint in. He was a great gardener, like Celia Furse, and she took him round the garden at Halsdon. It was strawberry time, and he asked if he could take some back for my children, but she said, 'Oh, no, they have plenty in London.' 'But it would be so nice for them to have strawberries from their grandmother.' She still would not give him any, so he bought punnets at the station and said they were from Halsdon.

* * *

At the beginning of September 1949, Pat and I left the babies with Françoise and took off for France, Italy and Yugoslavia, mostly by hitchhiking. A letter from Pat to Henry comes to the aid of accuracy here: 'We had the two heaviest packs since Sisyphus . . . At Fontainebleau, we were picked up by a Frenchman born in Australia, who drove like Jehu by day, and totally blind at night – the axle was broken charging a level crossing. A lorry full of copper took us to Lyon, thence to Vienne.' Pat noted that 'the countryside is lovely, but the people, at the moment at any rate, are not. Prices are terribly high, even for the lorrymen. The cheapest meal costs nearly a tenth of the average weekly wage (£5). We had to pay for our lifts – and the drivers drove a hard bargain. In Paris someone told us '*Nous sommes une race de Juifs – on vend et on achète pour n'importe qui.*' And this was only four years after the world found out what had been done to the Jews in the death camps.

We caught a lorry full of zinc bound for Marseille, which already had another hitchhiker, a Swiss jazz clarinettist going to Algeria. In Marseille, we visited Les Presentines.

> E took me to see her old cell. The prison is now whitewashed and used for storage, but we were shown round by some most obliging *sapeurs pompiers* (military firemen). Then we found a lorry driven by a wonderful old man, a partner in Dragon et Tardif, who was so intent on showing us the beauties of Provence that he made a long detour, and finally deposited us on a scorching stretch of deserted road, opposite the Mont St Victoire, near Aix . . . I found that Cézanne is entirely correct in painting his trees so heavily accented, 'like a blind man feeling over them'.

We headed east, catching a wine-trailer, then a lorry loaded with sheet glass, and then a local bus to Antibes, where we spent a lazy week with a female cousin of Pat's. The train to Venice took fourteen hours in teeming rain. This was the beginning of my love affair with Venice, and Pat's too. He wrote in a letter that Venice was:

> a dream of beauty, yet intensely *real*, since it is full of hard-working people who still live by the skills of their hands –

leather-work, shoes, glass, gloves, clothes, silk, furniture, all very cheap, and in beautiful taste, apart from some horrible modernistic styles that resembled the bogus ceramiques à la Picasso in the Castle Museum at Antibes . . . France smelt really decadent. What we have seen of Italy is far more vigorous, poorer but prouder (this may only be conceptual). But they are definitely not a broken people.

Anthony Elliott joined us from Belgrade, where he was Second Secretary at the Embassy, and we travelled on. At one point we had so little money that I exchanged Pat's army socks for a meal, and we went through Yugoslavia exchanging things like that for food. All they had was black bread, tea, jam and some kind of bean stew, but they were marvellous. We came back through Venice again. We walked along a beach and saw some working people cooking their meal on seaweed – two fishes they had just caught. They stretched out their arms and said 'Join us.' They were three and we were three, and we shared the two fish, a large loaf of bread, and some wine. I will never forget that meal.

Venice gave me pride in being a human being. The Venetians are hard people, tough because they are a mixed race – Oriental, Roman, Judaean. They are a real mixture of Europe and the world. Venice is beautiful, the nearest to a dream life and eternal peace, no cars, trams, buses, only the shiny canals, the shapes of incredibly lovely buildings against a dark and transparent sky with stars popping out. But it is the spirit of Venice that gets to me. Later I dragged my children there, and said, 'You are here to see the finest thing humans have made. Man built this miracle with his hands out of the water to save himself from persecution and destruction by the Huns. Whatever happens, you will have this pride.' I felt part of it. Venice is the expression of European civilisation – intelligence, taste, thought, and working artisans – the application of heart and hand together. In Venice, everything drops off me: it's the next best thing to being pregnant. Nothing hurts. The people there are so generous to the old and kind to the young. England is civilised and France is cultured, but Venice is both. I breathe it and I live it. I want to die there.

As a child and young person I looked forward to dying. It is the Slav in me. I used to hide in cemeteries. I found it peaceful sitting there reading, but I wanted to be dead, I wanted to be buried. All through my life I said 'I'll die young.' One day when I was over fifty Anthony Elliott said, 'You've missed the boat.'

When we got back to London, Pat showed some ballet sketches in an exhibition with Oliver Messel at the Wildenstein Gallery. Pat himself was really an artisan but he wanted to be an artist. There was a revival of enamelling as an art form, led by Stefan Knapp, and from him Pat learnt the technique, which suited his talent. Henry Swanzy wrote in his diary about finding him in Trevor Square producing plaques by the French process *verre églomisé*. 'The four examples he showed me were charming: a rose, a formal flowerpot, a doodle, a jagged modernism.'

In the spring of 1950 I went with a film team to Austria. In Vienna they expected war within two years, and wanted it – not an atomic war, but to roll back the Slavs. In the autumn I was in Sweden working on an escape story. A dishonest former RAF man sold the black and white film we had taken along to do our tests before using colour. Sometimes I travelled on my own. In the spring of 1951 I went from Folkestone through Paris to Milan (where I went 'to make quite sure that the Duomo is as ugly and impossible as ever', I wrote to Henry Swanzy) and on through Verona and Padua to Venice. From Venice, I went to Trieste (one night's rest in a brothel) and into the Russian zone, north to Vienna and then home by the same route. I told Henry:

> Neither in France, Italy nor Austria can the people, the intelligentsia, the professional classes, manage to eat properly and dress properly, though all the resources are there. The churches are crowded – and the Communist meetings are too. There is nothing else: only the religion of the Red creed or the Papal. All that is in between, or intelligent, is crushed or in the process of being crushed. This extremism makes me miss our crumbling but oh so kindly and still so gentle England. I feel like a child must feel, parted from its mother.

I had just heard that Henry's wife Tirzah had died, which was the reason for my long letter.

> People, harassed and persecuted by fear, throw one into the depths of despair. And behind all that, you appear constantly in my thoughts. Never have I felt you nearer and dearer to me,

> and gladly would I take some of your own heartbreak off you – although sometimes I feel that even I cannot carry on producing laughter and warmth and joy. I am almost suffocated by those who live off me, as they should – the children, Pat, the house, the Movement (I was still in the Labour Party), the Elliotts and others – you are the only one who does not whine and want me, and you are the only one I would so much like to give to.

But at least we had our house. Then, at the end of 1951, we lost that: Harrods said we had to repair and redecorate it and negotiate a new lease. We could not afford to, so we were homeless, after five years in Trevor Square.

For six months the family was split up. Anthony was at Gordonstoun school in Scotland, and stayed with Auntie Forbes in the holidays; Johnny and Katya lived with our daily nurse Eileen in Battersea; Pat was with his cousin Peter Newbolt; and I was at Aunt Gladys's. Then I found a cheap little house in Bourne Street, near Sloane Square, with a shop attached, where a lovely old couple sold antiques. The lease was £2,000 for twenty years. Pat went to his parents to try to borrow the money and discovered that for several years he had been entitled to some family money they had not told him about. So in the spring of 1952 we bought the lease of 3 Bourne Street. I loved it – two up, two down, a real old workman's cottage in Belgravia, beautifully shabby and well lived in.

I felt I was doing more than my share for our little family, but Henry Swanzy stuck up for Pat. I wrote to Henry:

> I should be glad if you would realise that Pat is neither misunderstood nor frustrated by me, but that he suffers, as all his family do, from a lack of vitality and drive and ambition. For Pat to be 'understood' too much would be fatal, because it would make him more self-centred and self-involved than he is already. I have a strong feeling that you believe in artists having to be 'understood', or to be excused responsibility. I am sure that you understood Tirzah – but I am also sure that Tirzah had a contempt for it, and rather preferred to feel isolated and 'misunderstood'.

To make Pat happy, I said we would have a little art gallery in the shop. We painted our names over the door: 'E. & P.

Furse Ltd, Engravings, Prints, Pictures'. We sold Pat's ballet drawings, old prints and sometimes enamels. We had room for one lodger.

I found out how to do the washing for this household cheaply: I piled it in our Marmet pram and pushed it to the magnificent public laundry in Buckingham Palace Road. It had huge copper cauldrons, sinks with scrubbing boards, drying cupboards, mangles and ironing machines. I saw tramps there who undressed down to their underpants and waited in a sheet while their rags were washed. The other women were not friendly. One said, 'Why do you come here? It's not for the likes of you. You're a nob.' The large graceful pram rubbed it in for them.

Our au pair at the time was a charming Dutch girl, Henriette van Eeghen, a cousin of Maurits Sillem who had lodged at Trevor Square. I had found flats and ties and flatmates for Henry Swanzy: what he needed now was a wife. I wrote to him in May 1952:

> I am off with my lot on Friday to the cottage, and will stay there until Wednesday or even later, then off to Austria (film) on the 11th June and back in 4-5 weeks. We have decided that it would be best to send Henriette and the children to the cottage, where life is easy and healthy, and also to avoid Henriette's getting overworked in more ways than one, with looking after Pat, the children and the inevitable hangers-on, which involves cleaning, shopping, washing and the endless preoccupation with Pat. The main thing is that she ought to be happy down there and not get frustrated. Why the hell do all my girls get involved and frustrated? Sometimes they seem to me to be more of a liability, moral and otherwise, than the children. I wish you would take some weekends, or even a week off, to visit them. It would give me terrific peace of mind. God bless you, darling – and do not lose your confidence and self-respect. You are too good for that.

Henriette and Henry got married in July, but Henry told me firmly that although I had always been his fairy godmother and he had found his bride under my roof, he had set his heart on her before I started my machinations. That year, 1952, Pat joined me in the film world. He won a competition in a film magazine and got a place as an art trainee at Ealing, under Sandy MacKendrick.

But he did not like film work and left in a few months and went back to buying and selling prints. The gallery did not do well, so we turned it into an antique shop. Pat found the stock to sell, but the shop was not a success either. I was very glad I had continuity work.

19

In the Studios and on Location, 1946–53

Almost all the studios were to the west – at Shepperton, Ealing, Elstree, Denham and Pinewood. I got a Green Line bus from Knightsbridge and hitchhiked the rest of the way to save two shillings, I was so poor. It was marvellous, being so poor. I used to get jobs at Elstree, where the Americans made films, and at Shepperton. American studios did not suit me: they were too factory-like, and you had to clock in. I much preferred Shepperton, with Alexander Korda. I liked it so much that one day I met Korda on the set and said, 'I wish I could work for you for nothing, I am so happy here.' Korda loved women and babies, so I was allowed to be pregnant to my heart's content and bring a baby to work if I needed to.

Film-making meant the spirit of a unit, the feeling of one for another. I was a misfit, though. I never took the work seriously, it was too much fun. Everyone was my friend, from the people on the studio floor to the cutting-room. I never understood what the camera was doing: all the lenses and measuring and the sound-boxes were a mystery to me. The cutting-room has to have enough shots to work with, and when the director asked me 'Are we covered?' I pretended I knew. But I did understand the actors and the director, which was how I could help. I made them feel good and did the dialogue work with the actors and prompted them. I was also the audience. I used to cry at emotional scenes and soak my notebook, forgetting my duty to note the details, which the cutting-room and the other technicians had to help me with later.

You could study a director's personality by the way he shot and cut his film. The timing of a shot made it cheap or expensive: I first realised this in 1935, when I worked for Gabriel Pascal, a Hungarian Jew who had just arrived in Britain – he was the most irritating and vulgar of all. He would stand with his back to the set and time the shooting with his stop-watch and scream at me 'How many minutes done today?' To work for him was morally degrading. The union did not like him either. After *Caesar and Cleopatra* (1945), which took too long, cost too much and was too wearing on everybody, they passed a resolution that he should not be allowed to make films in England except 'subject to special control'.

I worked with Sam Spiegel, who produced *The African Queen* (1951). He wore brown and white co-respondent shoes with white trousers and I loathed him: so common and vulgar. Most film moguls were like a mixture of street vendor and Mafia. There was a great deal of money involved, and they had little feeling for the people who actually made the films.

Alex Korda was civilised. He arrived in a Rolls-Royce with his stars and always looked what he was, a tall Hungarian Jewish gentleman in business. Churchill had given him a knighthood in 1942 for his help during the war – the first film-maker knight. His brother Vincent was small, almost white-haired, and very absent-minded: he was the art director. The third brother, Zoltan, worked a lot in Hollywood and a bit in England, in editing and sound. He spent hours and hours perfecting it. It was strange that one womb should produce three such different boys, but they worked well together and were totally loyal to each other, like the Renoirs.

Alex Korda was impressed by an Estonian woman with a Russian background, Moura Budberg, who never let you forget she was a baroness. She sometimes floated through the studios in furs and good clothes, doing the job he had given her of translating and script-reading. We called her 'Moura Woodwork', because she had come out of that to do nobody knew quite what. She had been Gorky's mistress and was H. G. Wells's mistress until Wells died in 1946. Moura Budberg had spied for both sides in the early days of the Bolsheviks in Russia, and liked it to be thought that she had gone on to become an important informant for the NKVD. She told Anthony West she had been forced to spy – the opposite of me, whom people accuse of being an agent when I was never one. She did everything to be noticed. The Kordas were proud to have her at their parties. She played the *grande dame*.

I did not like the comedians, because I do not like to be made to laugh: I like spontaneous esprit, wit and humour. All the comedians I worked with – Bud Flanagan, Arthur Askey, Max Miller – were mean, miserable men dreaming of playing straight roles like Hamlet. Straight actors, on the other hand, longed to get into comedy. Olivier achieved a dream when he played Archie Rice in *The Entertainer* (the film came out in 1957). A comedian comes in the end to resent being laughed at; when they tell jokes, their eyes weep. I have the feeling they hate the audiences who pay them for laughter.

I was fascinated by Chaplin, who made *A King in New York* at Shepperton in 1956. I don't believe continuity matters much, but Chaplin told me he did not believe in continuity at all. He would deliberately change backgrounds because, he said, the actors were the important thing and nothing else mattered. I did not like him as a person: he was full of self-love, vanity, saccharine and schmaltz. Even at a private party, he was acting. He had to be Number One always.

Other directors were very keen on continuity. Carol Reed and David Lean were extremely precise. Ann Todd, Lean's wife, I found unsympathetic. She made *The Sound Barrier* (1952) at Shepperton for him, with two child actors, and I saw her pulling them around. David Lean was himself tough. His brother Tangye was a friend of Peter Haden-Guest's, so we knew them.

I liked Ava Gardner, who was nice, very beautiful, not corrupt. Real sex hardly entered her life, but she was fascinated by Freud. She carried one of his books around the set of *Mogambo* (1954) at Elstree, asking the sparks and chippies what they knew about libido. She was utterly innocent. Anna Neagle was another nice girl: no tartiness, no sex stuff, just pleasant and dependable. Her first film was *Goodnight Vienna* in 1932 for Herbert Wilcox, whom she married and made many films for; there was nothing exciting to learn about her.

Elizabeth Taylor was arrogant. She was demanding and showed off while she was filming *Ivanhoe* at Elstree in 1951 (the sets were by Roger Furse, Pat's cousin). But she was only nineteen. She was being courted by Michael Wilding; we all watched with interest – it was better than the film. Robert Taylor was in *Ivanhoe* too. There was this huge, sexy lump of a man, and all he did was drink tea: he could not live without it.

Robert Taylor and Elizabeth Taylor had made an earlier film together at Elstree, *Conspirator* (1949), about a guards officer who was a Communist spy, based on the novel by my old friend Humphrey Slater. Humphrey had left the Party in 1939 and gone into the army; he was at long last disillusioned about Communism. He edited a right-wing intellectual journal, *Polemic*, for Rodney Phillips in the late forties and early fifties, and wrote *Who Rules Russia?*. He was married three times, twice to rich wives, and died in 1958, in Spain, of drink, disenchantment, despair – I don't know what. Two of his novels were published after his death: *The Malefactor* was described by the *Evening Standard* as 'almost Orwellian'.

Ralph Richardson, who starred in *The Sound Barrier*, was quite a normal man, pleasant to work with, a real trouper. Michael Redgrave, though not a great actor, was professional and friendly on the set. James Mason was much more introverted and on his dignity.

Some of the stars, both men and women, weren't actors, they were performers. They did what the director said, and it came out quite well. Jean Simmons, who was in *Uncle Silas* (1947), and even Vivien Leigh was like that. The British can act without being artists. If they come from a suburban or working-class background, they often have a natural talent. Real actors are quite different. I saw them go into a sort of trance. Actors are frightened people: everything has to be right for them or they lose their confidence, so they depended on the make-up people, the costumières, and all the rest of us. I like actors and know the challenge every performance is for them. I like their sensitivity and insecurity.

At Christmas 1952 our third child, Anna, was born. Before she arrived I was making *Heights of Danger*, a children's film about the Alpine Rally, shot in Nice, Switzerland and Austria. I got in a friend, Michael Alexander (they called him second assistant director), and he drove us out in his large open Renault. It was short of a gear and the brakes were not good, but we drove riskily up and down the thirteen curves of the Grossglockner. The car finally did turn over, but at the bottom and with only Michael and his girlfriend in it. The technicians found it rather a trial to be looking after a pregnant woman. I argued with them, saying, 'Boys, my family has to eat.' I got that film finished without giving birth, and moved on to *The Beggar's Opera* with Laurence Olivier as Macheath. We were shooting the barn scene, and Bill O'Brien, Alexander Korda's publicity man, begged me to produce the baby before they struck the set so he could get some headlines about a Christmas baby born practically in a manger at Shepperton.

They had to strike the set on 20 December. I felt the baby starting that day but went on working; the day's report still had to be made. I couldn't finish typing it. I said, 'Sorry, boys, the water is breaking.' That scared them, and they fetched an ambulance and sent me home. Anna arrived two days later, on 22 December in Bourne Street. So she *was* born in a kind of Bethlehem, under a Christmas tree.

Her christening was in the spring, at Chelsea Old Church. The godparents were Henriette Swanzy, Roger Furse, James Wells who had been our lodger at Trevor Square, and that strangely wonderful sculptress Fiore de Henriques. Beautifully mediaeval, she distributed warmth, colour and Mediterranean morsels of wisdom in her deep voice. I had met her two weeks before, and immediately realised that she must be Anna's godmother: we almost fell on each other's neck. She is a great big dark woman, half Spanish, like a man in many ways. Her work is impressive – heads of children at that time. She was a friend of Epstein and Augustus John.

Pat had rejected an offer of a job. Henry Swanzy put it kindly, in his diary for 28 January 1953: 'Pat, with his rather splendid pride, has turned down a TV job, £1,000 a year for three years.'

Then I realised that I had to give up location work, which is better paid than the studio. On location you get double bubble, or triple bubble for Saturdays and Sundays. But an anonymous message was pushed through the letterbox: 'YOUR HUSBAND SLEEPS WITH THE SECRETARY NEXT DOOR.' At first I thought it was a joke. I showed it to Pat, and he tried to excuse himself, saying I was away so much. He was very upset and repentant. But I felt betrayed. In a letter to James Wells, I said what I thought: 'You must have witnessed Pat taking on other ladies, for he was so very sensuous and needed a woman in bed all the time – well, he had so much unspent energy – and no one, but no one, had ever said to him: But Pat, you can't do that.'

I stayed in London and did release scripts and standby, and second unit for David Lean. The release script is the complete transcript which is issued with the film, for dubbing and so that it can be described when being sold. To make the release script, you run the finished film through the Moviola, checking with the original script. As you turn it back and forth, you notice how it was shot. Herbert Wilcox, for instance in *Lilacs in the Spring* (1954), tracked and panned and I knew he could shoot a whole scene in ten minutes. Carol Reed, who was making *The Man Between* (1953) about Berlin, with James Mason and Claire Bloom, would cut three or four frames very quickly, and that was expensive.

Reed had poise. He noticed people and was a very good film-maker, who had had a huge success with *The Third Man* in 1949. He started in the cutting-room, like David Lean and most of the good directors. Guy Hamilton (*The Intruder*, 1953) had been Carol Reed's assistant, but before that was in the cutting-room. Guy was nice and so was his wife Kerima, an unknown student whom Carol Reed found to star in *An Outcast of the Islands* (1951). John Hawksworth, who went on to make the *Upstairs Downstairs* films for TV, was a director who started in the art department. I never came across Hitchcock, who was in Hollywood, but people told me that working with him was like working with a machine.

The sparks (electricians), chippies (carpenters) and all the rest had their own unions and their own rules. They imposed their rules with heartbreaking consequences sometimes. The director would be struggling with the actors to get a particular shot, take after take after take, and almost have it, when the sparks called 'Lunch!' The director would ask for another three minutes' work, the sparks refuse and the scene be lost.

The power of the unions was what eventually broke the British film industry. They asked for too much money and imposed too many restrictions. The greed of the workers was matched by the greed of the producers. Together they destroyed a wonderful industry. The British are good at film-making and theatre, it is one of their great gifts; but too much greed, and not enough generosity, got in the way.

At the studios, they couldn't make me out. At lunchtime, when they were all at the bar, I was eating my sandwich and darning socks or going out to shop. Film people live very much by the bar at lunch and after shooting: it's where they pass on news and jobs. They knew I was a Furse, related to Roger Furse, who was a high and mighty art director and married to the great costumière Maggie Furse: but I carried babies around and hitchhiked to work. I was a puzzle to them – and to a great many other people. I still am. I didn't belong. I have never belonged.

20

Early Days of the Bistro, 1953–63

I still loved Pat, and needed him. I had always learned through men, and Pat knew everything, particularly about art. And he had a fantastic sense of humour, so elegant. He kept me in stitches, and he took the mickey out of me, which maintained the balance between us.

But I earned less by not going on location: how could I make the money up? There was food to buy and the children to educate. I was getting a small allowance from Peter, who had a job at the United Nations. Anthony was still at Gordonstoun. Johnny was down for Spyway and Eton.

I decided to turn the shop into a bistro. In all cities on the Continent there are places where you can read a newspaper, have a cup of coffee and a pastry, and talk to people. Most bistros come to life in the evenings, so I could combine it with film work. I could come home, take a bath, have the children round me, then start my second job. I told Pat, who usually let me do as I pleased. He agreed, although he was not used to bistros. Ours was the first in Britain.

I got an evenings-only coffee-house licence from Westminster Council and went to the Army and Navy auction rooms for furniture. I was after the French quality of talk but not French discomfort. I wanted the bistro to be in Viennese-Venetian taste – pale blue, red plush and gold. I had £70; I bought red plush seats for 25 shillings, and a lovely old spinet for 5 shillings that Pat cut up to make table tops – we could use any old thing for the legs. The shop had a bow window that I draped with heavy ruby-red velvet curtains I got cheap, and on the walls I put piano lamps that cost a shilling each. Stools came from the market. The central feature was a big three-cornered sofa, a 'sociable', that cost £2. We hung up signs, 'English spoken here' and '*Je suis tendre*' (from a Paris butcher) and 'Prints for sale'. On the door was 'The Bistro. E. & P. Furse Ltd', and in small letters 'Prints and Pictures'.

We bought cups and saucers, and a second-hand refrigerator and stove. Pat made a kitchen counter. The most expensive thing was a Gaggia coffee machine for £12: they had just arrived in Britain. Pat discovered where to buy the coffee cheap in Soho, and Fritzi Anzarut, the wife of my producer friend Ray, offered to make real Austrian *Linzertorte*.

In November 1953 we put an advertisement in the Chelsea Classic cinema in the King's Road. We set up chess boards on the tables, lit the candles in the piano lamps, and waited. The only person who came was a young lawyer; he perched on the edge of his seat, gulped his coffee and bolted. On the second night, two or three of my friends from the studio came. On the third, some young people from the King's Road in duffel coats stopped in for coffee and stayed until the early hours. In our first week, we took £18. For a while it seemed that the duffel coats were to be our main customers. It was tiring for us and they hardly spent any money. I let them in because I didn't yet know how to cope with the Bistro. My social antennae were not developed, and I wasn't in a position to be choosy. I didn't tell many friends we had opened a bistro – people were already shocked that I worked during the day, so I only told people I was close to. But others we knew began to come – schoolfriends of Pat's, our Trevor Square lodgers and their circles.

My sense of discrimination took over. I bought three signs saying 'Reserved' and plonked them on tables. That meant that when someone came in from the street I could choose whether to say 'Do sit down' or 'Sorry, all reserved'. And then the Bistro began its chemical growth.

Many people have told me I was tyrannical; one journalist wrote that I was 'the rudest woman in London'. It is true that when a stranger appeared, I always asked myself 'Would I go underground with you? Would I live and die with you?' I only admitted those I thought I would go into battle with. I brought to the Bistro my need of comradeship and my experience in judging character when it means life or death. In that sense, I may have been a tyrant. If people passed the test, they could come in and even bring friends. But I let in plenty without introductions. When I asked one young American 'Who sent you?', he said 'Jesus Christ, ma'am.' I let him in.

People need to feel smug, so they went around saying I'd thrown them out or let them in . . . they exaggerated my remarks. Elizabeth Dickson says she was brought by a boyfriend, and when I saw her green dress I called out 'No poison green!' I hate being told how I turned people away and was rude to them, but I suppose I did sometimes. You have to take into account that I got very little sleep. I never remember what I have said. People tell me, and I am astonished.

I turned a few away who came back. When I found out that I was wrong, I'd say 'I'm sorry.' I like being wrong, and to apologise. I'm bored with being right. Soon after we opened, the writer James Pope-Hennessy came in with a lorry driver from Sheffield, who I was told was his bodyguard. Our friends pointed out afterwards how naïve I was. I thought I'd be sharper when Emlyn Williams, who had been in *Ivanhoe*, dropped in with two young men. 'Oh God,' I said from the kitchen, 'there he is with his boys.' A voice corrected me: 'These boys, Elisabeth, happen to be my sons.' The one thing I could never tolerate was drunkenness. Sarah Churchill would come straight from the pub, swaying, and say, 'You bloody Russian woman, you *will* let me in.' I liked her, even if I sometimes would not let her in.

Coffee cost threepence and cake fourpence. We were not making much money, so we decided to offer food as well. The menu, written in Pat's beautiful hand, was soup (3d), spaghetti (6d), omelette (9d), goulash (9d), steak (1s 3d), salad and several cheeses. Our puddings were Mont Blanc (tinned chestnut purée and cream) or tinned lychees and cream. People brought their own wine. Later we got some cheap wine that we offered, illegally. The prices were what I thought people could afford. If they were rich, they paid extra for steak and salad. If they were broke, I gave them spaghetti for nothing. Girls on their own didn't pay. I used an old tea caddy as a money-box. Bills were made out only to newcomers. There was no cover charge and no corkage and certainly no tips. I could not be a restaurateur: I was the hostess and they were the guests.

People had to sit where I told them, and they were allowed to stay as long as they were talking intelligently – until two or three in the morning, if the discussion was good. But if they were just drinking and silly I sent them home. I made sure the car owners gave the footers a lift.

The leader of the late people was Milton Shulman, drama critic of the *Evening Standard*, who came in half an hour before midnight, after he had seen the play and written his review at the *Standard*. He was much respected for his solid presence and big wise head, his Canadian common sense and dry wit. Politicians also came in late when the House was sitting, and sometimes acted like released schoolboys, to the disapproval of the young Labour and Liberal journalists.

Most of the Bistro journalists were just starting their careers. Peter Jenkins, outspoken and gesticulating, was on the *Financial Times* and then industrial correspondent on the *Guardian*; he said later that he came to the Bistro because he liked talking to Pat about current affairs. We had David Spanier on *The Times*, preoccupied with poker; Alan Williams on the *Express*, one of Emlyn's sons, shouting out what he believed in, from fighting in Hungary to fighting in Vietnam – he became an adventure novelist; Johnny Moynihan on the *Evening Standard*: he was the son of the painter Rodrigo Moynihan. We saw self-confident young Jocelyn Stevens occasionally, and Mark Boxer a lot – the two were just down from Cambridge, and made the *Queen* the smartest magazine from 1957: Annie Trehearne, its fashion editor, used to come – a pretty girl with bubbly curls. Two other Cambridge people in their first jobs were Nicholas Harman at the *Economist* and Andrew Mulligan, the British Lions player who captained Ireland at rugby, at De La Rue. Andrew went on to the *Daily Telegraph* and the *Observer*, then into television. The Jolliffes and the Chancellors came, on the way from university into journalism. Bobby Birch was the last editor of *Picture Post*, and started Mandrake on the *Sunday Telegraph*. He married seven times, including two Bistro girls, Venetia Murray and Susan Stocken. Venetia was originally on *Picture Post*. She became a novelist.

We had a contingent from the *Observer*, where David Astor had recruited a talented and strange group from the services and universities: Ken Obank the managing editor, who was there almost every night; Mark Frankland, self-contained and silent, a novelist and foreign correspondent; Neal Ascherson, with a silvery intellect and a deep interest in Poland; dandyish Kenneth Tynan, drama critic. Loyal, reserved Terry Kilmartin, in charge of literature, came a few times, with his wife Joanna. We got foreign journalists too. Ricardo Arragno from the *Corriere della Sera*, a sweet little man, came with his sweet little girlfriend, and for a time the Agence France Presse descended almost *en bloc*.

There were several people from the new medium, television. British commercial television began in 1955. The BBC had been broadcasting some television programmes since the thirties, but telly was still not intellectually respectable: this gave a chance to clever young people, and many got important jobs in their twenties.

The telly boys (not many girls) could come to the Bistro and exchange ideas with the journalists, politicians and diplomats. Michael Peacock was working on the first edition of a current affairs programme to be called *Panorama*. We all went to the first showing at BBC Television Centre in 1956. He founded BBC2 in 1963. Cynthia Judah worked for *Highlight*, the BBC's ten minutes of current affairs which grew into *Tonight* (she married another broadcaster, Robert Kee). Humphrey Burton was musical; he edited *Monitor* and became head of BBC music and arts programmes in 1965; then he became head of drama, music and arts for London Weekend Television; then the BBC got him back – higher and higher. Desmond Wilcox was on *This Week* at ITV from 1960, moved to *Man Alive* on the BBC, then became head of the BBC's general features; he was particularly kind and considerate. David Frost led the BBC satire programme *That Was the Week That Was* (1962 to 1963) and *Not So Much a Programme, More a Way of Life* which followed it. The satire movement had just begun – *Private Eye* started in 1961. Other Bistro broadcasters were Bill Morton, who started *Man Alive* with Desmond Wilcox, and John Morgan, who was on *Panorama*, and deputy editor of the *New Statesman* for ten years.

When Johnny was ten, in 1957, we sent him to Spyway in Langton Matravers, the same prep school as Anthony, which was owned by two brothers, Eric and Geoffrey Warner, former Harlequin rugby players. The boys wore white shirts and grey shorts instead of those horrible caps and blazers. From the school, fields sloped to the cliffs above a famous shelf of rock, Dancing Ledge. The brothers had dynamited a pool in the Ledge where the boys learned to swim before tackling the open sea. I used to take the train to Wareham, hitchhike to near the school, change in the pub, and walk up to the front door looking like a respectable mother. I got on well with the boys and the masters. Johnny said, 'You know, Mama, although you are a foreigner you are really quite popular.' I could never visit Anthony after he went to Gordonstoun: the fare was too expensive.

In 1962 a young man called Roger Graef arrived from New York to direct a play at the Royal Court. He was brought to the Bistro on his third night in London by beautiful Clare Peploe and her boyfriend Jo Menell, who was then on *The Times Educational Supplement*. At about two in the morning, he asked me whether I was tired. I loved him from that moment – nobody had thought of asking me. Roger got his first film job through the Bistro. He went on to develop his ideas about television *vérité*, filming real people at work; his series on the police made him famous.

Willy Peploe, of the Lefevre Gallery, lived in Chapel Street, and all his children came in their teens – Mark, Clare and Cloe. Lizzie Spender came at sixteen, also with Jo Menell. Cloe married the writer James Fox and Clare married Bernardo Bertolucci and became a film-maker. Mark won an Oscar in 1988 for his script for Bertolucci's film *The Last Emperor*. Lizzie Spender became a writer and married Barry Humphries.

Sometimes I quarrelled with the Bistro guests. Roger Graef stayed away for eighteen months after I scolded him for criticising British judges. He said he could understand someone being invincibly ignorant but not that they would boast about it.

Milton Shulman and I often disagreed. Once he stormed through the Bistro shouting 'Why oh why is she so unselfconscious?' We had our final falling out over television. I got a set for the basement, where the children could watch it, in 1963. One of the first things they saw was the assassination of President Kennedy. Later I moved the TV up to the Bistro and I always sat at a little corner table to be able to see it. Milton sat where he could not see it. He said it destroyed conversation and that the programmes were of a low standard. I told him he did not know enough about it to judge. He said there wasn't much to know: it was intended for bored old ladies. I knew he meant me.

I loved television from the start. I don't understand how it is made, except where it resembles films, but there is much knowledge to be gained from that little screen. It lets you study people and their mannerisms, and it does not lie, for the people on the screen cannot disguise their nervous ticks and movements for long, even if they have been to television school. I watch all the current affairs and news and twentieth-century history, and often my heart goes boum-boum because I see David Owen or some other friend.

At the beginning of the Bistro, Pat cooked. His friends often tied on an apron and mucked in: Denis Dangan (later Cowley), Marye Rous, her sister Penelope, who was married to Ian Forbes. Titles were not used in the Bistro. I helped with the cooking. Pat was good at it, but as the customers soon pointed out, I was not. When one polite person said 'This steak is excellent,' I was taken aback. I said, 'That's ridiculous. No one comes here for the food.'

Ian Forbes once called out 'There's a nail in my goulash.' I said 'Iron is good for you.' Caroline Coombe from *Vogue* said, 'I'm amazed no one's had food poisoning,' and I answered, 'They will, one day.' Marye Rous worked for us until she rebelled against the way I put bits left on people's plates into the next day's soup. I think hygiene is the preoccupation of people who have too much – I have despised it ever since my mother set it up as a god. In prison camp we ate mouldy bread and maggoty rice and never got ill. Yet people who eat in restaurants come back with food poisoning. I think if the body really needs nourishment it fights off the germs.

Finally Clement Freud decided to teach me to make an omelette and grill steak. He had trained at the Dorchester and was running the Royal Court Theatre's restaurant. I was grateful for his lessons, but annoyed when I heard he was calling the Bistro 'that little room where fifteen people live off five seats'. His puncturing quips were a trademark when he became a Liberal MP and a broadcaster. Clement may have been asked to teach me by the actors. The Royal Court company made Sloane Square the centre of the theatre world with John Osborne's *Look Back in Anger* in 1956. George Devine, Tony Richardson, Osborne and his future wife Mary Ure, Claire Bloom and Jocelyn Herbert all ate with us. They seemed strangely obsessed by class. One day they were attacking public schools, and I said, 'Just because you went to minor public schools, that's no reason to take it out on the bigger ones.' My impatience leads me to say sharp things I don't exactly regret, but I regret the consequences if it ends a friendship.

The Bistro was too small for big personalities. Actors were too flashy: Mary Ure and Claire Bloom were the only ones who sat quietly and minded their own business. Peter Finch used to come in now and again, and Albert Finney. Christopher Lee became the king of horror film actors after *Dracula* in 1958. He sang Spanish folk songs and bits of opera and bounced the children on his knee. Olivier never came, because he preferred discreet, elegant places, but Vivien Leigh came once or twice. I knew her, but she was so neurotic it was difficult to be with her – like anyone who is tense and self-absorbed. She was deeply self-pitying. There was never any joy emanating from her, no blood. She was a cold orchid.

Clive Bossom, who was at Eton with Pat, and his wife Barbara lived opposite us in Cliveden Place. Clive dropped in every night when he was supposed to be walking Brandy the dog, and made everyone laugh with his dry wit. A well-known Labour couple, Aneurin Bevan and Jennie Lee, also lived in Cliveden Place, but I believe the shabbiness and discomfort of the Bistro put them off. The Wyndham brothers often came: Pat had fagged at Eton for the elder, John, and his brother Mark had fagged for Pat. Clive Bossom once remarked, 'What, only three earls and two viscounts this evening?'

In about 1957, Gerald Bridgeman came in and murmured to me, 'I have PM in the car.' I said, 'What, Macmillan?' 'No, Princess Margaret. Can I bring her in incognito?' I said, 'We are all incognito here.' 'I know, but you would have to call her "Ma'am".' I said, 'There is only one ma'am here. I can only treat her the same as I treat all of you.' He did not bring her in. But I did feed her brother-in-law. Two men came in, one fair, the other smaller and dark. I looked at them and said, 'You've been here before.' They said, 'No.' I said, 'I'm sure I recognise you.' They said it was their first time, but I let them in and they ordered omelettes. After they left I was told they were the Duke of Edinburgh and his cousin David Milford Haven.

Junior diplomats used to come: Martin Morland, Michael Butler, Iain Sutherland, David Duncan, Michael Adeane, Christopher Mallaby and of course Anthony Elliott. We got some foreign diplomats, especially from the American Embassy. The Bistro was often at the very heart of Britain's diplomacy: Richard Kershaw, who was resident clerk in the Commonwealth Office in 1958 and lived in a flat at the top, ate with us every night and told the switchboard to contact him at Sloane 8626. He went on being a regular through stints on the *Financial Times*, the *Scotsman*, editing *Africa Confidential*, and in television from 1961; and through several girlfriends and a wife, Venetia Murray.

The relationships were fascinating. I sat Tory MPs beside left-wingers, merchant bankers with actors, film directors with doctors, a general – Michael West – with artists. I am told that a lot of affairs started at the Bistro, with my au pairs and other girls, but I did not know about all the beds at the time. My life was rich again, for besides my work in the studios, I was giving myself heart and soul to my family at the Bistro. I trained myself to need only four hours in bed. I used to sleep standing against the wall, waiting for the last guests to leave.

Clive Bossom, who became a Conservative MP in 1959, said I was breaking the law in all directions, and what if he was there when the police raided me? Michael von Raben, another regular, was a special constable – a spare-time policeman – and once he and the local bobby did pass the Bistro well after midnight and the bobby said, 'See that place? Chief says mustn't touch it – nobs' place.' The British police have changed. Policemen are the sons of their people. A gendarme behaves like a Frenchman first and then a policeman. The British policeman used to be called 'bobby' and now is called 'pig', because the people have become violent. When I arrived from Europe sixty years ago, fearing the police, I found the bobby was someone I did not need to fear.

My son Johnny says the Bistro filled a gap for the people who had gone to the war without growing up:

> They went from adolescence to adulthood without maturity. My mother is very heavily armed with historical baggage, and played a potent role, very attractive. She was instant history. She could talk about the twenties, thirties and forties – provide a continuum in a fractured world. She is a person who contains the tribal stories. Her stories brought the European experience to the British. She had a powerful mythical role. She sat at her small corner table acting as moral judge of her friends and the world – a moral arbiter with a very black and white view. A mixture of witch, village gossip and storyteller.
>
> It was not easy for her children. We felt inferior to the friends she lost in the war. She has volcanic energies. She always had a huge number of people around who loved and worshippped her and were dependent on her, like acolytes.

I know the Bistro did not believe all my stories. But one day Michael West, who had become commander of the British Corps in Germany, told them, 'We've all had our suspicions, but I can confirm that everything she says is true – or almost everything.

I've seen her file.' I loved both Michael and Christine West. Henry Swanzy remarked cattily that Christine was one of the few Bistro wives I got on with. During Suez, in 1956, Michael and Christine and Pat and I were against war and the door was shut to the people who were for it. In October and November 1956, when the Hungarians rose and the Russians invaded and crushed them, it seemed that half the young of the Bistro left to help them resist. Peter Jenkins, Hugh Millais and Alan Williams went; Alan said, 'The Bistro will be the last barricade.'

The Bistro was very political. We had Labour, but we had more Tories. I agreed with Macmillan's speech in 1957, when he said 'You've never had it so good.' It was perfectly true. I didn't take the student rising of 1968 seriously because I thought they had it *too* good.

In 1957 or thereabouts, in came a group of racing drivers led by Lance Macklin, Pat's Eton contemporary, who affected an Etonian boredom. I asked him why he raced, and he said he loved the technology. That was probably what saved him: most of them died, including blond, sexy Mike Hawthorn and Ronnie Flockhart, all Scottish precision and tactics. The racing drivers brought with them the model girls: shy Sally Crichton-Stuart, who married the Aga Khan; Fiona Campbell-Walter, haughty and witty, who married Baron Thyssen; Sandra Paul, an intelligent observer who married the journalist Robin Douglas-Home; Jennifer Hocking, Australian and friendly, who went on to be fashion editor of *Harpers & Queen* and then a dress designer; Deborah Dixon, an American who looked like a Roman statue; sweet-tempered Roz Watkins, who married Brinsley Black; Bronwen Pugh, with green eyes, who married Lord Astor; Nena von Schlebrugge, a Swedish baroness who married Timothy Leary.

They were all beautiful and they in turn brought in the photographers: Claude Virgin, Dmtri Kasterine, Lester Bookbinder, Michel Molinare, David Montgomery and a young Etonian, Anthony Armstrong-Jones, who used to arrive with his friends Jeremy Fry and Andy Garnett. Claude, who worked for *Vogue*, always had lovely girls. He brought a beautiful half-Indian girl called Janet Aiyar whom he christened Tiger, and it stuck. She married two Bistro boys, Denis Cowley and Piers Dixon.

Fashion people go to wherever is fashionable. We had Audrey Withers, the editor of *Vogue*; Mary Quant and her husband, Alexander Plunket Greene, of the shop Bazaar; the clothes designer

Caroline Charles, very shy and elfin-like; Barry Sainsbury, on the way to becoming a fashion tycoon; Barbara Hulanicki who started Biba; Clare Rendlesham of the *Queen* who later ran Yves Saint Laurent's shops in London. Clare and Tony Rendlesham came in after the theatre one night and Clare said, 'Why did we go all that way to see *Mother Courage* when she's right here?'

We also had people who did not notice fashion: kindly, tolerant Carly Tufnell, Pat's schoolfriend, who had been in the Guards; John Meade, ex Royal Navy but like an eighteenth-century knight; and Ian Forbes, also Navy, scarred and noble, who had come back from a Japanese prison camp in Singapore emaciated. Those three men occupied a corner every night, occasionally joined by their wives. Giles Romilly and Michael Alexander, my pal of the Grossglockner, had been prisoners of war together in Germany. They were the first of Colditz's *Prominente* – people the Germans hoped to use as bargaining counters. Giles was Churchill's nephew and the Germans believed Michael to be General Alexander's. Actually he was a distant relation but had saved his life by claiming closeness.

Several people who could afford anything sat in the Bistro in crowded discomfort full of anticipation of the company. Douglas Collins, who founded Gala cosmetics with £100 after the war and made millions, came to show me his new Bentley and parked it beside my pram. He made me press its buttons, and presto – a cocktail cabinet opened, a television set appeared, the windows zoomed up and down. Hugh Wontner, the owner of the Savoy, walked in one night and became a regular. He said my goulash was a change from his lobsters and oysters. James Sainsbury came, and the young Sainsburys who had been at Spyway with Anthony.

One business success almost started, we all felt, in the Bistro. A shy young American, Christopher Columbus O'Donnell, wandered in with his borzoi, and although I did not allow dogs normally, he seemed so dependent on it that I let him in. Christopher was the nephew of Huntington Hartford, the American grocery millionaire, and after a few nights he told us he had been sent over to open the first supermarket in Britain. 'What is a supermarket?' we asked. 'You will see.' It was the A & P in Edgware Road. This was not the first self-service store in Britain – Tesco and Sainsbury's and little grocers had tried out the idea with some shops – but the end of meat rationing in 1954 had opened the way to supermarkets like those in America.

Christopher broke several hearts in London, and when Eartha Kitt came over to the Café de Paris in 1956 he brought her to the Bistro. He then left to develop Paradise Island in the Bahamas.

I am surprised I softened over the dog. I have never kept pets. I only recognise animals as working people: cows in the field, dogs in the kennel, cats in the barn chasing mice, horses taking you from one place to another. Chickens to be eaten. Every animal has a function, even to be eaten: as we have a function to be eaten. Worms have to live, we can't deprive them.

Felix Fenton and Charles Clore came, and the Greek shipping boys, the Goulandrises, Mavroleons and Zervudachis. The Greeks would flit from the Bistro to dance at Annabel's. Olga Deterding, tense and excitable, whose father was one of the founders of Shell, often came too and talked in her loud low monotonous voice. Nolly Zervudachi, who worked for Niarchos, became a particular friend, and so did his wife Carolyn, a witty Irish girl who had modelled as Carolyn Gorman; she sometimes played the guitar for us.

Rex Harrison's son Noel played guitar duets with Theo Bikel. Carly Tufnell's beautiful wife Sarah married Noel (and then David Salmon). One night when Eartha Kitt came in with Christopher Columbus O'Donnell after her show she sang for us, which got reported in the *Express*. I banned the reporter in future. I said the Bistro was a safe house: people were as at home. I was proud of that. Jimmy Goldsmith came with Isabel Patino while they were eloping, on their way to get married in Scotland. Dominic Elwes used us as a bolt-hole when he ran away with Tessa Kennedy. When Tony Armstrong-Jones became engaged to Princess Margaret in 1960, the American press rang me up and offered me lots of money; I opened the door into the Bistro so that the eaters could hear me say that all I knew was he liked omelettes.

For his best man, Tony wanted his old friend Jeremy Fry, who had an engineering business called Rotork, or his other old friend Andy Garnett, who worked in it, and they all three went to stay at Balmoral. When Jeremy and Andy came back we pressed them: 'What are they like?' 'Very nice, very chintzy,' said Jeremy. 'What else?' 'Nothing else. Very nice, very chintzy. Just like everybody else.' 'Well . . .' said Andy in his slow voice, 'chintzy: all right. Like everybody else: all right. But there is a difference. When we would fart, they seem to blow soap bubbles.' The royal family must have asked Tony if he had no serious friends in respectable professions, because Dr Roger Gilliatt was best man in the end.

My Polish friends came, and a Russian professor of yoga. General Challe, who mutinied against de Gaulle in Algeria in 1960, came once (I was on de Gaulle's side). The French film director Louis Malle said you didn't find a single country at the Bistro but all Europe. Other continents, too. King Freddy of Buganda, who was in exile, used to come, brought by Willy Peploe – I can't think how I allowed it, because I remember I did not like him.

We had a group of medical students and doctors. Gordon Simpson was very good-looking and helped pay for his studies by modelling; Nicholas Maclean was a young naval reservist who became what the others called a clap doctor – I occasionally sent Bistro boys to him. I consulted Nick about some brown spots on my hands. He said, 'We call them grave spots.'

A doctor from my past came occasionally: my Uncle Ilya, my father's cousin, who had been a doctor in Gdansk and was now a GP in Lydd in Kent. Milton pretended he didn't believe I had an uncle – 'What will she be telling us next?' The Bistro asked Uncle Ilya what I was like as a child, and he said, 'Exactly the same, only smaller.' He had a saying that impressed Nicky Maclean: if you are not aware of your lungs or heart or stomach or any part of your body you are healthy, but if you are aware of any part you should go to a doctor.

The Bistro was like a family in that almost everyone went to the same doctor, Lionel King-Lewis; lawyer, Reggie Freed; accountant, David Lyon-Maris; and architect, Julian St Leger. The Furses did not come, except a cousin, John Redcliffe-Maud, the civil servant and diplomat, and his children.

It's easy to drop names when talking about the Bistro, because the Bistro was a comradeship of names. Every name can be dropped equally: the Bistro was a fellowship, a community, it was equality on the basis of wit, intelligence, good humour and goodness. There were those who made it in the world and those who didn't – but many who didn't make it are closer to me, because they had the right reasons for so-called failure. They had the ability, but they simply could not be bothered to make it, because they enjoyed life and living more than using their brains or their talents to the full. I very much like that nonchalance, that effortless living. Those who did not make it to the top had more interesting things to do, perhaps. Then, too, there were people of little intellect in the Bistro – but with lots of humanity, which made them welcome. We had a life-and-death belonging and warmth which was very special. Mountain climbers have it, and soldiers during a war.

I could not stop Alexei Poklewski-Koziell drinking himself to death, although I fought his death wish, and screamed at him, put him up, threw him out, refused him drink for years. The night after he left us, it was quiet in the Bistro. All who had filled his glass and patted him tenderly wept in their souls: Claude Virgin and Michael Alexander and Milton Shulman and Clive Bossom and Penelope Forbes and the rest. There was a strange tender silence and sorrow in that shabby little room. And then Claude said, 'I am angry with Alex, I really am. He should not have done this to us,' and his eyes were very misty. And I shouted, 'But you helped him to it, for you let him drink.' Then they all said, 'But he wanted to do away with himself – what was ahead of him?' With Alexei went part of my own life, the smell of all that we had known together before we were born, the tough of it all and the nostalgia of it all.

The British regard me as a meddler. But if I meddled, it was because I cared. The Bistro was successful because I meddled. Some said it more bluntly – that I interfered – but of course it would strike some in that way. The English, at both ends of the social spectrum, are secretive and exclusive. The Furses were, and so are the working class. I dislike the English lack of passion, their lack of involvement, and their lack of real friendship. I don't think the English trust each other with their very selves. Everyone who is given something feels that he or she has to make a return of the gift. To me, that attitude seems petty and calculating. It has no real generosity or largeness in it. The English only rise in response to extremes – extreme need or extreme peril. Then they come into their own. Otherwise, they merely smoulder along. Extremes don't arise often enough to provoke them. Dunkirk was such – the Blitz was too; maybe the Falklands too.

My Bistro family were imaginative in their kindness to me. Before Christmas in 1957 I had noticed Alex Sterling and Claude Virgin going round the tables whispering. I just thought they were telling dirty stories. But on Christmas Eve they blindfolded me, carried me out to the street and sat me in a car. Then they took the blindfold off and cried 'This is yours, from us all.' They had clubbed together to buy a beautiful roadster, open to all weather as I love, a black and white Mercedes with a dicky seat. 'You need a car,' they said. 'Enough of your pram pushing.' Nolly Zervudachi proudly said, 'I am the wheel', so Peter Jenkins, Alan Williams and Hugh and Suzy Millais shouted 'We are the screws.'

Then in the summer, David Goschen asked me where I was going for a holiday. I said, 'Guess, David? 3 Bourne Street,' and at the end of the evening I found in the money box a cheque for £50 with a piece of paper: 'E – please go away and enjoy yourself.' I shall love David Goschen forever for that *beau geste*.

I have to love people – I cannot 'like' and be 'fond of'. Love them I did, and let them stay on into the small hours, sometimes until five in the morning, to talk and talk and leave their loneliness behind. Then I would go to the studio happy because they were happier. Those nights were a strong link. Many regulars could not afford spaghetti even, but they were beautiful to me, for they could drink fearlessly (someone always brought along a bottle of plonk for the late-night sessions). At the weekend, I gave Sunday luncheon that lasted all afternoon. Twenty-five people would often sit down, counting the children and au pair, among them the lonely and the lost. They had to be my comrades and my non-existing family. How many jobs were given among them, how many loves were found among them – and sometimes lost – how many clothes, cleaners, cooks and nannies were passed around among them! I forced them to help each other, and they did.

21

Bringing up Children on Top of the Bistro

I have been pregnant fourteen times in my life. Five produced children, the others were lost through miscarriages or abortions, mostly when I was working in Berlin. In February 1957, when I was forty-six, I had our last child, Sara.

The same wonderful nurse, Wheatie, came to me who had seen me through the first days of Johnny, Katya and Anna. Wheatie said, 'You are not strong. You need a good nanny, and I will choose her.' She found an Austrian girl, Anni Geschwandner, and told me, 'She's very capable, but you will never be able to put your arms around her and call her darling as you do me and everybody else.' Anni was a trained nurse, the daughter of a carpenter and a midwife. After three years she told me she wanted to give up nursing because she could never love another child as she loved Sara and my others. I helped her to become a medical secretary. She also did some work for Pat. I noticed they liked each other.

At the beginning of the sixties, two young loners often came to the Bistro. Both were tall, both draped their legs over a table and read newspapers, but they were different in all other ways. One was Christopher MacLehose, who got a job on the *Glasgow Herald*, then on the *Scotsman*. Later, he came back to London and went into publishing at Barrie & Jenkins, then Chatto, then Collins. The other was a medical student at St Thomas's, David Owen.

David was uncompromising. He came to the Bistro to study and to talk politics. He was generous – he rode a motorcycle and lived on a houseboat in Chelsea, and he constantly offered to let me stay on his boat if I wanted a change. Then he acquired a Morris Minor, and said I could borrow it any time. And that is how he is today. I was so impressed by him that after he qualified I asked him to become guardian to my children. He was only twenty-three, a houseman at St Thomas's. The rest of the Bistro said, 'Are you crazy – that arrogant little bastard?' I said, 'Yes, that "arrogant little bastard" is going to take the right decisions.' And he did. The children could always go to him with their problems, and he was always there to help and advise. There is a kind of arrogance that comes from impatience. David is very quick and ambitious: quick thinkers and doers are impatient with the slow ones and even easily contemptuous. I am impatient too. Most people do not understand how impatience sharpens behaviour.

In the same week that David Owen qualified, in the spring of 1962, he agreed to be put forward for the Labour candidacy in Torrington. He said the reason he thought he could manage it on top of his long hours as a junior hospital doctor was that he could borrow my cottage in the constituency. He got the nomination and began to travel back and forth to Devon. The Conservatives would not legally have to call an election until 1964.

Johnny was down for Eton, because he was a Furse, but we had no money to transport him there or equip him properly. In 1960, a place suddenly became free and he was told to come. Young Johnny Sterling, who was at the Bistro every night, asked when he was going. 'Tomorrow,' I said. 'Has he got everything he needs?' 'No. He hasn't a rug or a chair.' The Eton boys furnish their own rooms. At seven-thirty next morning, Johnny Sterling was in Bourne Street with a rug and a chair. The roadster was out of action, so I rang up Richard Lund, who immediately offered his car. Richard was always the most generous and kindest. And so we got Johnny to Eton.

I didn't have to send my children to these private schools, but I had no right to declass them. I had no right not to give them the same education as their fathers and I had had. I did not have to give them the same space or so many servants, but I had no right to declass them intellectually. A friend worked out that I saved the State at least £370,000 by giving my children a private education. Johnny was helped to go to Eton by a bursary given for his father's war service. He went to an interview, and passed. His grandfather paid the rest of the fees. Auntie Forbes paid for Anthony's education. But the holidays and clothes and extras are almost as much as the fees, and I paid for them. The only peasants

I have met in England were at Eton. I was amazed at how on 4 June the families and friends of Etonians throw themselves on the damp grass and sit there having their picnics – admittedly the food is not peasant food. They behave like people of the earth. I have not observed it elsewhere – English village fêtes are urban, not earthy. The English are an urban people.

I treated my children as naturally as I treat anything else. I dropped them like rabbits and somehow they grew up. I spanked them, cuddled them, coddled them. They did know that if they were in trouble they could come to me. I was working all the time, and was hoping for the best. I got away with everything because of being a foreigner. To act the English mother would have been ridiculous.

I was never a 'Mummy', only a mother – a provider and protector. I am not a good mother: I did not make jellies and tell stories. I sang to them, only because I like to sing. I always sing, almost more when my heart is heavy. 'If you want the moon to play with, the stars to run away with, they'll come if you don't cry.' '*Guten Abend, gute Nacht, mit Röslein bedacht . . .*' '*Frère Jacques, Frère Jacques, dormez-vous?*' I sang them to my children every night. Now my daughter Katya sings them to her children.

I was against conventional nurses or nannies, and in any case I could only afford au pair girls. The au pairs were French, Dutch, Swiss, Italian, Spanish or Russian, but I preferred French so the children would grow up bilingual. And I was very keen on manners – the children thank me for that now. Manners are a bridge on which people can walk to and fro and meet and acquaint. I believe in manners from the young to the old and from men to women. All that equality talk is crap. People who behave like equals are equals.

The au pairs eventually went home, which gave the children and me staging posts in Europe. Most of our helpers were beloved, but Sara tells me that Wheatie hit her on the head with a spoon and yanked her pigtail for having spilt a glass of milk.

I dislike the state of childhood intensely – it may have something to do with the aloneness I felt when young. A person is not attractive to me simply because he is small and cannot earn his living. I know too well children's fantastic ability to lead their very mature lives away from prying grown-ups, their sophisticated knowledge of grown-ups, their vulnerability, their capacity to hurt. Babies I love, the young have always bored me by their arrogance and lack of humility. I hated being young myself and always made myself older. What I love are old and wise people, at whose feet I can sit. Maybe I have never really grown up.

My girls were not going to wear a uniform. I wanted them to work at lessons with a governess in the morning and do painting and dancing and music in the afternoon. I found Mrs Palmer, Kirsty, a semi-retired governess. She said, 'What do you want me to teach your children?' I said, 'The love of learning.' She did that beautifully, coming to us from nine to twelve. With a governess, whatever she likes you learn, which is why I know American literature and Scandinavian literature. Mrs Palmer liked museums and architecture, and by the time the children were four or five they had been to every museum and knew a lot about architecture. One day Sara and I were going past a mews with an arch, and she said, 'That is a cornerstone.' 'What is that, darling?' 'Mrs Palmer said it holds everything together, like you.' When Katya was ten, Miss Goldsmid, called Goldie, took over. She was a cousin of Aunt Gladys's and Carmel's. Katya did very well with her O levels at fourteen, and A levels between sixteen and eighteen.

The education I gave the girls concentrated on the arts: I never thought about science and mathematics, because I had never been any good at them. Perhaps I was wrong not to send the older girls to a conventional school, but Katya did not mind. I did not like the idea of school so I did not send them. I never gave it a second thought. I just do things. I practically never have a conscience.

In the afternoon, the girls went to Madame Vacani's dancing school in Brompton Road near Harrods – Johnny refused. Betty Vacani, the niece of the founder, taught the royal family as well as most of the upper class. I took my girls in their nice dresses and white gloves, and at first Miss Vacani thought I was a servant, because they were so well dressed and I was not. Betty Vacani was egalitarian. She gave some children from a poor background free lessons. But her favourite was Prince Charles, who won her heart as a small boy when she went to Buckingham Palace to teach him and a group of children. She asked them to line up and hold hands, and Prince Charles would not. She coaxed him, and at last he looked up at her solemnly with his blue eyes and said, 'If you hold my hand, Miss Vacani, I will try.' She says, 'All his life he will be like that. He is such a lovely pure human being; almost too good.' She later taught the younger royal children, and also Lady Diana Spencer, but did not find any more royal saints.

Upper-class girls cannot dance – I could not believe how wooden they were. Upper-class British girls are too constrained. My girls could dance because of their Russian blood. Betty Vacani called them 'an example to others', and soon I did not have to pay. Both Francis Holland and Lady Eden's school offered to take my clever Furses free (Lady Eden told me she was short of children of originality and talent), but I stuck to dear Mrs Palmer. Both Katya and Anna went on to the Royal Ballet School, Katya to the senior part at Baron's Court, Anna as a daygirl to the junior at White Lodge in Richmond Park. Katya had a grant and Anna an ILEA scholarship, but I bought their shoes. Three pairs of point-shoes cost £9 a week.

I could not have afforded to live anywhere but in Belgravia. I had a real relationship with John Arnold, of J. Wood, the butcher in Elizabeth Street. He had been a sailor and loved the sea and Kipling, like me. I said, 'Mr John, what do you do with what's left over when you cut up a carcass?' He said, 'We sell it for dogs.' I said, 'Sell it to dogs called Furse. Scrag end, knuckle bones – whatever is left, put it in a box and price it for me.' My box sometimes contained chops or steak. I gave him books – Byron, Burns or Kipling.

Bill Bainborough, the greengrocer, was less of an intimate friend, though he too approved of my husbandry. Every day he put out a box for us – spotted avocados, black bananas, bruised pears and apples, everything Belgravia didn't want. The colour of my avocados was a joke in the Bistro.

The Misses Beaton had a baker's shop in the King's Road. They were neat, tough, middle-aged ladies. The home-made bread, buns, cakes and sausage rolls they sold me were never stale, but again what Belgravia turned up its nose at. It was always a wonderful excitement when I fetched the boxes and we saw what we were going to eat.

Every Christmas I wrapped over three hundred parcels, for friends, bank porters, bank managers, postmen, dustmen, bus men, electricity men, telephone men, fishmongers, butchers, bakers, greengrocers, lawyers and doctors. All who help family and friends to survive and work and live, I look after in my own little way, because I am truly glad for their existence and grateful to them, and when I ask them down for eats or give them little things, it is because I like them, and to me they are part of us. Yet I am often misunderstood. In the Middle Ages, I am sure I would have been burned as a witch: I was burned on the tongues of Belgravia.

One year John Arnold asked if I ever took the children to the seaside. I said, 'Sometimes we go for a picnic to Cuckmere Haven near Eastbourne.' He sent an artist down to draw it and gave it to me at Christmas – 'For all your kindness to me and the staff at Woods.'

For clothes, I went to second-hand shops, and dressed my children beautifully. Clare Rendlesham sold her children's clothes to As Good As New and I bought them: I thought it was a pity she did not sell them to me direct. For flowers, I sent the children out to Belgrave Square and Eaton Square, saying, 'We steal the squares' flowers because every house needs flowers and we can't afford them. But remember, it is *wrong*.'

I love the close shaves of frugality. Occasionally my thrift has got me into trouble. In my eighties, I go every Monday morning to a greengrocer in Fulham Road to collect the rejects they leave out for me. I don't pay – I give the men who work there little presents at Christmas. On the way, I pass a health shop. I noticed a big plastic bag full of bread outside it, so I took two loaves for my twin girl lodgers. I don't eat bread, but they were living on a small allowance, and were very glad of it every Monday. But one Monday a man grabbed me and said, 'I have got you now. You have been stealing my bread. I shall take you to the police station.' I said I was very sorry, I hadn't realised the bread was a delivery, I was so used to taking things left outside shops for me. 'Please do take me to the police,' I said, 'and I will explain it all.' He was not very nice about it. I sent him a postal order for £10 for the bread I had taken. I should have felt embarrassed, but I was amused. Every week I go by bus to two street markets – it used to be four. My Sunday morning market is Brick Lane in Bethnal Green, where I get little things to give people. The market traders say, 'Where will you sell them?' They can't understand that I am buying for my family and to give away, and they resent it.

In the fifties and sixties, the doctor said my children were the healthiest in Belgravia. Poverty kept them healthy, like little animals. They drank milk or water, they filled up on goulash or spaghetti and ate as much as they wanted of fresh fruit. They never had Coca-Cola or fizzy lemonade or sweets or crisps or tins.

For holidays, the children went to Devon or to Auntie Forbes at St Briac. She would rent a house for them and their au pair near the château. I took them over and brought them back. And when I was not shooting at Shepperton or on the Continent, I would take them on Saturday mornings to Covent Garden vegetable and flower market and pretend we were in the country picking flowers and plants – though ours had fallen off the stalls. So we lived from rich men's dustbins, like the Untouchables of India.

I found modelling work for Katya and Anna. They hated it, but gritted their teeth because Johnny needed a new uniform and they adored their big brother. They modelled for Fleetway Publications – children's annuals and magazines – and Ford cars, and in the *Tatler*, and bought Johnny's uniform and also ballet tights and shoes for themselves. Their modelling paid for a piece of carpet leading up to the nurseries in the brightest of all reds. The rest of the stairs were shabby old green stuff and horrid brownish stuff and some grey stuff, but their flight was the pride of the family. Anna modelled from when she was eight to when she was twelve. She complained that it interfered with her ballet classes.

They were never deprived children – they saw everything, heard all the music, read all the books and went everywhere. I would take all four to Zermatt or Venice, travelling at night and buying only two adult tickets, for myself and the au pair, and one child's ticket, pretending the others were babies in arms so could travel free. When the ticket collector came round I hid them under rugs and said the babies were sleeping. I enjoy risks. The children remember that just before the train left, I always got off to buy rolls or something, and they were terrified I would miss it. We stayed at youth hostels which cost one franc a night. In Venice, they slept like sardines in one room, and we lived off bread and cheese and fruit, surrounded by heavenly beauty. I took them to my favourite island, San Pietro, where I love to swim off the rocks. They sat on the shore crying 'Mama, Mama, please don't swim so far!' In Zermatt I bought two ski-lift tickets for six, but we all got to the top. We survived, and more than survived – we flourished.

I don't know how I brought up five children on no money – I just did. I have always had energy and strength. I am grateful to my mother for being so determined to give her children health. She did well, considering I have survived TB, hunger, internment camps, prison and overwork. Energy, of course, is also based on love, and I love life. I love love, and I love living. I have energy for love and for life.

* * *

Pat and I were not getting on well. There were arguments and tensions, particularly when I was carrying Sara. The double life I was leading exhausted me. And I did not like to see Pat cooking, because I had married an artist and I respect art. It seemed to me he was using the cooking and the family as an excuse. He had done some good sculpture, and given it up. Whenever Pat came near success in anything, he gave it up. He was not even self-destructive, more self-denying. He told other people how to get work and helped them, but did not get work himself.

Rest was an important word in the Furse family: it was a word I did not understand. Pat's lack of energy came from the Furses. It was not his fault that he was slow. He talked a great deal, very wittily, and he was much loved by everyone because he was very intelligent, good-humoured, handsome and beautifully behaved. One of the things that kept our marriage going was his lovely manners. And he thought beautifully. He lived in his head. The Furses are noble people. They are clever and rare, but Pat's heart was only big enough to love one person. That person had to be there to listen to him and be with him – but I was so much away, working during the day and in the Bistro in the evenings. He wanted one woman to listen to his thoughts. But what I wanted was lots of children, lots of friends, lots of people, lots of life.

In 1959 I had a kind of bleeding womb, and the doctor said it was possibly pre-cancerous. I had treatment, but I was scared for the children because they had no security. I found a house vacant near us at 17 Chesham Street, and Reggie Freed, the Bistro's lawyer, bought the freehold for £11,000. He converted the building into flats so as to sell long leases, but considered the basement hopeless. The surveyor said the basement was worth £1,400. Pat had been left about £2,000 by a relation and gave me the £1,400. So I got a ninety-nine-year lease from Reggie. I divided the basement into two flats, and let them. Julian St Leger from the Bistro was the architect. Eventually Bistro friends lived in them: Roger Graef, David Owen, Shane Alexander. We went on living at Bourne Street.

If I had not had to work so hard, and if we had had more room to live together as a family, our marriage would have been all right. But I was so tired all the time I could not be a wife or a mistress to Pat. I loved Pat, and we enjoyed life together. But we needed time, time to talk and time to listen, and time is money they say. So money, or lack of it, helped to break us. I didn't break the marriage – life did. I wrote to my father- and mother-in-law telling them we needed a little money. They did not even answer. They would not 'meddle', as they put it. They would not become involved. They were typical English people who brushed everything under the carpet. They would never talk about anything. They could have saved our marriage.

I respected the fact that Pat put art before the children and me. He had exhibitions, he was given permission to sketch and paint in the wings at Covent Garden, but nothing happened. He said family life held him back. I said, 'All right, Pat, go and prove to me and the children and the world that you can make it without us.' In 1960 Pat went to live in a studio in Battersea. I more or less pushed him out. The children were very upset; I did not realise how much. Johnny says that the last time he saw Pat and me together was when we drove him to Eton in January 1960 for his first day there. Only after Pat left us did he become a teacher at the Central School. He was a wonderful teacher, though he had refused to do it all those years. While I was keeping the whole thing going, he was able to live in his dream of art for art's sake.

Art for art's sake was the way of thinking in his family. Laurence Whistler wrote in his book about Jill, *The Initials in the Heart*, 'it was accepted that art was supreme and great work must be achieved by us all . . . Pat would paint, Theresa would write . . .'

Sex, for a woman, is more strenuous than for a man. A woman has to work herself into the right frame of mind, she has to have a bath, she has to feel good, look good and smell good. A man can do it anywhere, standing up or lying down – he gets rid of something, but a woman has to prepare herself for reception. That is the tragic difference between the sexes.

Peter Haden-Guest had married an American, Puji Hindes, in 1945, and he stayed over there. He worked for the United Nations in New York for nearly thirty years. He and Puji had two sons and a daughter: Christopher and Nicholas Guest, who became film and television actors, and Elissa, a writer. Christopher went to Hollywood and married the actress Jamie Lee Curtis. Peter became Baron Haden-Guest in 1987 and Christopher will inherit the title. Peter and Pat were both enchanting. They were lovers: I married lovers – poets, artists – not husbands or fathers. I wanted it all, I was greedy. I wanted lovers who might also become husbands and fathers, but you can't get all three in one. I know only two couples who managed it all.

At the Bistro, I must have been the most kissed woman in London – every night everyone kissed me hello and goodbye. I had everything except a man of my own. I sublimated my eroticism in work and in music – I always had music playing: Beethoven, Bach, Piaf, Jacques Brel, Dietrich, Yves Montand, Jean and Germaine Sablon, Weill's 'Mahagonny', Sinatra singing 'Love and Marriage'. Eroticism was always in the air, but it was never a threat.

I did fall in love with Ian Douglas, who came to the Bistro. I am definitely attracted to a particular kind of man – aesthetic, intelligent, and poetic. I had to be with a man who saw the moon even when it was not there. He was a Scottish biochemist, specialising in diseases of the blood. He painted and played the piano beautifully and was very good on French politics. He had done extremely well at Cambridge. He knew the names of flowers and insects, and he was wonderful with the children. In his way, he was rather a loner and he wanted to go out into the world and find adventure. Pat said to him, 'I love Elisabeth and the children, and I'd be very glad if you could make them happy.' For several months, from June 1961, the children and I lived with Ian in a rented house in Bloomfield Terrace near the Bistro.

Through me, he got a job in Intelligence. But there were difficulties, thanks to my past, and he had to make a choice between the job and me. Being a man, he chose the job. I agreed that he was doing the right thing, but it hurt. The children, too, were upset again. I heard from him thirty years later, and he said there had been a deep void in his perceptions ever since leaving me. He reminded me of a song I had sung, 'Les Chevaliers de la Table Ronde'.

Men like me, women don't. I had a telephone call from Georgie Galitzine after years of not hearing from him. I told him, 'I think your marriage is in trouble.' He said, 'How did you know?' I said, 'Because you are telephoning to me.'

The children had always hoped Pat would come back. Johnny wrote later:

> We were incredibly upset by the failure of our parents' relationship. At the time, Mama could not help but attribute the failure to the supposed flaws in my father's character. It took

some years for me to realise the rather tragic truth that so many of the key men in her life, not just my father but also Peter Haden-Guest, Anthony and myself, had in a sense to fail her. All of us at various stages were placed in the gilded frames of her own romantic longings or moral imperatives, which we could not possibly fulfil. (This in fact applies to my sisters and many many of her friends as well as to us men!)

I vividly remember sometime around 1971, after another furious row between us, having this flash that there was some failing in her relationship with her own father which might have caused the pattern. When I said this, she collapsed over the table crying, and asked for some brandy. I laid her on the bed next door and telephoned David Owen: I thought she was having a heart attack. David, who has always been an incredibly loyal friend to her and the family, came round at half-past one in the morning.

Over the years since then, not only I but also my sisters have built great understanding with my father, Antonia, Peter and Puji Haden-Guest and Anthony. My father says of my mother with characteristic grace and fairness: 'She is the bravest person I have ever met . . .' He too seems to understand why someone from her background living through the terrible events she did should have felt the need to reinvent parts of her life in order to survive.

Without wishing to be too cod-psychological about it, it does seem that there is a pattern of anger and rejection which keeps on being repeated. For many years I have had an image in my mind of the little girl inside her screaming for the love and attention which she felt she never received. Her almost childlike sense of right and wrong, friend and foe and the depth of her romantic longings and disappointments in the world seem all of a piece with this: as do her frequent rejections of the people and behaviour around her. So many of us have in turn felt terribly hurt and angered by her at various stages: it is unfortunate that so few have had the opportunity to perceive what may have produced this. I may be wrong, but this seems to me a hidden and rather tragic leitmotif in her life.

22

Cold War Travels, Berlin, USA, Canada, 1962–63

The idea of the Berlin Wall shocked me when the Communists built it in 1961. I wanted to see it, and all that it implied. In 1962 I went back to Germany, taking Sara, who was five, as my prop and decoy. The war and the loss of so many people I loved had never left my mind. I kept telling myself I was going to a different Germany from the one I had known. We travelled by train, which I prefer, because people talk to one another. Sara was happy: it was a great thing for her to be alone with Mama for once. As we came into Germany, the country looked prosperous and busy. Factory chimneys poured smoke and we saw masses of cars.

In the carriage, the conversation was political. It went something like this: 'Why don't the Americans march into Berlin and get rid of the Red murderers?' 'Ach, they have sold out.' The British husband of a German woman said, 'How can you want to risk a world war for the sake of Berlin?' 'Na,' a youngish man said, 'the West is only using us as a pawn.' I said, 'If it hadn't been for the war you started, none of this would have happened.' They replied, '*We* did not start the war. England did. Hitler and Chamberlain could have settled everything peacefully at Munich.' I talked of the violent occupation of the Saar, Austria, Czechoslovakia. The reply was, 'All these territories belonged to Germany once.' When I talked about the extermination of the minorities, they said, 'The Americans have done worse to the Red Indians and the Negroes, and the Australians to the Aborigines.' I reminded them of the concentration camps. 'The British started them in the South African War.' The trump card was: 'No one can accuse *us* of Hiroshima.' An elderly man appeared at the door of our compartment and before I could pick up my sleeping Sara, he ordered, 'Take the child up. I want to sit down.'

We went through the East Zone and arrived in West Berlin. I was surprised to see so many old people walking about with white sticks and yellow armbands. The Kaiser Wilhelms Gedächtniskirche had been left in ruins blackened by fire, as though to accuse *us* of what we had done to *them*. Beside it stood a new church, a symbol of modern Germany – an oval building in metallic grey with tiny little blue glass squares for windows.

The Berlin Wall was nothing of the sort, but sixty kilometres of bricked-up windows, street barriers and barbed wire. Children were playing a game like leapfrog, except that behind the leaping children was another row of children shooting with toy guns, and in front of them a further row pretending to hold blankets. The aim was to reach the blankets: if you didn't, you lay flat on the road pretending to be shot. Then I saw a woman in an apartment on our side of the street, waving a handkerchief. I couldn't see who was waving back at her from a window on the other side – perhaps it was a sister or a friend. They were one street apart, but separated. It seemed to shame everything we had fought for.

I went to a nightclub with friends, and everything about the young West Berliners who were dancing seemed more pronounced than in the rest of Europe – their glasses were darker and bigger, their jeans tighter, their faces more bitter, their movements clumsier. They were not as naïve as the British, or as elegant as the French, or as merry as the Italians. A young woman asked me where I came from. 'England.' She said, 'We thought you were a spy,' and told me that there were seven thousand paid spies in Berlin.

We visited the East Zone through Checkpoint Charlie. Here all was silent empty streets. At some kind of shopping centre, people in nondescript clothes were queueing for potatoes. Uniformed young men in boots stomped by with stony faces. We went into a grey little café and drank greenish coffee. On the wall was a photograph of my old friend Walter Ulbricht with his pointed beard, looking exceedingly cunning. I was glad to get back to the Checkpoint, where Sara asked the guard why he had a gun and such a 'house'. The guard said, 'We are trying to build peace here, but the others will not let us, so we had to build the wall, to live and work in peace.'

We went home, and in October 1962 came the Cuba crisis. It felt like Munich all over again. People in London said, 'At least we'll all go together.' That thought of 'together' was so soothing that parents' faces looked sadly blissful. Usually I am a strict mother, but that week they never had it so good. They got the extra bun, the second banana, the new petticoat, because it might be their last. At night I bent over their beds to hear them breathing. Listening to Kennedy's speech, I thought: Why should we in Britain sit in sweet togetherness and expect to be wiped out because of Cuba? The least concerned seemed to be the childless people. The angry ones were the parents of young children. All of us turned isolationist, if not definitely anti-American. I puzzled over what made Americans so fearful and therefore aggressive.

I had never had any desire to leave Europe. I hated to go, but off I went. I insured my life, health and luggage for the first time and set off alone by Boeing. The children were terrified because of the saying 'Boeing, Boeing, Bang'. When I landed in New York, I felt worlds away from Europe. A cemetery on the road from the airport stretched for quite a while and then melted into a factory yard. I thought of the cemetries I knew, walled like a garden and green. A beautiful peaceful cemetry makes people happier about their friends being dead. Then I found a delicatessen with barrels full of herrings, pickles, sauerkraut, and all the different sausages and cheeses of Europe – it was an ordinary New York grocer's shop, but in London it exists only in Soho. In Paris you might find it in the Jewish sector. It gave me the feeling of home.

I visited Hede Massing, who had converted me to Communism when I was eighteen. Paul Massing was dead. Hede had an elegant flat in Washington Square: she told me she loved ornaments and bourgeois comforts as a reaction from years of despising them. Hede's trusted boss in the NKVD had been purged by NKVD assassins, shot in Switzerland in 1937, and she thought it her duty to try to detach people from Communism. She said it was harder than recruiting them. She had been the most important witness in Alger Hiss's conviction as a Soviet agent in 1950, and she also testified at the McCarthy hearings against Hollywood Communists. McCarthy's prosecutors were right – Hollywood was riddled with Communists. But they accused them of silly things. Americans have a talent for meaning right and doing wrong.

At Thanksgiving, I went to a party in the suburbs, outside Lake Forrest, Chicago, where families live surrounded by their lawns –

nothing shared about it. I lay down and stuck my face into the earth and found that the earth in the States does not smell; or only faintly. The people at the party were middle-class professionals, all very earnest and dedicated. I said, 'I have come looking for hope for my children. I cannot see why they should be blown to bits – I cannot accept it.' They said they were prepared to die for freedom in the fight against the dark hordes of Communism. Cuba had proved they were a mature people who could match their minds and their bombs with the Soviets. Europeans must rely on the United States and let Americans act for them. Europe was on its feet only because of the Marshall Plan which had brought American help.

I reminded them of the political and economic blunders Washington had committed since the end of the war. I pointed to their phenomenal fear of Communism. They retorted that they had learnt from us, and would not let Communism near their own doorstep, would keep it out of their hemisphere. I said that Communism only took root or power in a country where there was open political and economic disorder; I asked, 'How can I trust people who seem so insecure in themselves? Whose children are raised as though they were adults, whose women are as spoilt as though there were only one woman to twenty men, who waste good food, good cars, good clothes, who are all so busy becoming materially "secure" they have no time to say "No" to wives or children?' American children look bored, as though there is nothing left to dream of.

In Chicago I stayed with James Wells, Anna's godfather. I went to Hollywood to stay with Michael Gough, the English actor, and to Washington to Michael and Christine West: he was representing Britain on the Military Committee of NATO. Through the Wests I met members of the Administration – more gentle, civilised, hospitable people, who listened politely and said they knew what they were doing. What really frightened me in the government were the men born in Europe but now super-American, adding to their new patriotism a hatred of the people and places they had been forced to leave. We have the same phenomenon in Europe, but there latecomers rarely rise so quickly to positions of power. In Washington these disaffected émigrés carried weight.

When I look at Americans I recognise in them the Norwegian, the Swede, the German, the Jew, the Irish or the Italian, and I realise that when a human leaves his soil, he takes with him many roots, dangling along, and when he strikes new soil with his old roots, the roots seem to grow stronger and stronger in reaction to the rerooting. And I find that therefore the American Jews are more Jewish than any Jew in Europe, the Irish live their worst Irishness away from Ireland, the Italians' craftiness blooms in the Mafia, and so on. Americans are emotional, but I find their emotional behaviour very superficial, like the taste of the vegetables and fruit in the States. Everything is so big and so bloated with water it loses its fragrance and intensity.

I left Washington anxious about those fine minds working round the clock trying to sort out the problems of the old worlds of Europe, Africa and Asia, with so little actual connection with those countries – the world of material plenty facing the worlds of emotional and philosophical plenties. I wondered whether the Americans could be as much inspired by a faith in democracy as they seemed to be by fear of Communism.

I went up to Canada, to see Carolyn Zervudachi's brother in Montreal and to visit the Laurentian mountains. At the back of my mind I was looking for a refuge for my children. I have always wanted a shack in the mountains: I looked in the Alps, in Vermont, and in the Laurentians. The Canadian forests had the things I loved in my childhood – pines, birches, blueberries – but I never found my shack.

After I got back to London in 1962, I was invited to a 'mediaeval' fancy dress party on New Year's Eve held at mediaeval Crosby Hall by Anthony and Bunty Kinsman and Michael and Sarah Alexander (Michael had married a clever girl, Sarah Wignall). For my costume, my greengrocer gave me three potato sacks and I made a cross out of two sticks. I went as a witch and carried on my back the cross and a bundle of firewood to burn myself with (fir branches left over from Christmas). I was the only woman who dared go as herself, bar the owners of big houses who went as châtelaines. The ladies who had excellent legs and less money went as pageboys, in black tights and their ski jackets. The most undressed was Bunty Kinsman – a few feathers round her fanny, a few diamonds round her tits and masses of delicious sunburnt flesh and whacking bunny teeth, as a unicorn. I wrote to Christine West in Washington on the first day of 1963:

> They all thought my get-up was 'out of this world', when I only went as my very self. There is a popular conception that witches were bad women. They were good – rebellious debunkers of

> the system of their time, with a hell of a lot of perception and intelligence, which is always feared. I tried to explain this to various of our mutual friends, that the Bistro is not a witch's queendom but the kingdom of all those who have an honest heart, an open mind and the courage of their conviction or their complexes.

I was alone in Bourne Street with the cooking and practical jobs I am so bad at. Then I was rescued. In the summer, a tall young Australian of twenty-one, Lance Dyson, arrived at the door saying he had heard there was a room to let. He had worked his passage from Australia and did not know anywhere in London except the King's Road, so he headed there and inquired about lodgings from the newsagent in Sloane Square. He was on his way to Venice. His father was a Venetian peasant and his mother came from a 'good' English family who had gone to Australia. Lance was two people. He had a face like a sixteenth-century aristocrat but hands and feet like bunches of bananas. His personality was noble and sensitive and intelligent, but his voice could suddenly turn rough and his thinking coarse.

He did not tell me that after seeing his father's birthplace he intended to commit suicide. I gave him a room in exchange for two hours' work a day. He soon saw I needed more help than that. He postponed his plan of dying and offered to stay and save us. He stayed with us for twenty years and did everything – cooking, shopping, mending, the accounts, driving the Bedford Dormobile and gradually becoming father to the children, or an older brother – Johnny was only five years younger. Lance was a much better cook than me, and the Bistro people liked him. David Owen said he would try to kill me one day, but I did not believe him.

23

From Bistro Boys to Lodgers, 1963–70

The children had grown too big for our little house: double-decker bunks were all right when they were small. Johnny liked coming home from boarding school to a place so cosy and full of life (a child who lived near us, a millionaire's daughter, was envious). Katya, at fourteen, had some Bistro *copains* and used to flirt with Christopher Lee; he wrote on a napkin 'I'll wait till you grow up', and she kept it. But she didn't like the drinkers, and none of them liked the noise that went on until after midnight. Anna and Sara were the two who really didn't like the Bistro, even though Anna enjoyed sneaking down to the big table on Sundays after Katya had put her to bed and plaiting Reggie Freed's hair. The children could never have friends to stay. They were also missing Pat. They told me, 'We need a father.' I said, 'I can't buy you one.' So Lance Dyson became the man they treated as a father.

One afternoon in 1963 I went to Betty Vacani's to fetch Anna and Sara from their dancing class. We walked home past Harrods estate office; it was five past five, nearly closing time. Some instinct told me to walk in. I said to the man, 'I want a very cheap house between Hyde Park Corner and Victoria.' He said, 'We have had 22 Chapel Street on our books for two years. The Honourable Mrs Clark.' It was £14,000 for a twenty-year lease. He gave me the keys and we walked to Chapel Street.

The house had a portico, and in the basement kitchen there was a lovely memory of the maids making jam – it may have been the jars or the smell, but I remember thinking: jam was made here. The rooms were all light, musty and friendly, yet each had a different character. The girls slid down the banisters, shrieking 'Mama, Mama, yes, please!'

I went home and rang up Reggie Freed. He did not think it impossible. I went to see Mr Hallam of Lloyds Bank in St James's, who had been extraordinarily kind to me over the American trip: he seemed to regard me as a kind of modern saint. I explained that the Entschädigungsamt in Berlin, the Reparations Office, had sent me a cheque for 28,000 Deutschmarks as compensation for my war experiences. The Americans gave the Germans Marshall Aid on condition that they compensate the victims of Nazism: so much a day for prison or camp, for loss of profession or study, for health (I did not claim under that), for being politically or racially or sexually persecuted – the Jews, gypsies and homosexuals.

I went to see Mrs Clark, who was living in Cadogan Square. She was a charming old lady of eighty-two. She asked, 'Are you related to Bishop Furse?' 'Yes, he is my husband's great-uncle.' 'Ah. He married me and he baptised my children.' She said she would halve the asking price. I rushed in to Mr Hallam again. He said 'All right, Mrs Furse.' He would let me have a mortgage and lend me £20,000 to do up the house and finish the Chesham Street basement flats. I said, 'Why do you say "All right"?' He said, 'Here are your bank statements. You have only been overdrawn once, for £3 12s 6d. You will have to pay back £100 a month.' I went to tell Mr Caplan of the Grosvenor Estates, because they owned the freehold of Chapel Street (and Bourne Street). He asked, 'How are you going to find £100 a month?' I said, 'I have twelve rooms. I shall have PGs.' 'What are PGs?' 'In plain English, lodgers.' He said, 'I did not hear that, Mrs Furse.' The Grosvenor Estates does not allow its beautiful residences to be turned into lodging-houses.

I needed a few thousand more. David Owen bought the long lease of one of my two basement flats for £5,000. It was a good investment: in 1966 he sold it to Reggie Freed for £6,000 to buy a house in Limehouse. Reggie sold the flat back to me for £5,000, losing £1,000; he was very good. He said he wanted me to have both basement flats for security.

The Chapel Street house had no central heating, so I had it put in with my reparations money – I said, 'This boiler is my political past.' The furniture came from the wonderfully shabby auction rooms in Lots Road in Chelsea: I filled the twelve rooms with beds, tables, chairs and old carpets for about £100. We had a music-room and a dining-room. Henry Swanzy wrote that he found me 'clad in purple, directing half a dozen workmen'. Leslie Benson gave me the stair carpet as a house-warming present. I chose mauve, I did not know why. Later a friend of my family's told me that my mother had liked mauve and worn a lot of it in Berlin. Jeremy Fry arrived with a long refectory table for my vast and lovely kitchen. It seated fourteen, and he had had it made in his workshops in the West Country. The house-warming party was on 19 December 1963. I had an enormous Christmas tree decorated with angels' hair and real candles. Henry Swanzy called it the biggest fire hazard in London.

I went to Vera Traill's bureau in Walton Street, and London University, International House and other language schools to ask for lodgers. It became a students' house. I had two au pairs, one for the children, one for the house. I slept in the short leg of the L-shaped drawing-room but had a dressing-room for my clothes.

My real life is always where my table is. Outside the kitchen window was a stump of a buddleia bush we later christened 'Czecho' because it shot up on the day the Russians went in to put down the uprising, 20 August 1968. It defied plants' usual verdict on me and pushed up through the area railings.

Chapel Street was another kind of Bistro – a place where people came and left richer. I went in for foreign students partly because I could speak their languages, and partly because I wanted my children to learn about different nationalities. Through the Bistro and Chapel Street, I gave my temperament what it needed: I was a mother, a provider. I always said my children were part of everything else – of the Bistro, of my life, of their father's life, of the world. They were human beings who were only mine in so far as I was responsible for their wellbeing – not to the point of giving up my own beliefs, personality and way of living.

The children sometimes resented all the others – they wanted to be alone with me. But I wanted everyone to share our food and shelter. One of the lodgers, Tim Husband, became a sixth child to me, I put so much of my strength and effort into him. He is now associate curator of the Cloister Museum in New York. Danielle Tilkin, who came to us to look after Sara, also grew into part of the family; she has since run art galleries in New York and the Canary Islands. My blood children complained about the time I gave to others. They made remarks like 'We can never reach your standard of ethics and morals.' But through me the children had to learn to live with others, otherwise they would have lived like their father, who sat and talked beautifully about people but never had any real contact with them.

I wonder how I would have felt, having a mother like me. Though I do believe that parents are born to be wrong so that children can cut their mental and moral teeth on them. Of course, there are families where there is no friction between parents and children: when I hear that, I ask questions. David Owen once said, 'My family comes first, Elisabeth.' I had a shock. For a socialist, the family is part of everyone else. In the name of 'family', so many crimes have been committed, even by me. It is just too easy to say 'for the sake of the children and my wife . . .'

I have been told that I do not understand family loyalty. That is true. I call it blind family loyalty. I do not believe that blood is thicker than water, except physically – perhaps because I had nothing in common with my own family. Why should family pretence be above truth? I often write to people and tell them what I think of their husband or wife or sister or brother or son or mother. And they get angry. But I think I speak out as a friend, to try to help, and I cannot see why a family drawbridge should be pulled up against me as I stand outside, having come to rescue them.

Some of my lodgers were the traditional enemies of others. The ones who were likely to hate each other I put in the same room. Soon the Arab and the Israeli were best friends. The Israelis were enchanting – intelligent, proud, charming. I had every kind of Arab that exists, and they were impossible – shrewd and clever, but unintelligent. They knew how to drive a car, smoke, put on a shirt, but could not behave by my standards. They were terribly immature. The Christian Arabs were better. The Moslems either bullied or wept.

Henry Swanzy says I generalise ridiculously and that my views on race were an embarrassment to him when be became a Third World affairs broadcaster at the BBC and then editor of *African Affairs*. I admit I do believe in racial characteristics. When the University accommodation bureau first asked if I had any preferred lodgers and any I would *not* want, I said, 'No Germans, Spaniards, Flemish, Swedes, Czechs (even though they are Slavs) and no Arabs, if only because their culture is so remote and hard to grasp.' I did not keep to this.

The Japanese make me furious with their cleanliness and single-track minds – just like my mother. The Chinese I love, the French

I feel good with for their intelligence and taste, despite their ruthlessness, the Italians make me laugh with them, Russians I love of course, but Romanians bore me with their vanity and Hungarians with their slickness. The Austrians have their charm, but Germans frighten me. My best friends have been Scots, whom I love, love, love. I don't love the Welsh, all those bushy eyebrows and singsong voices. I don't like the Irish, too sweet and too violent, also you never know what they are thinking. Nearer home, I like the people from South London but not from North London.

What am I? I am a FOREIGNER. My soul lives in Venice, my mind in France, my heart in Russia and my security in England. I belong to where I am needed and to who needs me.

I was not afraid of work. I slept on the bus, in the train, in the bath, talking to people. I made myself into a little fakir. I loved my children, I loved being a mother.

I gave the whole family – children, au pairs and lodgers – breakfast at the big kitchen table, to be in regular daily contact, and also for tax reasons. In the evening, Lance and I set off in the white van with the food for the Bistro. The first regulars of the Bistro had had babies and moved away from Chelsea, or had risen so high their evenings weren't free. They were replaced by new people, all nice, very bright and interesting, but the spontaneous unpredictable character seemed to have gone.

Hussein Shariffe of the Sudanese ruling family, related to the Mahdi, came – until I banned him for some reason. We had several of the Ethiopian royal family: Molly and Colly Messai Andargatchew, Haile Selassie's granddaughters (Molly was a girlfriend of Jo Menell's), and a favourite grandson, Prince Merid Beyene, who always brought beautiful girls. He came in with Christine Keeler in 1963, just after she had told a newspaper all about her affair with Jack Profumo, the War Minister. I said I did not want to talk to anyone who sold her friends. She said I was an ugly, jealous old bitch. I said, 'I may be old and ugly, but I am certainly not jealous of you.' That scandal helped cause Macmillan to resign, and Sir Alec Douglas-Home won the grubby battle to take over as Prime Minister.

In October 1964, he called an election. This was what David Owen had been working towards as the Labour candidate for Torrington. David's headquarters was our cottage and I helped him all I could; it was not popular with the Furses, who supported the Conservatives. The real fight at Torrington was between the Liberals and the Conservatives, and the Liberals said David would split the vote. The Liberal candidate was Mark Bonham-Carter, married to the daughter of my friend Leslie Benson. One night when David was to speak at Dolton village hall there was a power cut, so we lit candles and the butcher put on his white coat and shepherded people in, saying, 'I don't agree with his politics, but the boy deserves a chance.' David complains that I berated him afterwards for talking about sheep prices and not big issues.

The Conservative won, Mark Bonham-Carter came second and David third. When it was known that David had saved his deposit, the Tories cheered. Labour got in with a majority of five and Harold Wilson became Prime Minister. David Owen won Plymouth in the general election two years later, when Labour improved their majority to 97. He was soon given a rung on the ladder, as Parliamentary Private Secretary to the Minister of Defence in 1967.

In January 1965, Aunt Gladys died, so I and the children lost almost a mother and a grandmother. Her heart was so strong it went on beating when everything else had stopped.

But I found my dear governess Bächlein again. She had come to live in London and was the same kind, literature-mad person she had always been, with new writers I had never heard of to discuss and praise. My children loved her. She became head of languages at Pitman's College and lived in a one-room flat in Bloomsbury. I don't think she finished her Moissi book. Her new passion among performances was ballet, and she often spent the small hours queueing so as to be near when the ticket window opened. Katya and Anna sometimes queued with her. Katya had come home from ballet school in Copenhagen. Bächlein died in hospital a week after she had had a heart attack. On the last day, a nurse telephoned me to say it would only be a few hours, and I took my girls to say goodbye. Bächlein opened the little cupboard beside her and said, 'You forgot your gloves as usual. You never take care of your things, do you.' She left me her bed and some of her books – she had one other friend.

The Bistro was not in tune with the 'swinging London' that developed in the early sixties half a mile away in the King's Road. Those were less intellectual young people who had never known the war; they invented the permissive society. The Italian film director Antonioni, a small frustrated man panting to keep up with youth, did come to the Bistro for several weeks, and my son Anthony introduced him to friends in that set and to Claude Virgin, who was the inspiration for *Blow Up* (1967) with David Hemmings and Vanessa Redgrave, about a fashion photographer and upper-class druggies and a murder. Anthony had become a magazine writer and was working for the *Queen* and the *Daily Telegraph Magazine*. His first book was about the commercial culture of America, *Down the Programmed Rabbit Hole* (called *The Paradise Program* in America): it came out in 1971. (He eventually moved to New York, and worked on *New York Magazine*, which was just starting.)

I did not like pop culture. I described what was going on to Anthony Elliott in Hong Kong, where he was political adviser, at Easter 1967:

> The ridicule the English raise! In the XIX century they exported rickets, *la maladie anglaise*, *die Englische Krankheit*, from the undernourished working kids. Now there is a new English disease, the undernourished intelligence of the young – Mary Quant, the Beatles MBE (they had been given it in 1965).
>
> I am bitter and angry, and when anything in a superminiskirt or a Guards uniform under long hair hoves in sight I scare the pants off them. It is not funny, and it is not a phase, it is a disease, not even tragic. For money, the young are encouraged to destroy the drama of life and living. If you knew the heartbreak most parents suffer from their teenagers!
>
> As for our David (Owen), he is too influenced by the glamour of the House, and George Brown sucking up to the young. He (David) comes here for pummelling from me, and that at least helps. What a mediocre world.
>
> It is almost morning. The night is very old, and the day is as young – and I have come home from work and watched and listened fearfully to the News. U Thant has said again that we have entered the first stage of the Third World War. If a man in his position in the UN says so repeatedly, it must mean that all hope has left him of solving peacefully the various problems of the human species' peaceful cohabitation. The children are away in the country, it is Bank Holiday, and gladly would I wish them to stay there forever, or until I am sure that there is peace . . .
>
> I feel smaller and smaller as they start looking down on me, grabbing my shoulder and sometimes saying, 'I am getting taller

than you, Mama.' They have pains and aches and stitches in their tummies and groins and heads, and Doctor says 'growing pains'. I have pains in the same place, and Doctor says 'wear and tear'.

Yet all is as it should be, except for this dreadful, dreadful threat, Total War, Holy War, War for This and That, Against This and That. And there is our own beautiful life of daily challenge and response, full of the well-measured insecurity of those who live from day to day, a struggle we can easily cope with. Shall Katya have a new pair of shoes? Will we have stew or maybe fish? Is it *Panorama* on television, or shall we queue for the gallery at the ballet? Will there be buns for tea or just bread and peanut butter?

But I am starting to crave peace again, so as to be able to meet my children's eyes. I saw that look in the last war and, full of absolute faith, could say, 'We are fighting the most terrible danger that there has ever been.' Yet now the same question is asked from Israel, from Egypt, Vietnam, the States, as once from Cuba, Korea, Berlin, ever since that marvellous peace broke out 22 years ago, only to be followed by wars, one after another.

Yet in those famous thirties, as I remember, while we were marching for peace, we really loved the smell of conflict – I remember that feeling of elation when the bullets flew on the Place de la Concorde. . . And how are you? I shall soon be in Hong Kong. Are you frightened?? Tell the truth!!

In 1968, David Owen married an enchanting American girl, Debbie Schabert, and she set up a literary agency in his house on the Thames at Limehouse. David and his friend from St Thomas's, Michael Barraclough, lived beside each other on the river years before skyscrapers and big business arrived. Michael left medicine for a type of human politics. He built with his own hands a beautiful house in steps on the Isle of Dogs for his wife Jenny, the television producer, and their children and went on to organise the development of his neighbourhood into a co-operative.

One day in 1968, Anna came back from school and said she could not understand other people's jokes. Nor indeed could I: I never laugh at Chaplin, who uses *Schadenfreude*, amusement at other people's misfortunes; I am not unloving, therefore do not know the fun of someone's comeuppance; I am not clever, and therefore do not use irony; I am not bitter, therefore do not know sarcasm; and I am not sad enough to produce serious humour. Slavs laugh, but at different things.

I realised my children had inherited more from the Slavs than graceful movements. The White Russians used to gather every summer at La Colline Russe at La Favière on the Riviera near Le Lavandou – four generations, from America, France, everywhere, the old in huts, the young in tents. It was run by the Prokovskys (the father was a scientist, the mother an opera singer, and their son André was a well-known ballet dancer). Prince Obolensky had a café in La Favière. I took Anna and Sara down there and left them. They were the only ones from England, but they loved it. Many musicians from the Paris cabarets went. The teenagers could work and have the holiday free, and Anna did that three years running. I believe the Russians still gather there, though their white blood has been diluted by marriage.

I sent Sara to Bousfield, the local state primary school, but the children were rough. Some came to school without breakfast and made Sara feel bad for having eaten. I took her away and sent her to Queen's Gate, where all the children had breakfast. She went on to Heathfield in Berkshire, where Diana Ladas, whose son had been at Eton with Johnny, was the headmistress. I could not afford Heathfield, so it was suggested to the Inner London Education Authority that Sara might be in danger because she was the only child in a house full of lodgers. The inspectors came round and said immediately that she must go to boarding school. The ILEA also had a policy of preventing a child falling behind its brothers and sisters educationally, so Sara qualified for a 90 per cent grant. She did not like Heathfield, and says the matrons sometimes reminded her she was on a grant. She came back to Queen's Gate for A levels.

Johnny went into Gulliver Films in 1966, after Eton. I asked Roger Graef to take him to Paris for his first brothel visit, but Roger decided to give him a job instead. So he later worked with Roger on his big television series, *The Space Between Words* – in fact, the title of the series was Johnny's idea, and he also gave me the title for this book. I had asked all the Bistro film-makers about work for him: we fed several people in that industry. Michael Luke, a writer and producer, made *Oedipus the King* with Orson Welles in 1968; David Cammell and Hugh Hudson had the top company making commercials, Cammell, Hudson & Brownjohn. David Cammell produced *Performance*, written by his brother

Donald, which starred Mick Jagger. Both Cammells came to the Bistro. I remember David bringing Deborah Wood, of Deborah & Clare – all the smart young Bistro men had a Deborah & Clare ruffled cream silk shirt for grand parties. Donald came in with Anita Pallenberg and Michele Breton from the film; they inspired Clive Bossom to even greater wit than usual.

Peter Jenkins wrote about the Bistro in 1968 in *Nova*, the magazine that was in touch with the new kind of people. He said it was 'a club, a hideaway, an emotional poste restante, a debating society, a womb to climb back into, an intellectuals' employment exchange, and a Salvation Army soup kitchen for down-and-out Old Etonians . . . in short, a state of mind, not a catering establishment.' Of me, he said, 'She oscillates emotionally and noisily between wild misinformation and error, and – almost cruelly – truth and perception, mostly about people, and particularly about the English. In London SW1 she performs the useful function of a Mittel European poltergeist.' I was still going there every night. I suppose I had £10 a week clear profit, sometimes £20, from the Bistro. To me that was a lot of money. I cooked at Chapel Street, worked in the Bistro, let the rooms over the Bistro, and was able to reduce the amount of film work because the income from the rents more or less covered my expenses and the monthly mortgage.

In 1969, my divorce from Pat came through. Pat married Anni, our children's nanny, and they have lived happily ever since. They had no children of their own. Anni changed her name to Antonia because it was confusing having two Anna Furses. Pat paints and does his beautiful enamelling and craft work, Antonia is a jeweller. She does not like me. Peter's wife does not like me either. Would you like me if you were them?

Lance and I fed many more men than women at Bourne Street, but some women came without having to be brought, for instance Helen Montague, then directing at the Royal Court, and Vivien Pickles, who was in John Osborne's *Plays for England* at the Royal Court in 1963 and became famous as Isadora Duncan in Ken Russell's TV film of 1966. Vivien married the actor Gordon Gostelow. Both Edwina and Celia Sandys were Bistro girls. Edwina married Piers Dixon, who became Conservative MP for Truro in 1970.

Michael Peacock was still a regular, now with his lovely wife Daphne. He had become controller of BBC1 in 1965 and moved over to run London Weekend Television. Richard Kershaw was at the BBC on *Panorama*, Andrew Mulligan was on ITN's *News at Ten*, then *Panorama*. Jo Menell had also gone into TV: he edited *This Week* and produced *Panorama*; he was filming in Chile when Allende was overthrown by the Pinochet military coup in 1973, and just got out.

There were as many journalists as ever: Nicholas de Jongh of the *Guardian*, Richard Casement, Dudley Fishburn and David Gordon of the *Economist*, Mark Schreiber, director of the Conservatives' Public Sector Research Unit, on his way to the *Economist*, Simon Jenkins of the *Evening Standard* (who ended up as editor of *The Times* in 1990) and Polly Toynbee, who started as a reporter on the *Observer* at twenty-two in 1968 and married Peter Jenkins two years later. His first wife, Charlotte Strachey, had died. Polly became Social Affairs editor of the BBC in 1988. Nicky Harman went from the *Economist* to the *Sunday Times* and *Panorama*, then to BBC current affairs full-time, then back to the *Economist* as Latin American editor.

Dudley Fishburn had been coming to the Bistro since he was at Eton. I realised he was a schoolboy, but I let him stay because I liked him. He became the MP for Kensington in 1988. Michael Shea had been at Gordonstoun with my son Anthony; he was in the Foreign Office. One of my great prides was always the mixture: we had added to it schoolmasters from Eton and Gordonstoun, monks from Ampleforth and the girls' dancing and art mistresses.

Lance was respected no end and everyone asked his opinion. One evening the Bistro was discussing a man who though brilliant was small, bald, pot-bellied and piggy-eyed, and wondering how he got such beautiful girls. Lance's voice was heard from the kitchen: 'He must be a demon in the cot.' Demons in cots was our description of it from that day. Lance himself said sex was only for making babies. I always put my foot down when anyone tried to call the Bistro 'Elisabeth's'. It wasn't mine – it was theirs. After I left the Communist Party I needed another group of comrades to whom I could give myself entirely: that is why I became so rich in my emotional life.

At Christmas 1970 the Bistro closed after just over seventeen years; our house in Bourne Street was to be demolished. We tried to move the Bistro to a room in the Nag's Head in Kinnerton Street, but the Bistro people were not natural pub people and liked to bring their own wine, which did not suit the publican. When we closed, I wrote to the regulars:

The Bistro lived in its quintessential meaning as a place where people came, sure to see people they liked or hated, agreed with or disagreed with, where they brought their hearts and minds, and sometimes their souls, in need of others. It was a free gathering of free people who liked one another's presence without having to become wholly involved. I knew it would come to an end, and I sat and watched and wondered what would happen. Would anyone miss it? Was there a real need for it?

I thought about all those who came and stayed on and came and came again. All those I knew and loved and still love and will always love, with the kind of love that would make me go into battle with any of you and die with you. I would face whatever you had to face with you. That is the kind of tenderness I feel, however much momentary resentments may creep in – we were, and are, dependent upon one another. At night, there you all were with your gladnesses and sadnesses, your successes and your failures, your loves and your hates, your marriages and your divorces, your careers or lack of careers. I was near you always and gave what little I could – compassion, anger, love, and sadness. Deliberately, I kept almost all contact with you within the four walls of that little room. I tried very much indeed to help you all, and to make all of you help all the rest – and you all did help one another, you all did splendidly whatever, whenever, you could.

We all affect everyone. That little room was a powerful room, full of growing talent, full of people who had a purpose. They filled the room until that room overflowed. That room was life for seventeen years.

24

A Convicted Witch, Switzerland, Finland, Israel, 1971–76

I still had Chapel Street to run, and I often brought people together to eat in the basement kitchen. I don't ask an equal number of men and women and I don't plan the numbers. If too many people come they have to sit behind the others – I ask friends with cars to bring their own chairs. I have seen three rows of people sitting happily round my table. They dined with me and their problems dined with them: it is the most wonderful thing in the world to succeed in helping others. Jenny Morland, who had married my Bistro boy Martin, says I'm selfish and I do good because it makes me feel good. I say I prefer the selfishness of those who try to help than the selfishness of those who don't.

I do not care whether it comes from selfishness, vanity, power: without boasting I can say that I have saved lives, yes lives, by finding love, work, homes, safe houses and schools. If I have not achieved a professional success of some kind it is because I gave it all to the children and others – willingly, happily and easily. But I did not get enough serious discussions after the Bistro closed. I suffered the agony of mental solitude and a dreadful silence – after spiritual and intellectual and emotional exchanges twenty-four hours of the day and night.

The miners went on strike in January 1972, defying Mr Heath. It was an angry time politically, and cold and dark because of the power cuts. Later in the spring of 1972, I went to Switzerland to smell the snow and ice again, and to be with Roger Graef and his wife Karen. I had arranged for them to rent the chalet of a friend at Leysin, near Geneva: Karen had bronchitis and Leysin has the purest of pure air. Then I thought: I will follow them. The chalet had no telephone. Roger says that he had been surprised on arriving at the station in a blizzard to find that the house was a mile and a half's walk away. In the clear air of next morning he saw that the chalet was perched on an alp. That evening, it was snowing again, and he suddenly said to Karen: 'Elisabeth is here.' He set out for the village to fetch me, and there I was, in the café.

When we all left to return to London, I wanted to visit friends in Geneva so I said I would join the Graefs' night train at the next station. They looked up and down the train for me and realised I had missed it. When they arrived at the Gare de Lyon in Paris at five in the morning, Roger said to Karen again: 'Elisabeth is here.' The trains shunted apart and there I was: I had caught an express. Roger says that I am a witch and that I know it.

In 1973, my beloved father-in-law Sir Ralph Furse became bedridden. I had talks with him while he lingered on. He told me he had seen the best and the worst of England. 'What is the worst, Didda?' 'Hypocrisy.' He was buried in August 1973 with his cavalry sword and under the Union Jack. In church, the children and I sat at the back, Pat and Anni at the front. That night I went to the grave and lay across it and talked to the man I had known and loved. Pat inherited the estate.

The diplomats and politicians who had come to the Bistro were out in the world representing Britain. Michael Shea became head of Chancery in Bucharest in 1973, and went from there to the British Information Services in New York; Christopher Mallaby was at the British Trade Office in New York. Christopher was the one who nicknamed the Bistro regulars 'Bistrots', pronounced 'Bistrott'. Andrew Mulligan left *Panorama* to become head of the General Reports of the EEC in Brussels from 1973 to 1974, and director of Press and Information of the delegation of the European Communities to the US in Washington in 1975. David Duncan became ambassador to Nicaragua in 1974, Anthony Elliott ambassador in Helsinki in 1973, Iain Sutherland minister in Moscow in 1974; Martin Morland was counsellor in Rome. There they were, being 'His Excellency' from morning to night. What an awful job – party after party after party. I have never been a diplomatist – putting off the truth for another parler, another nice meeting, another let-us-put-it-off. Many diplomats, such as Anthony Elliott, are valuable people, but they are no longer of great use, except to keep the little conferences going and masses of secretaries in jobs and hotels filled and themselves bored and worried and morally vexed.

In August 1975 I joined Anthony Elliott in Helsinki for an important conference he had organised, the summit meeting on *détente*. One day we drove into the Finnish forests, and there among the pines and birches of my childhood he told me the truth about myself. I said, 'Ant, I am a good wife, a good mother, a good mistress, a good friend and a good hostess – why am I alone?' He answered, 'You are an impossible mixture of colossal strength and utter dependence. The two do not go together. They frighten the British. We are basically homosexual – not physically but mentally. We like nannies. We like our women to be strong and independent, and to stay out of our real lives.' So from then on I knew my fate – to be forever too much for British men.

On 28 March 1976, Ian Garrow died. I had only seen him once since Marseille, but I felt his presence in the background whether I saw him or not, the man who had risked his life for me, who never changed, always calm, wonderfully brave and most of all *intelligent* and able to correct me. He said in one of his letters:

> You talk of 'disillusionment' and 'bitterness'. I am conscious of neither. The strongest wording used was 'disappointment', and that was only because Pat had placed his reputation into the hands of an indifferent craftsman for his biography. You must not read any more into my words. I did not denigrate the French Resistance, but tried to make you understand that the will to resist was not stirred by any martyrs but was the active expression of the conviction held by the nameless millions that June 1940 was not the end of the story. It was quantity as well as quality that gave the movement its strength and vitality.
>
> I quite agree with you about *Le Silence de la Mer*, it was the first worthwhile book to come out of Occupied France. Mario Prassinos gave it to me just before he returned to France.

Ian Garrow was gone, but I still had Anthony Elliott, now ambassador in Tel Aviv. The Israeli novelist Amos Oz was another true friend: I had met him in London through Debbie Owen, his literary agent. I love Amos, for he has blue eyes and he smells of the desert and he is good with words and he is so passionate. I decided to make a trip to Israel.

I like to travel with men, because men know about history and art: I do not take in knowledge by reading, only by listening to a man and by living. Actually, I don't believe in the high importance of art. Skill I respect, but am not carried away by. Having been an amateur all my life in everything, I find that amateurism can take you a long way and allows for more freedom. I always preferred to watch a ballet class to Margot Fonteyn performing more or less perfectly. To me, to be a connoisseur, to be a collector, to be of knowledge – even of infinite knowledge – is not enough unless the scholarship helps living things. From my youth I always considered Bernard Berenson repulsive, for he dealt in art in a more vulgar way than any man could in kitsch, rags or food. And if beauty is what brings a Berenson into existence, then to hell with beautiful pictures and objects. Beauty and art should be part of living. Stanford Anderson, a professor of architecture at M.I.T. in Boston, who had once lived at Chapel Street, said he would join me in Israel. I invited a pretty American friend called Nancy to go with me. She was living in Belgravia with her rich husband – but I understood they had separate lives. Nancy was what the girls in my house called 'a Southern belle'. She was nicely generous to them, and I love generosity, for it allows me to be myself (so many people cripple one's need to give by their own meanness). She thoughtfully insisted on giving me the plane ticket to Israel.

In Jerusalem and in Israel in general, it was difficult to get away from religions. We went to Protestant, Armenian, Russian Orthodox and Greek Orthodox churches. The monastery of St Katarina in Sinai was outstanding Greek beauty, but the monks were absolutely pure, unlike the ones on Patmos, and resented tourists and non-believers. We were allowed into the holy of holies, the shrine of St Katarina, only because I looked like everybody's dear mother and Stanford Anderson was so serious. Everywhere in Israel people treated me as the archetypal mother, though I did most unholy-motherly things such as riding on dromedaries with my thighs showing. Even the Muslims smiled and spelled out 'MOTHER'. The passport officer had come from Russia, and when he saw my birth date and birthplace (which had become the USSR) he said in Russian, 'Only Russia can produce women like you,' and shook my hand and almost wept. We visited Amos Oz on his own kibbutz, Hulda. By that time I was sunburnt and healthy, having survived the desert and climbing Mount Sinai – not quite to the top. Nancy and I were rather helpless and very glad to have Stanford with us.

Two months after we got home, on 28 August 1976, came news

that Anthony Elliott was dead: drowned swimming in the sea off the lonely woods round Caesarea. He had had a seizure in the cold water. His wife Thea and two of his children were picnicking on the beach and did not notice anything wrong. I thought of our last evening with him in Tel Aviv. He put on the record of Mahler's 'Das Lied von der Erde', then jumped up suddenly and changed it for Louis Armstrong. We danced in the garden to hot jazz and he gave me the Israeli toast: 'To life!' Thea told me that when Anthony's body was waiting to be taken to England for burial, she saw Israeli friends waiting outside the house. They knew that the English do not like other people to share their grief, so they stayed in their cars, sitting quietly to express their love and sympathy, but not to embrace, nor hold hands with the family, as they would have done with one of their own.

With that tragedy of Anthony's almost irreplaceable loss for Britain and Israel and mankind in general (for he worked to help save this doomed civilisation), with Anthony dead and cold, and with him gone the most intimate person in my life – I felt ready to go too. Not because he was a particularly good man – not at all. But he KNEW THE TRUTH, always, and he could see right through any human being – but analysed nicely and tolerantly. And nothing could buy him, not even sex.

David Owen drove me to Anthony's funeral service in the family church at Taynton in Gloucestershire. Afterwards I wrote to him.

> Dear David, in all relationships, there are certain moments of proof. And on Wednesday, there was a real proof – and whatever dark shadows had been passing between us and probably still will, remains this deep feeling of trust and compassion – some kind of belonging. I will never be able to tell you what it meant to me to have you take me to that terrible, terrible service.
>
> The grief for Ant, who was not the goodest, nor the most generous of men – though generous intellectually, spiritually and in tolerance – the deep shock, the feeling of a great loss in that church, was beyond any I have ever known.
>
> Roy (Jenkins) weeping like a child behind his dark glasses, Michael Palliser wet-eyed and shaking, and so many others that knew Ant well or less well, all affected by his personality and all in the knowledge that an Englishman that could ill be spared was suddenly taken away. Thea and the children trembling with shock – and we were together afterwards and all we could say

> was: this is not possible, this is a kind of a film we are seeing or participating in, and he will walk in, bent and strong, and say: 'Huuuullo – what are you doing here?' Roy and I wept together, for we had known him longest, bar his family, and known him oh so well . . . and he was essential to Roy and myself, as a sort of guiding beacon . . . Enough, all will go on – please do not belittle him because of his need of me.

My friends have to deal with a very passionate being such as they have never known on this island, for they do not grow in British earth – they grow from far away and they hurt much and heal much. They do much and live much, and they never ever grow old, for they never ever resign, nor accept, nor appease, and they never ever sweep things under the carpet – any carpet. And they are very tiresome people, for they are irksome to people's conscience and people's awareness. For to be aware of all and everything is a kind of law to my kind of species – to be aware and involved.

25

Grim and Carefree Carnivals, Rottweil, Basel, Venice, 1977–81

In February 1977, David Owen became Foreign Secretary in Jim Callaghan's Government.

When Anthony Elliott died, everyone telephoned, wrote and came, holding my hand, my heart, my soul – my tears. When David got the Foreign Office, they did the same, just like a wake. 'Local boy makes good,' they said proudly, as though it was much due to me and to them too. And that is true, for David cut his political teeth in the Bistro. He often made me take important decisions, so in a way David was a bit like Ant, making me feel that my being mattered, politically and morally and somehow ethically. And that is good for anyone. Debbie and I trembled, for we knew how fast one goes up and also comes down. We decided to make the most of limousines, trips to Paris, and so on, and be prepared to go back on to the bikes any minute. I wrote to him:

> Please, please David, remember: the lower the backs, the bigger the daggers hidden in the bend. What a horrible vulgar way of putting it. Someone has just brought in *Private Eye* with you inside it. I dare not look.
>
> Here are two poems for Tristan and Gareth, to pin over their beds. I did over my children's, and unashamedly I say that 'If' is what I tried to live up to as a kind of commandment – I have always been checked by it when I behaved what might be called unconventionally. I think, in spite of that strange arrogant veneer, deep down you are an 'If' person too. Keep well, on this voyage – you will need all your

> clarity and humility to resist the corruption of power and success.

I have never known so much publicity over one young man and his wife and children. I was besieged for interviews. David would have made it under any government, any system, at any time in history, for he has it all – utter security, intelligence, quickness of mind, charm and looks. He just smelt of succeeding. Anthony Elliott had the same ingredients, though he was much more modest (Ant was a gentleman – David is not) and more intelligent, but had less energy and more hang-ups.

David Owen appointed Peter Jay ambassador to Washington. Peter was only forty, and a journalist not a diplomat, but he was married to Margaret Callaghan, the Prime Minister's daughter. I wrote:

> Well done, David – but what about the consequences? Though there is a twin quality about you and Peter J – is it the hair and the sweater? Not the same kind of brain, but the same 'ruthlessness', people call it. He is utterly anti-Common Market and you are supposed to be utterly pro – but you both play tennis. Or did you appoint him to strengthen the 'English look' and the sales in Jermyn Street? You, and Callaghan, and the rest, are playing Britain back against a wall called USA – and I am all for it, for it is the only hope Britain has for some decent survival.
>
> I know that looking good, and being daring and nonchalant and arrogant and risking all on some chips, is impressive and attractive, but you need much substance to sustain it. How will Peter J sustain his impeccable looks and intelligence without the positive human qualities, for instance care for others, not just thought? He has not got the touch. But maybe he will go to church with Carter and drink lemonade and make his wife cocu (a cuckold).

I was more than pleased to have a letter from Little Mac, Lewis MacDonald, my friend since the train to Marseille. He had married a Frenchwoman from Normandy, and after retiring from the Nigerian police he bought a pub in Stirlingshire. He wrote in the bitterly cold winter of 1977 from their house at Dunblane. I answered:

I always knew that you were tenderness-starved when you were a very young boy, Mac – do you remember telling me about the homes you went to and your mother never cuddling you? It is a terrible thing, this lack of tenderness. I suffered from it as a child, I had everything money could buy – but no tenderness, no physical touch, no LOVE. I discovered that you can get over almost anything in life except deprivations and sufferings in childhood. The craving, the need stays with you forever (I can never get enough love and tenderness – ever, ever), and whether it was the bicycle or the shoes you did not get, or the food, or the this and that – all your life, you will be crying for that bike and that pair of shoes.

That is why people who have been deprived in their childhood should never ever be in power. They will never forget nor forgive, and make other people pay forever.

Of course, the deaths of Anthony and Ian cut me down. Last year was really quite unbearable for all, and the children decided to accuse me of everything on earth, because all of them were miserable and in a fix (that is why I love to help people in any way, Mac – only because they do not hurt other people when they are reasonably 'happy'). And mine did lash out to the point when I decided to go miles away for good and die somewhere in Brazil or the Arctic, and only this Christmas have at least two of them turned a corner and returned to some kind of tender and civilised relationship.

Anyway, what is much more important than my little belly-aches is the international situation. Carter gives me the creeps, always did, the Irish make me feel sick, really sick, English people make me want to scream – and whenever you tell them about their laziness and greediness and what is going to happen to them because of it, they just laugh and call you a doomsday person and go in for another Social Security application. In Italy, corruption screams for Communism or Fascism – *les extrêmes se touchent, n'est-ce pas*? And the countries where people work and live a somehow decent life are being laughed at – and I am sorry to say that Germany is one of them.

But all the young are deprived of not being understood – and as they cannot bind about not being understood they will kill to be misunderstood.

Jimmy Carter, who became President in 1977, seemed to me a disaster, more dangerous than Nixon. At least Nixon was lucky and intelligent enough to choose the monstrous but oh-so-right Henry Kissinger as adviser on defence and disarmament – a German Jew, with all that a German Jew knows and understands. Kissinger could help the States into the world and into proper world politics: he flew around, dealing and fixing and succeeding. Jimmy Carter thought he should have the same sort of European adviser, so chose Zbigniew Brzezinski – but Brzezinski was a Pole. The Americans were courting suicide, given the Poles' national characteristics based on their miserable history. The Kissingers are survivors and wanting-to-livers, the Poles are always ready to die. I was very relieved when Reagan beat Carter in the 1980 election.

My children were all grown up, if not settled. Johnny looked like a wild man out of the woods and insisted on wearing cotton shirts in the middle of winter; he was working in films. Katya had finished film school in Boston and was planning a documentary on ballet. Anna had a degree in drama and French from Bristol, then studied film and theatre at the Sorbonne, and got a post-graduate certificate in education and drama from London in 1978 – all on grants. Sara had finished a course at Hornsey art college and was nursing physically disabled children at Chailey Heritage hospital near Brighton. Anthony was a well-known journalist in New York, utterly selfish and egocentric but clever. He was still working for *New York Magazine* and also for the *Sunday Telegraph* in London. In 1979 he got an American Emmy for writing and narrating a television programme called *The Affluent Immigrants*. In 1980 he was covered in glory by a book called *Bad Dreams* about the murder of a New York drug dealer by a racehorse trainer over a model. He signed up the girl before the trial. I was upset by the publicity but glad he would have money and feel more secure. They had all missed a father badly when growing up. In the teens, a father is much more important than a mother; when all the protection and hen stuff are over, the father's personality and *poids*, weight, are necessary.

In February 1978, I fell over a lump of ice outside the Brecht Theater in East Berlin and hurt my knee. I had to have cobalt treatment and ever after I walked on an aluminium crutch. I was declared officially disabled, which was quite useful, but I kept falling again. The kneecaps had gone, like footballers' knees.

After that ice sprawl in East Berlin, my life with pain and

painkillers began. The fall worsened arthritis I already had, and later came sciatica on both sides – pain down the back of my legs. I also have a tired heart; and I get bronchitis every year, a legacy of my TB, which left me with shrinking lungs – emphysema. I also have softening of the bones: in my eighties I was two inches shorter. My knees would crumple and drop me on the floor. But bodies wear out. In old age, there is no health, there is survival. I had a hard life and I never took care of myself.

In July 1979 I got a flat in Berlin, in Düsseldorferstrasse, and in January 1980 Katya became the first occupant. It means I can go to Berlin often, and also give friends a bed. Katya wrote to me:

> Darling Mama, I just want you to know how grateful I am to you for getting me all set up here with a home – and a pleasant one at that. It was wonderful to have you here when I arrived, really – I hope that you will not forget those few days we just spent together – that they will be a happy memory for you, unlike those of our last trip to Berlin together! I am sorry if I was a little irritable on the day you left, yesterday – it seems to be something that often, if not always, happens when people who care about each other are about to be separated, and in case you are not aware of it already, you yourself act differently just before a departure. I suppose it is a certain anxiety which produces this pricklyness – partly anxiety about being left, and partly about the departing person. Anyhow, I was sad to see you go.

But the most wonderful thing I did in 1979 was to discover carnivals and get inside my time, the Middle Ages. I know I would have died at the stake, but I love the darkness and the discomfort and companionship of those centuries before 1500. In February, I set off on a big trip in our Dormobile with Sue Collins, a friend from Australia. We drove through many countries on the way towards Turkey and back. We got into the Middle Ages by accident. We were driving from Belgium through Germany towards Zürich, and decided to stop at the mediaeval town of Rottweil in the mountains of the Black Forest. Rottweiler dogs came from there. We arrived in the evening. It was two days before Lent.

We wondered what the drumming was, drumming and drumming and reedy pipes. We saw a line of men and women in masks dancing to the drums in a line, man and woman, man and woman, hopping through the streets. They wore jesters' costumes, for this is the *Narrenfest*, the Feast of the Fools. They are handed the keys of the city by the mayor for two days, Rose Monday and *Fastnacht* (Shrove Tuesday) and they and their followers sing day and night: 'We are the Fools, we want you to be happy, we want you to laugh with us – we celebrate the Fool, for he is good.' Many of their masks and costumes have been passed down in the family for hundreds of years. The music is only drums and shepherds' pipes, purely mediaeval. It starts at eight on Monday morning at the Black Gate. The whole population begins dancing, which means hopping. They all jump or hop around the city – old and middle-aged and young and children – throwing oranges and sweets at onlookers and reading out the year's events in dialect, for which they are given food and drink. There must have been at least two thousand people hopping about, but there was no drunkenness or lasciviousness as happens in Munich during *Fasching* (carnival), where nothing done in the two days can be cited in divorce cases. Rottweil was open and joyful: they visited each other, danced and ate and drank and talked. This Feast of the Fools is for the sake of pure joy. That was the Roman Catholic carnival. We drove on to Basel for the Protestant carnival, which is always a week later.

It starts at four in the morning. The street lights of Basel go out and torches are lit; drums and pipes start the procession. This carnival is not spontaneous like Rottweil, but serious and sombre. Different groups each have to prepare a subject. One theme I saw was British, '*The Times*', which was then on the third month of what became a year's strike. A man on stilts, dressed as a Victorian aunt in leg-of-mutton sleeves, led men and women, draped in pages taken from the real *Times*, with on their heads little coffins lit inside by a battery. Another theme was 'Black is Beautiful' with 'black' people in nineteenth-century Mississipi costumes led by a beautiful girl, naturally black.

The Protestant celebrations were all thought and design and artfulness. Two years later I saw the Venice carnival, so I could compare the three. To the Catholics, carnival is religious and mediaeval, to the Protestants, intellectual and mindful, to the Venetians, theatrical, a show. The Venetians restarted their carnival after two hundred years in 1979, and with what panache and passionate involvement. In 1981 off I went the way I love to travel, by boat and train, for one meets the most extraordinary people – ordinary people travel by plane.

After visiting Colette and René Sanson in Paris, I took a train to see other friends in Maastricht in Holland: Hildegarde Schneider, who had lodged at Chapel Street, was a lecturer at Maastricht University, her husband René de Groot the professor of Common Market law. They lived in a sixteenth-century house with beams, tiny windows, creaking floorboards, a spiral wooden staircase and the right kind of furniture and candles.

The train from Paris stopped very early in Liège, and they took me to the Liège market on our way home. There we saw live ducks, geese, hens, cocks, rabbits, goats, peacocks, turkeys, pigeons, cats, dogs, birds, fishes – all animals bar horses – sold live and taken away in cardboard boxes (centre open for their heads). We went to Maastricht for breakfast and lunch and talked of politics, Russia, war, law, peace, books, old cutlery and music – mediaeval music, in which they are experts. The Groots are the best of Europe – compassionate, generous, highly intelligent, knowledgeable, linguists, musicians – all one loves in one's friends.

Then on to Venice, arriving on Monday, a brilliant morning of sun and blue skies and Bora (the wind from the Dalmatian mountains, the equivalent of the Mistral).The streets were full of people in unbelievably elaborate costumes. I saw a whole family of religiouses: grandfather a cardinal, son a bishop, grandson monk, granny Mother Superior, daughter nun, little girl novice. I saw any amount of clowns and Turks and Harlequins, and a circus animal-tamer holding on a long chain a lion, a tiger, a bear, a leopard. I saw Scotsmen, witches, saints, angels, devils (no God), Nazis, Bolsheviks, Chaplins. The most *risqué* were a group dressed as Martian footballers, with their jockstraps on top of their tights. In the Montin, my *locanda*, they had a night of folk music and we formed a chain and danced through the restaurant, the kitchen, the street. I just wandered around, watching and feeling so good that if time had stood still forever, it would have been right.

The next night I was invited to the Cipriani Hotel on the Giudecca. That seemed to be the carnival of the rich – British, Americans, Italians and Germans in oh-so-expensive but strangely unimaginative costumes, except for Pierre Cardin, who did impress as he stalked around decadent and arrogant as a mandarin, followed by Denise Lady Kilmarnock, six foot two in her socks, one of those giant Englishwomen, dressed in black 'sexy' tights with a leopard flung round her left shoulder. The duchesses and contessas wore silver wigs and eighteenth-century duchesses' and contessas' dresses from granny's wardrobe; their husbands were Doges. They danced demurely cheek to cheek. They blew little balls through pipes across the tables and threw confetti and paper snakes and tried so hard to enjoy themselves; but I was pining to get back to the people's feast across the water.

And I did get away, and saw in the arc lights human visions swirling round San Marco – people dressed entirely in gold and with faces painted gold, in icy blue and painted icy blue, in black and in white. It was breathtaking, and made me feel again that time has very little meaning and all our yesterdays are todays and probably tomorrows, if our civilisation holds out. At the end of the evening the restaurateurs for once were generous and gave us *Fastnacht Krapfen* – a sort of doughnut, pleasant and very light. The next morning, Venice returned to work and to tidiness and to ordinary clothes as if the carnival had never existed.

I took a boat to the Lido and walked along the sea, which was noisy and grey, and said goodbye to all that I loved there. I went to get the children shoes – a ritual in Venice – and bone combs, and caught the night train to Zürich. From there I took a little train to Chur (lovely Middle Ages town, lovely Gothic cathedral) and another little train to St Moritz, for I was pining for all that was cold and icy and white and quiet.

It was the middle of their carnival preparations (Protestant), and I found a room with a featherbed in a little old inn behind the station run by a tough Swiss lady of eighty-three. There was the usual whitewashed *Gaststube* with plants and timbered walls and heavy furniture, where a few Swiss were drinking beer and playing cards. I sat down with them and we talked. I discovered what they minded about the tourists: that tourists never want to find out what they are, what they think – and of course, it would not be easy, for who can speak and understand *Schwyzerdütsch*?

I came down from the white peaks and went to Basel for their carnival and then home, soul and eyes and ears and mind properly salved.

26

New Starts, Including the Social Democratic Party, 1981–83

In 1980, the opposition Labour Party, under Michael Foot, was moving to the left. I said to David Owen, 'You are surprised? I saw this coming thirty years ago. I told you Foot and Benn would get power, and what they would do with it.'

On 25 January 1981, four Labour MPs – David Owen, Roy Jenkins, Shirley Williams and Bill Rodgers – published the Limehouse Declaration, announcing a Council for Social Democracy. The papers were very excited about the so-called 'Gang of Four'. Everything was stale in politics and Britain had almost three million unemployed. There was obviously a chance to form a new party. I wrote to David in January suggesting New Independent Labour Party or New Socialist Party. I said:

> Everything has to be explained to the people in detail, for instance why our economy is worse than anyone else's in Europe. And why it is foolish to blame any particular government for unemployment when to blame are all governments anywhere who have not worked out a system by which, when computers and machines take over and make men redundant, the redundant man can be retrained and fitted into an equally interesting and well-paid job. You must explain and explain and explain. That is what you are about – where the others failed because they are preoccupied with staying in power.

David says he read all my letters, but he never answered my political points. I hope he found it helpful that I watched all the politicians on television and reported to him. When I want to say something special I use deep, deep blue writing paper, the colour of the sea and the Bistro walls. It's silly really, because the typing is hard to read against the dark blue. David Owen says that when he sees the blue paper he knows he is in for the high jump. Claude Virgin says he has kept all my letters on blue paper but never dared read one. Like Claude, I also do not read letters from certain people right away, for I am frightened of their contents; then I discover it is all nice and happy and positive.

In March 1981, twelve MPs including David and Bill Rodgers resigned the Labour whip. On 26 March they launched the Social Democratic Party. There seemed hope and energy in politics again. Thousands of the young and people who had not liked either of the two old parties joined the Social Democrats. David Steel, leader of the Liberals, wanted an alliance with the SDP. David Owen did not, but Roy Jenkins and the other two allowed it to happen. A formal partnership with the Liberals led by David Steel had to wait until the Liberals endorsed it at their assembly in September 1981, but it was obvious the Alliance was going to be powerful, and more Labour MPs transferred.

There was also a change in my own family that summer – the first wedding of one of my children. Katya got married in Boston to a Fulbright scholar and film-maker called Claude Chelli, a Frenchman from Tunisia. Anthony, Johnny, Anna, Sara and I went. The wedding luncheon was in a big Winthrop house in the country, lent to Katya by her friend Linzee Turner, whose father was a Winthrop. The Winthrops were Auntie Forbes's family, but she had died in 1970. I did not at first like Claude for Katya, because he was a left-winger and wore a beard and had a chip on his shoulder. Instead of emigrating to Israel, Claude had gone to the New World, where his fighting was for the arts. An old Communist like me can see that the arts and entertainment are encouraged and financed by Communist and Fascist governments as a barrier against thinking and finding out, as religion was for the old regimes. Ballet, opera, theatre, films and sport are the new opium of the people.

The SDP got their first elected member in a November by-election. Shirley Williams won what had been a safe Conservative seat, Crosby. When she went into the Commons she found twenty-three happy SDP faces already sitting there. At the end of 1981 the opinion polls said that the Alliance would win a general election.

The SDP held a first birthday dance on 25 January 1982 at Poplar Civic Centre. I took about twenty friends – Christine West, Roz Jenkinson (who had been Roz Watkins), Anita Brookner, John and Xenia White, Peter York, Stephen Winkworth, Hugh Vickers, lots of Social Democrat sympathisers. Three were *Harpers & Queen* writers, and together they wrote a rather mocking description for the magazine.

> Elisabeth Furse beamed at the scene benevolently. Mrs Furse is surely the mother of the SDP. Most of the guests were recognisable faces from up west.
>
> David Owen and Bill Rodgers arrived, with their wives. Silvia Rodgers had an eye to current fashion, but David Owen looked the best, the planes of his face young and definite, triumphant, vivid for his supporters like a film star. Deborah Owen, in ruffled flowered dress, was talking and greeting non-stop. Shirley Williams arrived on two sticks (after the toboggan accident), round and friendly-looking. 'Roy Jenkins went before Shirley arrived because they both want to be the leader.' Elisabeth Furse was advancing the theory that the SDP was founded on happy marriages: 'The SDP people I know have *good* marriages. They are happy with each other and have lots of children. Sane people, balanced people.'
>
> The other SDP leaders were dancing energetically. David Owen gave a speech. Bill Rodgers, in what looked like teddy-boy fancy dress – even a greasy lock right in the middle of his forehead – gave an even better one. He described how the Limehouse Declaration had been put together a year ago at David Owen's house in Narrow Street. The birthday party was here because it all began in Tower Hamlets. . . a new party. Clapping and happy faces.

There was a wonderful atmosphere those first two years. Everything seemed to be opening out, even clothes – this was the time when people began to jog. All my young friends were sweating through the streets unhealthily: I told them that what they should do instead was swim, for the sea is where it all started and two-foot locomotion came long after. Walking is socially pleasant – you can smile at people, perhaps help them with a bag; when you run you are isolated, pounding your ankles to pieces, not seeing the houses or trees or fellow humans.

In November 1982, Pat sold the remainder of the estate at Halsdon to the drummer of the Rolling Stones, Charlie Watts. Pat and Anni kept the home farm at Venton. When the money came through, Pat gave a share to each of the children. It was a terrible shock to me. With those cheques was destroyed my *raison d'être*. I felt stupidly redundant, not having to provide them any more with bicycles, typewriters, record-players, insurance, holidays. I had to try to find a new way of living in which the children had no need of me. I thought: I shall go and hang myself, with a message pinned on my outsize breast 'Am redundant – leaving you.'

I worried about what the money would do to the children. Life is all about stretching – not the stretching of your limbs in bed when you wake, though the effect seems the same release into action, but the stretching needed if you never have enough – and that is where my life has been and still is and I hope will never change. The price has been no growth or very little growth of the brain-matter, and some physical disadvantages – in medical terms, injuries – but what does that mean compared with almost always feeling elated and stretched and challenged?

The Conservatives won the election of June 1983 – it had been obvious Mrs Thatcher would get back in since she took back the Falkland Islands. Labour got 209 seats and the Alliance of the Liberals and SDP twenty-three. David Owen and Roy Jenkins won their seats but Shirley Williams and Bill Rodgers lost theirs. Four days later, Roy stood down as leader of the SDP. I must give him his exits – they were each well-timed and decently done: but then he is not an evil man, he is just RJ of SW1 and W11. What I had hoped for and been sure of happened: David became leader.

By the spring of 1983 Katya was pregnant. She had a scan and found out it was a boy. I wrote to her in April:

> I will not indulge any more in pretty little girl's things, darling Katya. It is very generous and thoughtful of you to telephone me, and so often.
>
> Be very careful as a young mother, Katya. The most important thing is to have a house with a few rooms to let if you must – it helps to bring in money for gas, electricity, rates etc, and an au pair for the baby so that you can work in peace. I will help you with whatever I have left over, and when I die, which will be soon, you will get a bit more from Chesham Street. But a house with a garden to grow vegetables in is the only safety,

and a job done well – but there is no safety in *that*, for soon they will be selling editing machines and films will be made automatically too.

Well, now I must tidy up for seven houseguests, with Lance down again (gastroenteritis). Yesterday I took René and Hildegarde de Groot, my friends from Maastricht, to see the Owens on one of those daffodil and pussy-willow days, with the wind doing its bit and moving everything to a lovely rhythm, the skies wild, clouds chasing all over, the blue very blue, the hills of Berkshire at their best. Though I do not really like spring because it is so noisy and showing off. I brought back eggs and flowers.

Anna and Sara have gone to Greenham, poor ducks. All such nice people, guided by Communists to demand disarmament. (That is what it should be, complete disarmament all over the world.) But you know my view about all *that*, the Communist takeover, the end of our civilisation, the robot life. But, oh dear, how dishonest and dangerous it is to blame a *government* for a civilisation that is dying. For that is a law of nature, all that has been been born must die. I am giving you this as a form of testament, knowing that you will not accept it, nor Claude either.

There is friction between me and Anna and Sara. Sara, complete with funny earrings, was the more belligerent, Anna quietly counts me out as 'poor Mama', but both seem otherwise in good fettle, and I think that that windfall from Halsdon has helped them towards a certain security and independence. Somehow, as I told you before, I now feel deprived and even resentful.

Well, darling Katya, it is all part of the tragedy of the species on two feet, which includes chickens, ducks, geese, turkeys, those horrible vain birds the peacocks, well, all birds really – and kangaroos.

It was such a hot summer I worried about Katya, with her big belly. In August she had her son, Sacha. It pleased my heart that my darling Katya had what would suit her so well. I searched for a proper teddy bear, not too big, with button eyes.

On her birthday, 26 September, I baked a cake (just guessing at the instructions – it dropped, of course) and put candles on it, and nicked a few blossoms round the square, because it was also the birthday of an Italian student in the house, Carla, and by giving her a feast and presents I felt close to Katya. I wrote to Katya as that day turned into the next.

> I think I was a good mother . . . slowly I hit the truth, survival of the fittest is still the law of all laws. As you told me yourselves, 'You are always right, Mama, but we must do it ourselves. Please let us be and make our own messes – please just step aside and let us destroy ourselves, hurt ourselves, cut ourselves into tiny pieces.' And that, Katya, was and is the most terrifying experience of all, to have to watch people, more so one's own, repeating the same mistakes as one made oneself, and I suppose generations before made, and stand by and swallow and accept and accept.
>
> So I am writing to you today my dearest daughter – my dream daughter, for I always dreamt of having a dozen little girls. Not boys – to rear boys worried me. I felt they belonged to the other side of the fence. But rearing little girls for the world, for love and pain and joy and work and – above all – to be women to men, was a kind of pipedream I had.
>
> So today is your birthday, and though you are not on speaking terms with me because of my anger with your husband, I do not consider that as most important. When I married your father I was going to write a book about a foreign bride and I was going to call it 'Thy People Shall Be My People', and I expect you feel the same. But be careful not to lose your roots, Katya, or ignore them – nothing can grow without roots. That is why (unlike Claude) I never ever pretended to be anything but a foreigner in this country and anywhere else.
>
> I am sure you will do – as you always did – what you think right. So goodbye, my dearest little baby girl – that is how you started and you always have been so very dear somehow to me, so good a friend.

David Owen was always on the TV screen – someone called him 'Wall to wall Owen'. But he was no longer everybody's blue-eyed boy, he was everybody's black sheep. At the Labour party conference in October, every member of the Shadow Cabinet slammed him. All the young at the conference and most of the old wanted complete disarmament, which is exactly what the Soviets wanted Britain to have. Labour people do not learn, in their effortless working-class superiority. And the delegates were so gross – wrong fat, new fat, and all the wrong shirts and the wrong hair; to look good on television you have to be thinner than for the naked eye.

David Owen, who always looks good on television, lost two stone by eating baked beans and baked potatoes. But I have to be fat. When one is frustrated for tenderness as I am, sweetness to eat replaces the sweetness of humans, and therefore I cannot not eat sweet things.

I was on bad terms with my son-in-law Claude, but my true friend David saved me from being small by writing six pages to me in green ink on House of Commons paper on 10 November 1983.

> Dearest Elisabeth, Thank you for your letter and all its generous feeling – I knew you would be annoyed by my remark about Katya's husband, but you are right when you sensed this was no throwaway remark, but carefully considered and timed. I delayed mentioning it until I felt you were strong enough to take it on board and to think about it. Your defence is true – after all I have never even met him. All your remarks seem justified in strict logic – but love overrides logic. Your attitude is causing unnecessary hurt, and you are bigger than that. Be generous in this as you are in everything, and it will bring happiness. There is too much sadness, hurt and bitterness around for you who are so warm and generous not to shift your position. It will certainly not diminish you, and will delight Katya. There was no point in making me the children's guardian if I wasn't to watch over them and occasionally, when I saw something, protect them.
>
> All children are ambivalent about their parents, the stronger the personalities the deeper the ambivalence. Why else are love and hate so closely linked – it is as if nature was designed to balance and we to live always strung between extremes, right and left, good and evil. Some settle for the anodyne, the blurred compromise of true balance. You and I live oscillating between the poles, finding no satisfaction in the blurring of the issues, believing in the distinctiveness of choice, not afraid of living with love one moment, hate the next, Right politically on some issues, Left politically on others. It makes for colour and for pain, but it does mean being prepared to move back when the polar extreme puts too great a strain on relationships. It is why we are both mobile, emotional, fluid. Not for us the

status quo, the boringness of predictability. Be unpredictable – write to Katya and make it clear you accept him because of her, and that you will not go on shutting him out. Be bigger than them and I will love you even more than I do. Yours, David.

27

Among the Writers, London 1982–83

I had met Rebecca West in the 1930s through the Committee for the Relief of the Victims of German Fascism. In the 1980s she was living in a flat near me in Kingston House on Hyde Park. I loved visiting her. We travelled back through fifty years and laughed a lot, for there was a lot to laugh about, and were angry a lot, for there was even more to be angry about.

I wear proudly the cast-off dresses Rebecca gave me. She bought clothes in the maternity shop Just Jane in Sloane Street. Old ladies are like babies – no waists, sloppy eaters. Old ladies have to go to maternity shops to find dresses and bathing suits that fit. Rebecca told me that she faced a new young sales-girl and asked for a pretty flowered frock that had caught her eye. The girl said 'Not for *you*, Madam?' eyes goggling. Rebecca answered icily 'Miracles do happen, my dear girl. Please fetch me a size 16.' She was eighty-nine. I get compliments on the dress whenever I wear it.

In the end, Rebecca became angry with me for seeing Anthony West, her son by H. G. Wells, when I was in the United States. I had known Anthony almost as long as I had known her, and he was my son Anthony's godfather, so it seemed natural to visit him on Fisher's Island, New England. I knew that mother and son detested each other. I did my best to mediate, but it did no good. She bore the mark of her class, the lack of a compassionate and loving heart. When she died in March 1983 at ninety, I could sob for her, but not weep. I sent a letter to Anthony West:

This, dear Anthony, is not a letter of condolence, but a kind of commiseration for all that could have been and should have been, as between mother and son. Did you know that Rebecca would not see me, or write again, so deep was her resentment when she learned that I had seen you on Fisher's Island? I also had a mother, and did not have her. As you once said to me, the trouble was probably that you were too much alike. . . All I hope is that you are not afflicted by the thought, *if only*. In the strange loneliness that I found in you when you were young, I wanted to show my affection, as I do now, and hold your hand, and shake it, and wish you peace.

P.S. Rebecca was a great pleasure to my mind, and a great hurt to my heart – I do not mean that she hurt *me*, only my sentiments. I loved her in a girlish way, and her writings more than I can say.

I had always wanted to be a writer. Several times I had planned a book: about northern Europe just before the war, which I was researching on my journey through Sweden; about my wartime experiences in France; about the countries shaping the post-war world – that was one reason I visited Germany and the United States in 1962. But I found writing difficult. Temperamentally I cannot concentrate, and beyond that is the fear. I revere words, and mine seem so watery and weak. Anthony Elliott always said 'Write, write!' but there was no one to push me. Christopher MacLehose got me to do it, years ago, when he was on the *Scotsman*. I wrote down my experiences, and he shaped my undisciplined words into articles.

After Christopher moved to Collins in London, I used to visit him at work and take the opportunity to use the copying machine. I don't understand the protocol of offices, and I treat them as places of dedication and comradeship. If it is a cold day I might pop in to bring the girls a cake, or on a hot day, choc-ices. I used to visit the staff of *Harpers & Queen* in London. Then men were installed behind a big barrier to stop people with no appointment. The editor, Willie Landels, told a Bistro boy it had all been done to keep me out (I still got in), but the deputy editor said it was to keep Willie in.

I often visited the SDP headquarters in Cowley Street. I had sent several volunteers and paid workers to David Owen, including young Hugo Dixon and Roland Rudd. But the atmosphere seemed to me too impersonal, like a Liberals' stronghold. I wrote my worries to David in December 1984:

> To sit in an office and think it all out does not make for people moving towards you and for you – they must be moved by a force of conviction – a force of feeling. It is not canvassing, it is *mobilising* people, ramming fire and passion into them. The Communists always welcomed all and made them feel always and immediately needed, wanted and welcome, and had the jobs ready.
>
> At the SDP Quarters they come and knock, only to be told that the converted are busy on important things. Old ladies may be tiresome, but they have nieces and nephews and grandchildren, so do not pooh-pooh them and their zest. The SDP cannot afford to lose the goodwill of a single person – or Benn and his boys will come in when Thatcher goes, which looks to me pretty soon. I know how many people I have converted, but soon I shall need more conversion myself, David, and might give up, and I am a good barometer for anything of that kind – it has always been so.

One day in the spring of 1982, I was with Christopher MacLehose at Collins when Ian Chapman, the managing director, came in. He said that he and his wife Marjory were going to Venice for the first time. I was thrilled. I went home and wrote Ian a long letter.

I told them to sit at the front of the vaporetto coming from the station so as to feel proud of European civilisation as its greatest creation slides past. I said that the best place to stay is Locanda Montin with Adriano and his family, or another family *pensione*, because you should not go to a smart hotel and just go round ticking off the famous pictures and sculpture. Venice is supreme not for the 'beauty' of this and that, which makes it the exultation of the dandy and the misanthrope and the art lover – it is supreme for a group of boys of thirteen or fourteen in San Barnaba, a lovely campo, shouting with enjoyment at blowing soap bubbles, as here only two- and three-year-olds do; for the Lido, with families strolling and swimming; for the vaporetto conductors heaving, practically carrying, the old off the boat, and the babies in their prams; for little boys rushing up to a person on a crutch and saying '*Poi?* May I help you, Signora?' In Venice you can still walk the streets at night fearlessly, and you can be old and handicapped and feel cared for and even honoured. Venice is beautiful and heroic for the reason of its people: their humanity. Venice for the soul, Florence for the mind.

Ian Chapman said I had helped them, so I went on talking to him on paper. On 26 August 1982, Christopher MacLehose wrote to me:

> Ian was enchanted by your letter, and cannot understand why we aren't publishing you. Why *aren't* we publishing you? What would happen if we commissioned you to write a thoughtful *pensée* every day for a year, and published it eighteen months from now under the title 'Don't Say I Didn't Tell You So'? Is this something which you would like to consider? I would.

He offered me a contract, and I wrote to Amos Oz about the commission. 'It is lovely because I have at last been helped to lose my fear of the word, and because it allows me to get rid of all that crammed thinking, discovering, finding out and analysing. My mind is always nice and clear now for more intake, just like eating and the bowels.'

Back from Israel came that encouragement I always need.

> My dear Elisabeth, wonderful. And just. And right. I remember yelping and screaming at you, in the Russian manner, in your own kitchen – that miraculous womb of yours – that you ought to write a book; that you are a teller and a witness and a big woman in a kindergarten. I said so, or shouted so at you, even though at the time I was 'clever' and 'sober' and slightly ironical about some of your insights and – all right – your prophecies. All right: I asked for your forgiveness and you forgave me.
>
> When you write letters, you teach and preach and laugh and cry and scream, because you are Jewish and Russian, and all your 'Western-ness' is like a tight, oppressing corset. So, away with that damn corset. You ought to write not with ink but with all your juices. Be shameless and cruel and merciful and angry and funny and don't even fear to be ridiculous when the tale needs it . . .

I started off happily, but I disappointed myself. At night, or when queueing for the bus, thoughts and the words to cover them ran round my head. By the time I got to the typewriter they had fled like bubbles. In the morning, after the bathroom ritual and the cup of coffee, everything became heavy, when at night it had floated feathery round my heart and soul. When I put it into words, it sounded so noisy, like Wagner, when it had been Mozart and Handel. I spent ten years trying to get the book done, and called on help from several people, especially Henry Swanzy. He sent me a letter of advice:

> Only total candour would explain the marvellous chaotic wisdom of your life. Incidentally, no one could accept your claim to empathy. Only among rare people do you know what really makes them tick, especially not the muted elliptical English upper classes. You say 'I do not remember ever having had a bad conscience.' The Japanese would agree on that . . .
>
> You will be, to the end of my time, my fairy godmother, dear E, with your Eastern eyes, so full of wisdom and so lacking in accurate Western detail. Yours till Hell freezes, Henry.

The Chapel Street lease was running out and Grosvenor Estates wanted £385,000 to renew it, so I was looking for a place to live. It had to have a kitchen big enough to take my refectory table and fourteen chairs and two hundred cups and thirty teapots and my Christmas tree. My kitchen is my workplace, my love place and my talk place. And it had to be within walking distance of Piccadilly.

Lance and I went to see a house in Halkin Street. Going up the basement steps, I tripped and fell and had to be taken to Westminster Hospital. I lost my sense of taste and smell and acquired a bad headache: suddenly I understood all those advertisements for aspirins, with people holding their heads, then smiling when they get the pill. I was thankful I had not lost my memory – I could remember the wondrous scent when I watched the leaves being burnt in Belgrave Square. My cooking became even worse: I made a risotto with so much salt no one could eat it. But I was the cheapest person to take out – dog biscuits were fine by me. And on Swiss trains, I could take that seat by the skis and the lavatory, which no one who can smell likes. I hoped all would be normal by Christmas, but the lost senses never came back. When April 1983 arrived, I surprised myself by not hurrying out to nick the lilacs; without their scent, I could resist them.

For six years, Lance had been different from the old, kind

Lance. I thought he was having a nervous breakdown. He had big Venetian bones like his father and he should have weighed twelve stone, but he starved himself to look like a Belsen inmate. He told me he did it because it made him feel lucid and Italian and took the Australian out of him. He cooked himself little meals of soya beans and vegetables twenty-four hours a day in the kitchen or in his room on Johnny's paraffin stove. He soaked and pounded legumes. Dreadful smells came from his pots. He would not talk to anyone and looked as though he might kill. He was such a good being and so generous and gentle – but when sick, he became mean, cruel and utterly destructive. I have three antique pewter plates which I loved and one of them he put on the fire to melt, just to hurt me. But if anyone else had hurt me he would have killed them.

I knew it was because he felt he should go back to his family in Adelaide and couldn't bear to leave. His mother had been extremely beautiful and young, his father was an alcoholic who left when he was seven, and his mother married again. Lance had a brother nine years older who he never talked about. Both boys treated their mother as a sister. Lance wouldn't let her go near his school because the other boys fancied her.

Lance said Britain did not offer him anything, but he stayed. He could have made many successful careers. He was offered jobs in computing and managing a restaurant but he turned them down, and he had given up architecture although he was one of the best students. He played the piano, guitar, squeezebox, balalaika, mandolin – he had half a dozen instruments. The Russian orchestra took him on for the balalaika, but he left immediately and never played again. His instruments sat in the corner useless and neglected; I still have three.

He suppressed all the normal activities of a man, and that must cause disruptions. Many women threw themselves at him but he was not interested. He was right out of Dostoevsky and the rest of literature that describes self-destructive genuises. He did everything for me and the family and the lodgers and the house and while we had it, the Bistro. He cooked, put new bags in the Hoover, and carried my chair when I could no longer lift things. He was in charge of the heating, the lights, the pipes, the doors, the keys and the television, every bolt and nail and plug and hammer.

He became even cleverer at frugality than me. He would go down Piccadilly at eight in the morning dressed in a raincoat and carpet slippers to find leftover food that had been put out by the restaurants. He brought back what he called 'wonderful materials', as though he was building, not cooking. A Green Park coffee bar was his favourite, until the owner grabbed him round the neck for driving away customers.

All the Bistro people liked Lance, but the one he identified with was Christopher MacLehose, because they were both withdrawn, subtle, mixed characters. Lance knew the inside of human beings – he could give me the perfect character formula for anyone. No one knew he was ill, because he was so intelligent he could disguise the disequilibrium.

Lance got so bad that I was physically frightened. He was sucking me dry emotionally. All my life, neurotic and elusive and secretive people have found me and taken possession of my stoicism. It is strange, because I am not interested in anybody so self-involved, I am only interested in people who are willing to take help. Help can be given, at this stage of history and medicine. When someone I know needs a flat or a job or a wife or a fridge or an au pair, I arrange it at once, whereas depression or any other psycho disease can't be cured by me and makes me impatient. I wrote to Lance one day when I was too angry to talk to him, saying that after all the unbearable suffering I had seen in Europe I had no patience with self-fabricated pain like his and Johnny's and Anna's. 'It really makes me feel that you are such wasters, such insulters of the very air you breathe, which is precious, and the very bread you eat, also precious.'

Lance seemed a hating ghost in the house, giving me his dark moods but being attractive and charming for strangers. He was often absent from the feasts that are so dear to my heart. I thought he liked to be alone – then I found out he was smiling and laughing at the tables of other people, people I looked upon as pretty transparent human beings. He liked one or two of the girls at Chapel Street, and wholeheartedly gave them tenderness, care, affection and himself, right in front of me. I knew I had taken the role of the old nagging peasant wife – you feed her and look after her and ignore her. I wrote to him:

> You are not to be there when Katya comes and act 'sweet' Lance. I will not let you get away with it again, for I will have another hysterical outburst and I hate that – one is quite enough in my lifetime. Someone must drag me to the lowest point to make me scream and shout like that. Pat did and he had to go forever –

> forever. He did apologise though, and tried to come back and make up, but I knew he couldn't change his personality, and kept him away.

I can't bear being ignoble in public. That is why I have very few real friends: they have seen me at my worst and can still care for me.

I thought I could make a friend of Anita Brookner. She had the same European background as me. I wanted to talk to her about writing. She had written a novel, *A Start in Life*, in her spare time while teaching history of art at the Courtauld Institute. It came out in 1981, and she wrote almost one a year after that. But she had no time to help me. When I telephoned she made me feel quite a nuisance. She spoke quickly, then 'God bless!' and hi-ho-here-we-go, and the real human contact did not exist. I wrote to her in disappointment. 'I have no real woman friend in this country – someone I can giggle with and nibble chocolates and talk about other people intimately and trustingly. I thought one could have that relationship with you and was looking forward to it – instead of which you were always so busy!'

Anita wrote me back very patient short letters in her beautiful hand, and invited me to parties; but I did not want to go to a gathering at the Courtauld to see her among lots of people, being elegant and charming and polite in a large halo. I wanted to sit down with her and discuss the writing of books and the deteriorating of Lance. I wrote:

> I do not accept your jealous possession of your time – that you cannot give to a friend and share because of your WORK – for I always believed and do believe that humans come before everything. That is why I am as I am and that is why you once liked me.
>
> I do not really know whether you understand my language, or want to understand it; indeed I really wonder whether anyone does in this country. I do know that my Russian friends and my Italian friends and my French friends, yes, my French friends, do understand. But in London I am inclined to shiver, and feel like joining Exit. One gives, one cares, one trembles for their security and wellbeing, and then one is alone, with a nice smile from some of them, until the next crisis, Dunkirk, or a fire, or dying. Then their hearts wake a little feebly, and there is a kind of convulsive movement of life. It must be the climate.

In 1984 *Hotel du Lac* won the Booker prize, and success assailed Anita. In 1987 she gave up the nine to five at the Courtauld which she had so enjoyed, and I trembled for her. London is a hard place for a solitary woman.

After Collins gave me a contract, I went to the Frankfurt Book Fair: I had always wanted to see it but felt too shy. There I was, a young and budding author of seventy-two, but I was still outside – everyone working, myself just visiting, and my friends' faces saying 'I wish I had seen Elisabeth approaching anywhere else but my publishing stand.' My old friend Jerry Kaplan, president of Macmillan in New York, had not even breakfast time free for me. Oh, that awful motto 'Time is money' – it has made it impossible for Americans ever to grow properly, to mature and understand the importance of manners. Growing takes time, sitting back and thinking and just *being*, and manners take time too. The French have a saying: 'Time takes its revenge for what is done without it.' People were becoming more and more self-involved and ruthless, racing through work to success, to more and more, and this mad roundabout was not moving to jolly music but to voices of threat and fear.

Jerry Kaplan went on chasing his impossible schedule and it led to a heart operation. I was worried, so I flew to New York to see him. I rushed to Macmillan without an appointment, and he was again too busy. I boiled over. At Christmas I wrote to him from London:

> Whatever I say I mean at the time and maybe forever – who knows? My anger over my last visit to New York and my pain was immense and I let you know – then, of course, arrived that vast Stilton which is so heavenly and makes so many happy. It goes on the table, still fresh and fat, and they all say: 'How, E?' and I say 'Jerry K, New York' – and they nod their heads and say 'Very, very nice and thoughtful', and then they eat delicious cheese.
>
> I know I barged into the office, Jerry, but then I never understand office workers. Remember I worked for 30 years in films, on the floor, and everyone 'barges' in. And I cannot see the difference between a president and a security man, if both of them are sympathetic and people I care for. Never ever

> has position, money, fame nor any kind of fortune affected my relationship to a human. To me they have always been utterly naked, and passionately lovable or not. I lack the sense of any effigy – no, maybe I have one effigy, and it is ANY MAN WHO LIVES AND DIES FOR OTHERS. I do not think they become presidents – they may become gods or saints or prophets or just corpses – but I love the men of that kind.

Am I wrong in how I behave? I know I have often brought happiness to others. My bank manager at Lloyds, Mr Hallam, wrote to thank me for a Christmas bottle for the staff: 'What a marvellous one you are. Whenever you visit St James's Street you fill the whole office with the spirit of your warm friendship and very vivid personality. Especially so at Christmas, which is a time which represents so well all that you stand for.'

The magazine office in New York where my son Anthony worked had just replaced several secretaries with computers that could even hyphenate words, mostly correctly. So my boy no longer had to grapple with the human beings working near him: he was cut off from human contact. When I see tiny children playing with these new information instruments I am awestruck, but not surprised when they ill-use their grannies and grandads.

I went to my insurance company to put a claim in. The girl who interviewed me could barely understand what I was saying. A man I knew in that office told me, 'Mrs Furse, our girls now cannot think, for they deal all day long with computers – that is the one link they have outside themselves, that and the gossip at lunch-time.' I suppose human beings will be made in bottles and will live their 'lives' from bottles to buttons, from labs to spacecraft. Our bodies and our brains do not work together. How wise the Greeks were about 'Mind over matter'.

In September 1983, I went to Venice for swimming and thinking. When I am at the end of my tether I creep, hop, train, plane to the sea and just walk in and stay in and my whole body moves around and finds peace. But Venice could not save me this time. I had another fall there, a very bad one, and did something to my ribcage and knees, and most of all to my morale. The hospital was like the Middle Ages – I told friends they used leeches.

Back in London we had an autumn full of wind and rain, which I love, except that it made the pain worse. I could not breathe without screaming sometimes, and my knees hurt too. It was worse than in Venice, for there to weep into the salt sea with salt tears made me feel good, it was so natural. The pain was really idiotically penetrating. I went to my doctor to ask for morphia. He smiled and said: 'It is osteoarthritis – very painful, progressive: it will slow you down. And I, for one, am glad, for I expected you to go in a heart attack any day. I am sure this arthritis will give you another ten years.'

It did slow me down. I had to be sure to use my crutch, or I forgot I was not eighteen and ran for the bus and jumped on and fell against the stairs with my tender ribs. Sometimes I wept, for I wanted to do so much more. But a body is a machine and machines wear out. Pain became a habit, as no-pain must be a habit. I would miss being in pain – it must be lonely.

The wild weather passed. In the mornings the dew and mist were countrylike in SW1 and the trees refused to turn their greens into yellows and reds, they refused to start to die – they seemed to be on strike.

Collins were feeding me with biographies and autobiographies to show me how to do mine. It did me no good. I have never learnt anything from reading. I have hardly read since the war, certainly not novels, because novels are too slow and thin compared with what is in my mind. Friends say 'but you read Primo Levi.' I say 'Primo Levi, Shakespeare, Dante, Vercors are not books – they are testaments.' Collins sent me one book which became to me a testament: *Eleni* by Nicholas Gage, a former *New York Times* reporter. Eleni was his mother, who was tortured and executed in 1948 by the Greek Communists for sending her five children away so they could not be taken behind the Iron Curtain. The Communists were abducting or conscripting peasant children as part of their struggle with the Nationalists. I identified with that woman utterly and entirely, and tried to make everyone read the book. I sent a copy to the Queen by Michael Shea, who had become her press attaché: 'From one mother to another.'

I am sure few people realise how hard it has been for the Queen to be a mother. Each one of her children is so different, just like mine. Her husband is also like my two, attractive and never to be taken for granted. I got a polite letter of thanks from the Queen's private secretary.

Lance broke down a few weeks before Christmas. He came out in a fever and saw ghosts and things coming out of the wall. He kept it secret from me and everyone else until the end, then he confided in Johnny. It was heartbreaking. Johnny made him see a doctor, who said that Lance was that rare thing, an adult male anorexic. Only 3 per cent of anorexics are male, and those almost all teenagers. Lance had been vomiting up the meals he had cooked. Johnny lent him money for the fare back to his mother. He left on Christmas Eve, the most important day of the year for me. There too he made me pay. The children helped him pack and he wanted to say goodbye to me but I locked myself in the bathroom. His final words were, 'We have had good times and we have had bad times' – after twenty years. Anna drove him to the airport. In Adelaide he admitted himself to hospital and was under treatment for months. He gave Johnny back the fare. Johnny wrote about Lance:

> He had arrived when my mother was still very upset about my father's departure. Our home life both at Bourne Street and later at Chapel Street, which had always been dominated by Mama's personality and moods and by her constant stream of friends and lodgers, was an emotional roller coaster. There seemed to be never fewer than eight lodgers at the breakfast table. In that highly charged atmosphere we children felt pretty skinless. Lance was terribly important for the girls when they were growing up because he was the man in the house. We were in turmoil and he was St Peter, the rock.
>
> Anna was terribly upset about Lance sharing Mama's bed, but he claimed it was platonic, and Anna and he came to terms with it. He told me that he did it because he couldn't bear to see my mother suddenly alone at the end of the day.
>
> He would not get involved in anyone's neuroses; he dealt with problems in a detached practical way, very male. To Sara he was like a stepfather. To Anna he started as stepfather and became brother. To Katya he was between the two. To me he was a soul brother – that is what he also called himself.
>
> As a teenager I looked up to him. I did not realise he had been a fish out of water in Australia, rather like my mother was a fish out of water in England. He held his wound closed, so that he could keep us and the Bistro going. He had a very, very deep dream of the European family with big Mama and dozens

of kids. He was always enamoured of Italy or anything to do with Europe – a romantic dream. Life with us and the Bistro fitted him like a glove.

The loss of the Bistro was a big loss to Lance. He was in love with it. I remember helping him to take it to bits. After losing the Bistro he began to open up. He then learned the balalaika and became far more curious about the world and introduced me to jazz and even started to watch television with Mama. He liked to see us grow and succeed. But as we grew up he grew down. We watched his wound open and open. It was worrying, but beautiful to see his feelings and vulnerability emerge.

He and I were particularly close from 1982 onwards. I was the only man he entrusted with his feelings. I was working in Wardour Street and used to go on coffee-bar runs with him. He'd want to sample, say liver and bacon in three Soho cafés to compare them. I didn't know he was vomiting it up. When he told me later, I realised he was ill, probably anorexic, and tried to persuade him to see a doctor. He would not listen at first, until food deprivation made him break down.

We had in common the experience of a false idea of our bodies. After I left Eton in December 1965, I had a prolonged breakdown which involved a condition I've seen called 'dysmorphobia' in which your self-image, body image, is completely distorted and shredded. I couldn't go out, I only felt any safety in the family. But people merely thought I was depressed.

I had tried to explain my physical self-disgust to Lance in the cottage in Devon when in the throes of the condition in 1966 and he said, 'Well, you are an ugly little bugger.' When I told him years later, he was very apologetic that he had not realised there was more wrong. He felt terribly remorseful.

That was our bond, our body illnesses. I knew how monstrously distorted one's mental image of one's body can become. It just takes hold of you: it takes you over. The same thing happens in hunger strikes.

My mother would not accept Lance was ill. She was worried about the move from Chapel Street and needed him to help with it. But he was dreading the pain of the last Christmas at Chapel Street, and he managed to avoid it by leaving on 23 December, three weeks after the specialist diagnosed him. There was a good anorexia unit in Adelaide and I thought it might cure him, especially as his mother was there. He knew the cause: that there was a seven-year-old inside him still desperate for attention.

So Johnny helped Lance to leave.

It would have been funny, how the house mourned him the week after he left – if Lance's 'death' had not left me feeling so futile and useless. All his bolts and nuts and plugs and hammers protested. The television aerial cable broke on New Year's Eve, the roof started to leak, the kitchen leaked, two fuses went and the keys got lost. I felt helpless in the face of their strike action. He had protected me against fuses blown, pipes bursting, bills to be paid and boiler clocks.

28

My Family and Other Maladies, 1984–85

I missed Lance's help, but I missed Lance himself more. I wrote to Johnny:

> The most important factor at the moment in my life is to have someone close to me to talk to and discuss things, decisions or whatsoever, as Lance did. He was THERE – in a destructive or constructive way. You removed Lance from me but did not take over a tiny little bit. A human being needs comfort and nearness and warmth – it does not involve much time – just the feeling and knowledge that the other knows of one's sufferings. Well – I have five children and am alone and that is that.

Johnny was still working on films; Katya was happy in Boston with her man and with film editing and with little Sacha; Anna was teaching at the Rose Bruford theatre school and had a fringe company, Bloodgroup. Later she became artistic director of the touring company Paines Plough. Sara had been in Newcastle for five years, studying and then working in the Side Gallery linked to Amber Films, and wanted to move to Australia. Anthony was in New York; in 1988 he joined *Vanity Fair*. In Tom Wolfe's novel *The Bonfire of the Vanities*, the drunken British journalist Fallow was said to be Anthony. Tom Wolfe denied it, but I saw the film, and I think Fallow *is* based on Anthony.

A friend reported that he asked Anthony 'How is your mother?' and Anthony answered 'I have no mother'. He has inherited a fine soul and the lack of a heart. He cannot feel. He cannot love and has never loved – neither did his two grandfathers. He is a very honest, brave person and very intelligent. He is also mean: he will never pay for anything. He is the result of his genetic structure and not to blame. I tell my children that no one can be accused of anything except not trying to improve on their genes.

My lease on Chapel Street was coming to an end in June 1984 despite postponements and my pleading. It was an extremely cold spring with lovely light blue days, wonderful for my arthritis, which needs either icy cold or heat. In my bed at night I travelled round looking for cold places for my joints burning with pain.

The miners, led by Arthur Scargill, went on strike in March. On 17 April, a young policewoman was shot dead from the Libyan Embassy in London. That poor little police girl. I was glad my body hurt together with the rest: that made it complete and one. The press called the Libyan leader Gadaffi 'mad', and they thought Arthur Scargill was a bit mad too. People used to call Hitler mad and that allowed them to be inactive against Nazism. Gadaffi and Scargill both knew only too well what they were doing.

I dislike the idea of madness, and that people are driven to do things because of dramas hidden in their minds. I have a friend called Gerald Reddington, a Bistro boy, very good-looking, with a wife and three children. He felt he had to escape from success as a stockbroker. I always say that with a heavy conscience of any kind, people join the Catholics or the Communists. He joined the highest of high Anglicans, with nuns and candles and white nightdresses, and after he was ordained was sent to a Wren church in the City. He also worked at the Centrepoint in Soho, for teenage drug addicts and the homeless. I like and respect this way of sublimation. At his church he ran a psychotherapeutical surgery. I had it out with him about psycho stuff in a letter in June 1984.

> I always feel angry over drunks, drug addicts, neurotics, for I feel that they are what they are and do what they do because they are egocentric, wrapped up in themselves, and this I simply loathe. I have known so many doing psychotherapy, and being done by it, all to no avail, a waste of time. I despise it: it makes a nothing out of friendship. All one needs to teach is the art of friendship, and then there will be a good comrade to listen to one's boo-hoos, and not a professional. But then you, I suppose, treat it more like a confessional, and that I am absolutely in agreement with, there is nothing more clever in any church,

when you can get all out of your system, clear all your guilts, without having to face the receiver.

I was spending a lot of time in churches – there is a church on the way to everywhere. The priests thought I was religious, but it was just that I needed a rest.

Jash Pomian, who was a friend from the Trevor Square days, tried to help my arthritis by paying for a course of acupuncture. It didn't work, but his tenderness raised my spirits. I wrote to him in June 1984:

> I feel that I should talk to you, Jash, and first of all to tell you what a wonderful joy it is to have you somewhere in my life. When I was a girl there were young men like yourself about, sending flowers and chocolates, taking one out, kissing one's hand, writing poems. In a way you are a man of my kind, at least of the same tradition and the same temperament and the same affinities.
>
> For the play on Wednesday, there are only two tickets, rows apart, but if I go to the box-office after 4 pm I shall get some returned tickets, and that will be my hour, and you must not spoil it by doing what comes naturally, i.e. getting two tickets for later on.
>
> So let me have my little triumph, since everyone says that you have to book at least three weeks in advance. I could not ever book anything – I arrive and tickets just happen and have to happen. So I shall be off for the fleshpots of Europe for precisely 30 hours, and when I get the returned tickets, I will hop on the bus and go back to the dump called 22 Chapel Street, and wash and change and put on a lipstick and my nicest scent and some dress that will easily cover my wickedly dilapidated body and wait for you with whisky, gin, vodka, and anything else that is on the kitchen table, of course with ice cubes.

I was not really going to the fleshpots, I was visiting a doctor in Berlin who I thought might be able to help me walk fast again and bend again. But telling friends one is in pain is a bore.

On 22 June I finally moved out of Chapel Street. After all my dreams of where I might go – to Venice, forests, mountains – I ended up in my own basement flat in Chesham Street, five minutes away. Christopher MacLehose and Roger Graef took me out to dinner the last night before the move, and the following night Hugo Dixon did the same thing. It is surprising how comforting I found this.

I did not like my new surroundings, a horrid little airless box, but change is always interesting. I wrote to Stuart Proffitt, my nice young editor at Collins:

> It is 5.30 in the morning and the night is decrepit and the day still a baby, and I am afraid of it, a grey little baby, and the only sound I can hear from this basement is the yowling of the cat, no cars, nothing, still as in the depths of the country, beautiful. I want to go to the square and nick some blooms and branches, under the watchful eye of our diplomatic police. What about it? Have taken tea and cornflakes and painkillers, so should be able to make it.
>
> I feel that I might get down today to what you are waiting for, the fluttering life of E, spasmodic, up and down, intense and passionate, all yes and no, hate and love, hunger and indulgence.
>
> But I think I feel fatigue creep into my body, and must do what my little policemen tell me. There are several that tell me what to do and how to live: when to drink tea or coffee, when to eat, when not to eat, when to stand or sit or lie, when to listen to my instinct. Oh, they are my best friends, they told me when to stop smoking, when to stop driving, they told me, and still tell me, whom to trust and whom not to trust. They often tell me what to do to make my life easier, but generally I do not listen to that kind of voice, because challenge is life. And now one of these little policemen says 'To bed, or you will muck up this Saturday, when there is so very much to do.'

I heard from Lance that his anorexia had got out of control and he was back in hospital in Adelaide, weighing seven stone. In his head, he was still looking after me: I had another bad fall in July 1984 and he wrote:

> I will tell you about your fall. As I saw you begin to tumble I knew it was going to be a bad one. For a moment I considered jumping the fence so that you would land on me – a cushion – but you had already hit the basement. I ran down and you

moaned from the next world. I knelt beside you and put my hand under the small of your back, put my head on your chest and wept. That you don't remember this is my only proof that you were unconscious for 1 or 2 minutes.

Only Lance understood my anguish over the children. I could let down my defences with him.

In March 1985, Katya brought Sacha to London. She and Claude were moving to Paris, where his parents lived; they hoped to get work in films. Sacha was full of charm and intelligence and desperately spoilt. Katya was as sweet as ever and would not come clean about the behaviour of her sisters and brothers. She was seeing many of my old friends, whom I had given up meeting for that reason. I knew it was easier for her to 'get out of my shadow', as she called it, if we were not talking to the same people, so I told them that I did not invite them because Katya preferred me not to. I withdrew because I wanted to free her. Then something upset me. I wrote to Lance:

I am at a loss – really and truly – and do not understand anything any more. Katya is having dinner tonight with Johnny. For the first time, after two weeks – and two days before leaving – she telephones, having been away in the country for three days, and wants to see me. Why do not they ask me to have dinner with them together, as we used to when they were small? When I said 'Shall I ask your brother and sisters to a fiesta?' she said 'No thank you, we do not get on together when we are all there.' Do you agree with that? Do you remember? What a desert of motherhood – have I been such a useless mother, Lance? You were the closest witness. I remember them asking that I should spend suppers with them when I was supposed to work – and they were right too, and I did let them down – did I? But then what parent does not let a child down – where are the saints? Except for David and Debbie, but they are two and work it together, really together, and they did not have nor do they have the problems I had to finance the family. Oh dear, oh dear – I really do not want to see them at all, for they only come because they say 'must see Mama' – I hate that. It is all very frightening. I feel like running away.

I felt very sad. Had I done this to my own children? I knew I had helped other people's children. A letter had just arrived from Widar Halen, a Norwegian art historian who had lived at Chapel Street as a student.

> My ever dear Mrs Furse, During my stay in Paris I met Glenn Russell, who told me that our home in Chapel Street has ceased to exist, and I suddenly felt such a yearning for staying there just one more time to say farewell to the dear old house which was my home in England for so many years. It was always 'the house', wasn't it – it was never you nor I but always the 'house', and it did so many things to all of us, and we all grew up and were blessed by the house and you. You were always there, and there was never a 'no' in your mouth, but always, 'We will find a way round of doing it' or 'We can put in an extra mattress.' I did well in England, thanks to the secure and warm home you gave me, and all the advice and comfort. And you never gave for pity, but from the abundance of your heart, as among good friends.
>
> In one single moment I can recall the house, and our first encounter in the study, when you said, 'You have got elegant socks; my father used to wear silk socks.' The songs you used to sing, I can hear them now. They have got some salt taste of tears in them, but at the same time a vigour, a curious sweetness and generosity. The house merged us all into a unity, so that we shall recognise each other on another planet, and the things still cry out to each other, my round table, the rocking horse, and your teapots.
>
> Many friends came to the house and went away again. They were never the kind of people who stay for a long time in the same place. They were not the kind of people who grow old. But they sat contented by your table, and when the house, closing around them, said, 'I will not let you go except you bless me,' they laughed and blessed it, and it let them go.
>
> When one says these words, then one must also agree and consent to let go that which has really given one its blessing. For it happens almost every day in our lives that a time, a circumstance, is past, we cannot struggle against that. But when one has received a blessing, one has that to keep, that can never be lost. The house blessed me and all my friends that came to stay, and I always felt that you blessed me as well. I never had to

pretend with you, or to prove something I could not prove, you blessed me as I was. There has never been one single moment in which my heart was not full of blessing towards you then, and I feel that there is still much light in the darkness around you. Yours ever, Widar XXX.

Primroses and daffodils were in flower, then a new wave of frost came down. I knew they would survive as usual, sticking their little heads high in the air. Suddenly in the same month of March came much good news – the end of the miners' strike, Mikhail Gorbachev taking over in the Soviet Union, and the best, Lance being allowed out of bed in the hospital for the first time after seven months and three weeks and gaining 27 kilograms. I wrote immediately.

Your letter arrived with that beautiful handwriting of yours and I wept and wept, as I did yesterday when I learnt that Johnny is going to a shrink. No one understands the heating and hot water, so I manage without the heating. I turn on the hot water and it comes boiling hot, and then I turn it off. I need three hot baths a day because of sciatica, so it is heat for sciatica and cold for arthritis and ice for thrombosis – I do not bother much – take the baths and move my legs a lot and take painkillers (as little as possible) and just am in pain.

I am moving around all the time, for I hate this flat so much – everything is topsy turvy and there is no room and I cannot bear the closeness of it all. Want still to go to Venice but have not got the energy nor the strength to househunt. I think I will just become an errant animal and leave everything in everyone's cellars plus the storage (£40 a week) till I die.

Roger and David have been the real standbys. Of course, they cannot arrange the heater, clean my bath and make my bed, which I could do but no longer, drive the car and change the typewriter ribbon – and be there to say good morning and good night to. I lock the door and creep into my bed and am really and truly ALONE. Well, I am always alone, for I am a loner like David – but to have no one to say good night to or good morning to hurts very much.

Twenty years you were here, Lance, and twenty years is a long time of being cared for even when being ill-treated and unfairly treated. I now know it all and know where your illness came from and it is mostly genes. Doctors can help to a point of healing but not cure. The only cure is to remake yourself. I did it – for that I feel very proud. I killed everything in myself or almost everything that I rejected in my parental genes. But I started early and was conscious of it all for I disliked them so much.

I know why you were so hating me for so long. I know it all and about the children, too – and why you must all hurt me and be bad to me. And I have to accept it somehow, somewhere. I do understand it with my brain but not with my soul and heart. It is interesting how the children will ring Australia and you and not me, is not it? I find that most people are only happy when they are hunting the impossible – dream – fantasy?

I never worry over flying these days – am always prepared to go down and under – which is a great relief, for all that anxiety over flying was pathetic. I plan gently to take a train via Poland into Moscow, into Outer Mongolia, into China, into Hong Kong, into Sydney, into the States and back – sort of six weeks in the autumn, if one is still around, with a lot of painkillers.

Lance was wanting to come back to live with me, yet he knew he had to cure his anorexia nervosa, which he called AN. He wrote one day when he was drunk.

How can I have you no further than a neighbour (perhaps domestic companion) and also retain my support system – pension, shrinks, doctors for new pains and malfunctions. AN for me is a stubborn return to 'childness' in order that *someone I trust* should grow me up properly (simple words but a book full of nuance and subtlety) to fulfil my birthright. At the same time I want to experience and live an unsophisticated but *intelligent* European life (forgive me but I see it in one of the myriad Italian villages which make us all cry when we see them – but then why not there, where my preferred blood originated).

How awful it is to be only partially intelligent – a kind of computer (my 'act') groping to find its program from the void of my absent Italian culture. See how it always turns out bullshit. I understand everything but can *do* nothing! One parade after another. My words are the footprints of an elephant when I want the Mona Lisa . . . I can see but there is no reference point, everything becomes confusing because there is no self, no me, no Lance, just an act, a camera, an observer – Lance is a screaming angry 7-year-old demanding to be grown up *properly*.

'I' believe that many cases of AN occur when there is a breakdown in a child's trust of one or both of his/her parents. Mum put me in harm's way, Dad never came to rescue me – they were both at fault. I have all the answers/excuses: how can one throw out the negative (nello words) and capitalise the positive? My bricks are OK, the *cement* is atrociously bad – weak – elastic: unsupportive. I find it impossible to be the container of all that is within me!

I know that at my best I am a useful member of society, at my worst a total unviable being. Mood changes hourly – how can I contain this confusion.

If you decide to come to Australia, do it for BIG reasons – China, Hong Kong, goodbye Oz, whatever. I will meet you in Sydney. But don't come just for me – my conscience won't allow this. Better I come to you – you decide, I will comply. Please let Johnny read this crap – I feel so close to him. I wonder if my words are stepping-stones to understanding the whole stream. I cry a lot these days – it's the only truly honest thing I do! THE ONLY WAY I CAN COPE IS WITH WINE (homemade Italian wine of course) – OBLIVION IS MY ONLY MOMENT OF PEACE – WHAT IS *ULTIMATE*/SUPREME OBLIVION – HA-HA-HA – I LOVE YOU! Lance

XXX *mi anima a tu*.

PS This was written unedited during gradual consumption of wine within 3 hours of my telephone call to you – dear *you*, Lise, salad girl (Bistro), cashmere sweater, skirt, and lovely stockings.

A HOUSE IS NOT A HOME – UNTIL?

DARLING – YOU KNOW WHAT IT'S LIKE TO BE A CHILD. YOU KNOW WHAT IT'S LIKE TO BE A FOREIGNER – YOU HAVE COPED WELL! I HAVE NOT. AMEN.

NOT EDITED – THIS IS IT – I LOVE YOU (WHO DOESN'T?).

29

Moscow, and a Benediction from Lance, 1984–93

Iain Sutherland had become ambassador to Moscow in 1982, but he seemed to have a bad effect on the Soviet leaders: they died like ninepins. Brezhnev was the first to topple over, in November after the Sutherlands arrived, and Andropov took power. Jeanne Sutherland wrote to me from the British Embassy.

> The funeral was extraordinary, but they say it was the normal 1st class type – nothing special. Now Brezhnev is mostly forgotten – no one mentions him. No wives were allowed at the funeral or the lying-in-state. And no ordinary people either – only groups from 'organisations' . . .
>
> I can write you a letter because I have made my pen work again by soaking it in the bath. Everything dries up here, even pens, and Andropov. He looks very dry and I suspect he is going to be dull and 'correct' by Soviet standards.

In February 1984 Andropov died and Chernenko took power. He was seventy-two, and so was President Reagan in the United States. I had a terrible idea: old people resent that the young have time ahead of them, and now Reagan and Chernenko were in a position to kill us all, so no one was alive when they weren't.

I was seventy-three. At such an age you should go through your life and say, 'Where did I miss out and where can I still catch up?' It is not quantity, it is quality. I decided to go to the land of my fathers and hear my lovely language spoken again, after fifty-three years. The Sutherlands had invited me.

When I am hopeful I want to travel. When I am in despair I want to travel too – it soothes all my moods, like singing. I like to live in what I call the dark, in basements or valleys, and then I go out into the world with wide eyes.

The day after Christmas 1984 I set off, and had a mishap immediately. Michael Alexander drove me to the airport in his vintage Toyota and at Heathrow I hastily opened its door, straight into a bus that carried it away. All Michael said was, 'Never mind – let us get you on the plane.'

I took British Airways to Berlin West, then went by bus across the Wall to Schönefeld, my first Communist airport. It was quite deserted except for two silent groups of West Germans going on holiday to Siberia: no shops, just dimly-lit desks.

Moscow airport was as deserted and as like an empty stadium as East Berlin. Nothing seemed to be happening, wheelchairs did not exist. Now and again a voice came over the loudspeakers. The duty free shop was closed, although it was early afternoon. All was utility, reminding me of the war; it pleased me, for austerity is full of possibilities. At passport control, the little KGB man stared into my eyes for a long time and I prepared for a tedious wait. But no, I was let through, and met by Iain Sutherland with his diplomatic pass and the Embassy car. We drove past birches and pine trees loaded with snow, and soon there were blocks of flats, then the onion domes of churches glistening in golden armour with snow like white fur, then the Kremlin wall, and on top of the Kremlin and the churches bright red stars, for it was dusk. When I saw all this, I said, 'Pinch me, Iain,' and he did. I could see the chauffeur looking through the mirror with interest.

I stood in my bedroom and looked out at the Kremlin and was overcome by emotion, thinking of those friends who came here in the 1930s never to return. Iceflowers on the windowpanes, snowflakes, an eerie silence (no bells), and the red star shining defiantly under the inky black sky.

Next morning, when I woke, I saw lorry after lorry driving past piled with Christmas trees. The Sutherlands told me they were not Christmas trees but 'New Year trees', which would be decorated with baubles and angels' hair by 28 December. Every building had one. The Russians had made Father Christmas into Uncle Holly. On top of every New Year tree would be a bright red star. So now our foundering civilisation is given three stars: the star of Bethlehem, the star of David, the red star of Communism.

Strangely, the Russians do not wear red – there were many stares at my scarlet shawl. Blue seems to soothe their anger and nervous systems.

In the next few days I drowned in ikons, which do not seem to me to be art so much as handicraft. Although I had two bad falls, the snow and ice made me very happy. We watched the queues at the GUM stores for special things: cheeses, sausages. Again, I had a political thought: queueing stops people thinking. (But it can also embitter them. The Czechs have a riddle: 'What is vegetarian and a mile long? A queue at the butcher.')

There seemed to be much more privilege than in the West. In one museum I saw seven exquisitely dressed children aged three to eight shepherded by five young nannies. The nannies and even the children were ugly, like most Muscovites – physically unattractive, colourless and shapeless. Except in the special shops, everything bore the mark of utility: clothes, food, medicines, furniture. As there was no unemployment, every shop and office was overstaffed. When I bought medicine, I picked it out with one girl, priced it with another, paid a third and got it wrapped by a fourth.

In the museums, every room had an old lady, generally shawled, sitting ready to wag a finger and say '*Niet*' if you got too close to a picture. Their ages were between fifty and a hundred, but seeing my crutch they offered their chair if I stood too long. The young guides in the museums seemed to be the great-granddaughters of the *ancien régime*, judging from their delicate noses, heart-shaped faces and haughtiness. They spoke very good English, French and German, and looked with contempt at the tourists, especially the unkempt Americans chewing gum. Young Muscovites try to look smart.

A memory from the plane that took me to Leningrad for a few days: a rich young couple and our conversation. The man's hair was beautifully cut in Western style, and he was good-looking *à la* Nureyev. He wore a fine suit and shirt and tie, sable hat, sable-lined coat, gold watch, even gold bracelet. She was very pretty in light blue leather trousers, a sable hat and, as they told me proudly, her coat was blue fox. Moreover, they were eating pears, unknown to the masses, especially at this time of year. They told me that they had a little girl and a nanny and a maid. I asked him his profession. 'Economist.' I said, 'Business?' 'Yes, shipping. Baltic shipping.' I was reminded of the Polish joke: 'Our trading relations with the Russians are excellent. We give them our coal and they take our meat.'

The Sutherlands took me to Peredelkino, the village outside Moscow hidden in birch groves and pine woods where loyal artists were given dachas, wooden villas, for weekends and holidays. We met the poet Yevtushenko, whom I did not like: he seemed ingratiating and in some way phoney and furtive.

In Moscow, I saw groups of people at the Bolshoi being handed tickets and money to act as a claque, applauding their own dancer and interrupting another. The performance was the worst I have ever seen – I was enchanted. To me perfection is always boring, unlike most of my friends, who demand it.

Museums, galleries, theatre, ballet, opera, concerts, films, books, discs, cassettes, newspapers were all cheap – anything that was controlled by the state and could form the minds of the people and keep them going. But anything that might cause controversy, doubts, questions was taboo. What a clever economy, I thought at the time, to keep your people entertained and hoping for material things, unlike the British Welfare State, that had overfed and over-cosseted its people so that the dream of my generation had largely turned into a nightmare.

It seems to me that the Welfare State is wrong as a concept, because human beings live by challenge and competition and hope, and a sufficiency is very deadly, and too muchness is a killer, and *too little* is what makes people grow and flex their muscles of body, mind and heart. So these Russian people, and all the Slavs, Bulgarians, Poles, Czechs, Slovaks, Slovenes, Croats, Serbs, were dreaming night and day of a better flat, a better coat, a better sausage, a better orange. The Muscovites had oranges, but awful ones, from Cuba – the skin hard and glued to the flesh, if you could call it flesh.

I had long talks with the servants at the Embassy. KGB or not, they were human beings, and our hearts beat at the same rhythm. None had more than one child. They talked of the niceness and the fairness of the British, but also of their coldness – of course they could not understand British reserve. For once, I had found people who laughed as I laughed and cried as I cried. I thought of the aunts and uncles and cousins on my father's side. Yes, I could get lost among my people there in Russia, and shed that awful shivering loneliness of England.

* * *

On 10 March 1985, soon after I got back to London, Chernenko died and was succeeded by Mikhail Gorbachev. I was coming to think that the Soviets put dying leaders into the saddle just so that no change could be made in policies; perhaps also they liked the cut of Iain Sutherland's funeral clothes and wanted to photograph him for the third time. On television, I saw David Owen and Iain standing together on Red Square and thought 'There goes the Bistro.'

The high hopes we had had of a new party that could win power melted in 1987 and stranded, temporarily, a few careers, including David Owen's. Perhaps his high-handedness contributed to the quarrels that split the SDP. He is not very good with people. I had always been afraid that the television satire programme *Spitting Image* would set David Steel against David Owen. The little mousy David Steel puppet was made to look so silly, always outsmarted and bullied by the big handsome David Owen puppet but still trying to squeeze into bed with him. I said, 'It's only puppets, but David Steel will want to have his own back and show he's not really David Owen's masochistic pet mouse.'

After Mrs Thatcher's victory in the 1987 election, in which the Alliance took only 23 per cent of the popular vote and lost five seats, David Steel called for the SDP and the Liberals to merge. Although the Liberals were sad to lose their noble old name, they agreed. The SDP split. The larger group, including three of the Gang of Four, joined the Liberals and David Owen took back the leadership of the tiny remaining SDP.

It was a sad end to the chance of new policies. Most people could not make out what had happened or remember the name of the new party (Social and Liberal Democrats) – they called it the Salads because it was green and flimsy. What they all knew was that there had been a lot of bad temper and bungling and that they were back in the grip of one or other of the two old parties, and that the Communists, and Labour's far left, the Militants, were very relieved.

When the Berlin Wall came down in November 1989 I was there: I have an excellent instinct. I had gone to Frankfurt to Margarete Buber-Neumann's funeral. I had known her for fifty-six years, since our Communist youth in Berlin. The Neumanns went to Moscow in 1937 and Heinz was executed, Margarete was sent to a labour camp. She was handed back to the Gestapo by the NKVD in 1940 and spent five years in Ravensbrück. I visited Margarete before she died, when she was in hospital with Alzheimer's disease. She told me that not all the nurses were kind to her. I said they were mean because they envied us our experiences, however terrible. I sang with her 'Die Gedanken sind frei' and the other old songs. She died on 6 November. Many people from those days came to the funeral, including the son of dear Willy Trostel, my Swiss contact of 1933.

I went on to Berlin for those days in November, and saw the jubilation at the dismantling of the Wall, but I was not convinced. The French anarchists had rushed to paint in large red letters '*VIVE L'ANARCHIE*' on top of the monument. Since then, the scream 'Freedom' has turned into the scream 'Money'.

Communism is not dead, as Christianity is not dead. For while there are the poor, there will be people who want to die for them. I knew there would be a coup against Gorbachev; he was strong enough to survive it in August 1991. He was trying to rule a country of people who had never known freedom. They are decent people, but politically they are serfs.

It is now over twenty years since the Bistro closed. During that time, I have given several dances so that the regulars can be together again. These 'Bistro balls', as they were nicknamed, take place in the basement of the French church, Notre Dame, off Leicester Square. I charge people who can afford it and give their money to charity. For two weeks beforehand I cook, and take the dishes to friends who have deep freezes. I send out about four hundred invitations.

The first Bistro ball was on 3 November 1978, the day *The Times* suspended publication. The girl who had been the ballet dancer Anya Linden asked whether she could send a cheque, and I said, 'Not *you*, Anya.' She answered, 'I can, now I'm Lady Sainsbury.' Henry Swanzy described the evening in his diary.

> E is in a psychedelic dress, and in the seventh heaven, Johnny sits at the door. An old couple (they were street musicians) play violin and accordeon; the MC is George Melly. In fact, the company is nearly all middle-aged, as befit survivors of the fifties and sixties. I talk to Robert Kee about his book on Ireland, *The*

Green Flag . . . The lion of the evening is David Owen. Asked by a journalist why he was there, he replies, 'When Elisabeth calls me, I come.'

I thought it would be the one and only and last time, but everyone seemed so glad to be together that I gave another party on 29 November 1979.

Simon Jenkins, who had become political editor of the *Economist* and married Gayle Hunnicutt, gave a party in October 1984 in Battersea Power Station and the Bistro was there in full force. It was a beautiful lofty setting, not like the shabby church basement, and perhaps that is what made it so strangely conventional. They were all there, all well dressed, well fed and well succeeded, and everyone stood waiting to be courted – on one side the Jonathan Aitkens, on the other the Peter Jays. The number of Bistro boys who had 'made it' was astonishing.

By 1991 Simon Jenkins was editor of *The Times*, and he and Gayle gave a party in the Tower of London, among all the corpses and guns. It was like watching television – politicians and Dimblebys and Attenboroughs and Pakenhams. I thought: perhaps I am actually sitting at home? Half the guests were Bistro people, and several came up to me and said, 'It's you! I haven't seen you for thirty years.' I felt almost known, like the rest.

I gave two more Bistro balls in the church hall, on 4 December 1986 and 11 December 1987. 'There will be the usual goulash, soup, salads etc and wine. Music (band), cheek-to-cheek dancing and maybe a bit more modern for the children, a disco. Cabaret of a kind produced by the young. Please come in your best bib and tucker. Please contribute £15 each (inflation since the last dance). I would love to see, as Nanny used to say, your dear little faces again, probably for the last time.' Shusha Guppy sang love songs, '*Que reste-t-il de nos amours?*' and 'Troubled Mind' and 'The Rose'. Kate Percival, daughter of my old friend from Vienna, Dorli, who was Carol Reed's secretary, sang Weill and Eisler, and that naughty one I love, 'Travelling Hands'. Hugo Dixon, son of Piers Dixon and Edwina Sandys from the Bistro, became a singer for the night instead of a *Financial Times* journalist and sang 'Money'. Somebody commented that all the older men were dancing with their illegitimate daughters. And the wonderful thing was that the middle-agedness that Henry commented on, and the frightening success, had melted away. Second-generation

Bistro and others in their twenties or thirties filled the hall with life and comradeship – people like Roland Rudd (son of Tony and Ethne), Andrew Gimson, Carinthia West (daughter of Michael and Christine), Edward Fox, Keith Raffan, Caroline Forbes (daughter of Ian and Penelope), Amy Jenkins (daughter of Peter and Polly), and Rachael and Gabriel and Daniel and Mikail Barraclough, and Laki, Paddy, Manuela and Tino Zervudachi . . . the Bistro had given birth to a whole new group of talents.

My old friends and my young friends gave a dinner at the Golden Duck for my eightieth birthday in August 1990, and Caroline Forbes, who is a very good photographer, brought a poem by Czeslaw Milosz to be read out. Another friend picked it up from the table and saved it. It's called 'Reading *Notebook* by Anna Kamienska'.

> Reading her, I realised how rich she was and myself,
>   how poor.
> Rich in love and suffering, in crying and dreams and prayer.
> She lived among her own people who were not very happy
>   but supported each other,
> And were bound by a pact between the dead and
> the living renewed at the graves.
> She was gladdened by herbs, wild roses, pines, potato
>   fields
> And the scents of the soil, familiar since childhood.
> She was not an eminent poet. But that was just:
> A good person will not learn the wiles of art.

I was very moved by my friends' tributes and their tender love.

John Major became Prime Minister in November 1990 at only forty-seven. I told Andrew Gimson, then a leader writer on the *Independent on Sunday*, that I used to watch Major on the box and encourage him as he grew: 'Well done, boy. One step further and I'll give you a biccie.' Andrew wrote a leader about an old lady's view of the Prime Minister.

I went to the European Community summit conference at Maastricht in December 1991 to see how John Major did. I got a journalist's pass and stayed with my professor friends the Groots.

I cannot keep away from history. People said, 'You are eighty-one – you will wear yourself out.' I said, 'I have to watch and feel such an event, and to go to Maastricht is to me as easy as going to my television.' I wanted to check on my love for Europe. At the end of your life, you feel like revisiting your great themes to see if you were right.

John Major did very well and the Europeans loved him. Douglas Hurd the Foreign Secretary nannied the negotiations through, kind and unselfish and a gent. I was the oldest so-called journalist, and the only one on a crutch and pushing a basket on wheels. All the Europeans wanted to photograph me and interview me, I was so old. I said, 'I am not sure this united Europe is the Europe we fought for.' At night, the journalists and politicians were together in a big hall. I went to bed at four and got up at six to catch the plane home. When I told my young British journalist friends about it, they asked who I had been representing. I said, 'All of *you*.'

These days I usually invite the children, not the parents, to my basement kitchen. When the parents come, they look at their watches and go home at eleven, not for any purpose but because they are set in their ways; the children are full of enthusiasm and get excited by each other and talk wonderfully and go home when the evening reaches its natural end. And I can help the children: the parents have everything.

My kitchen is like the Bistro – young journalists talk to the young politicians and television people and also meet other minds who have no interest in that swim. One new friend I met through the SDP is the chess player Nigel Short and his wife. When he beat Karpov in 1992 and only Kasparov stood between him and the world title, we had a celebration round my table.

Johnny used to hear from Lance quite often. He had met several of the Italian community in Adelaide and was living with a kind old lady called Nell Gretton, a friend of his mother's he had known since childhood.

At the end of 1990 Nell Gretton, who had Alzheimer's disease, had to move into a home. Lance agonised with Johnny about what to do: buy Nell's flat, move somewhere else in Adelaide, or come back to London.

At the end of June 1991 I was in great pain again with my arthritis, and thought I would go this time. Caroline Forbes came in every day to massage my neck. I usually sleep on my belly, but for four nights I lay on my back and folded my hands. I said that I was arranging myself before I went to sleep to save trouble for whoever found me.

Ten days later, I knew why I had rehearsed death. In those hours, Lance had been dying, weighing three and a half stone. His brother telephoned Johnny from Australia, and Johnny, Anna and Sara came to tell me. Lance had moved from Nell's into a male friend's house. When the friend came home the first evening, he found that Lance had taken twenty-nine sleeping pills. He was rushed to hospital and kept in because of his anorexia. His mother asked why he had tried to kill himself. Lance said, 'Well, it was such a nice sunny day.' He stopped eating and drinking. His mother visited him every day. He did not want anyone else to know. His mother told me: 'His last thought was for you, Mrs Furse. I wish you could have seen him in his coffin; he was so beautiful.' Lance had made a will dividing everything equally between me and the four children and his brother Max's children.

The children held a wake. Katya travelled from Paris, without her children (she had a second son, Alexis, in 1988). Tim Husband and Danielle Tilkin flew from America. Anthony telephoned. The other three were in London: Johnny and his wife Suki Dimpfl (they married in 1988), Anna and Sara. Sara could not go to her job at the photographers' co-operative Magnum for three days. She hugged me and told me she loved me. Roger Graef and his new wife Susan Richards came. He had arrived in England the year before Lance, and understood his life. I made it up with Fiore Henriques and Christopher MacLehose. Lance had healed many wounds.

When it comes to my funeral, I have asked Gerald Reddington to conduct it. I would love to be buried at sea, but it is too expensive, so I will be constructive: the worms will eat me and make more earth. I love earth, and that will be my chance to give something back to it. I have always been part of the grassroots politically. I am telling my children they can put me down for a pauper's grave – it only costs £75 for the whole thing. I might as well carry my beliefs through to the end. It would feel so good. I don't want anyone to put on a long face and wear it in the church for half an hour. Instead, love life and help each other, and light the candles – that will hide that the floor is not swept. And give with warm hands and a fiercely beating heart.

People Elisabeth Furse Fed at the Bistro

(She apologises to those she has misspelt, or even temporarily forgotten)

Jerry Adams, Michael Adeane, Jonathan Aitken, Tiger Aiyar, Jacintha Alexander, Michael Alexander, Shane Alexander, Liz Allsopp, Penny Allsopp, Pietro Annigoni,Michelangelo Antonioni, Fritzi Anzarut, Ray Anzarut, Jose Argadua, Tony Armstrong-Jones, Eve Arnold, Ricardo Arragno, Humphrey Arthure, Neal Ascherson, Diana Ash, Jane Aspinall, John Aspinall, Jeremy Banks, Michael Banks, Susan Banks, Ann Barr, Patrick Bashford, Sally Belfrage, John Bendon, David Benson, Leslie Benson, Robin Benson, Prince Merid Beyene, Theo Bikel, Bobby Birch, Brinsley Black, Anthony Blond, Peter Blond, Virginia Blond, Claire Bloom, Shirley Bloomer, Lester Bookbinder, Barbara Bossom, Clive Bossom, Doric Bossom, Ilinca Bossy, Anne Bowen, Mark Boxer, Robin Brackenbury, Jon Bradshaw, Christopher Brasher, Michele Breton, Gerald Bridgeman, Garech Browne, Robert Brownjohn, King Freddy of Buganda, Humphrey Burton, Michael Butler, Kiki Byrne, David Cammell, Donald Cammell, Jean Campbell, Fiona Campbell-Walter, Peter Carvell, Ann Casement, Richard Casement, General Challe, Jacqui Chan, Caroline Charles, Sarah Churchill, Charles Clore, Douglas Collins, Debbie Condon, Richard Condon, Caroline Coombe, Fleur Cowles, Vivian Craddock Williams, Richard Crewdson, Colin Crewe, Martha Crewe, Quentin Crewe, Sally Crewe, Sally Crichton-Stuart, Michael Crosfield, Denis Dangan, Gretel Davis, Nicholas de Jongh, Olga Deterding, George Devine, Marie Jose de Vine, Polly Devlin, Jessica de Wet, Elizabeth Dickson, Deborah Dixon, Piers Dixon, Mary-Rose Donaldson, Dorothy Donaldson Hudson (called Dorothy Dorothy), Hugh Donaldson Hudson (who became Hugh Hudson), Robin Douglas-Home, James Dreaper, Arthur Duckworth, Lila Duckworth, David Duncan, Elaine Dundy, Anne Dunhill, Gioa Dutch, Lene Eddowes, Michael Eddowes, John Eden, Philip Edinburgh, Anthony Elliott, Dominic Elwes, Jacob Epstein, David Evers, Felix Fenton, Sebastian de Ferranti, Peter Finch, Albert Finney, Dudley Fishburn, Stephen Fitzsimon, Ronnie Flockhart, Ian Forbes, Penelope Forbes, James Fox, Mark Frankland, Hugh Fraser, Reggie Freed, Clement Freud, David Frost, Camilla Fry, Jeremy Fry, Bill Fuller, George Galitzine, David Galloway, Andy Garnett, Ann Gaskell, Robin Geiger, Christopher Gibbs, Martin Gilbert, Robert Emmett Ginna, Jimmy Goldsmith, Teddy Goldsmith, David Gordon, Nicholas Gormanston, David Goschen, Gordon Gostelow, Michael Gough, John Goulandris, Grey Gowrie, Karen Graef, Roger Graef, Adrian Grant Morris, several Guinnesses, Nicholas Guppy, Shusha Guppy, Richenda Gurney, Guy Hamilton, Clive Hardcastle, Connie Harman, Nicholas Harman, Vere Harmsworth, Richard Harris, Noel Harrison, Mike Hawthorn, Christina Hellstedt, Fiore Henriques, Jocelyn Herbert, Sally Herbert, Pat Hearn, Jennifer Hocking, Walter von Hohenlohe, Tony Hubbard, Barbara Hulanicki, Maurice Hutton, Jill Ireland, Janey Ironside, Virginia Ironside, Peter Jancovic, John Jasper, Peter Jay, the Jay twins, Julian Jeffs, Peter Jenkins, Simon Jenkins, Toby Jessel, Paul Johnson, Cynthia Judah, Jerry Kaplan, Dmitri Kasterine, Irene Kasterine, Robert Kee, Tessa Kennedy, Richard Kershaw, Joanna Kilmartin, Terry Kilmartin, Lionel King-Lewis, Anthony Kinsman, Bunty Kinsman, Fleur Kirwan-Taylor, Nancy Kirwan-Taylor, Peter Kirwan-Taylor, Eartha Kitt, Stefan Knapp, Herbert Kretzmer, Diana Ladas, Millard Lampel, Angela Landels, Willie Landels, Philip Lasky, Henrietta Law, Frederic von Ledebur, Christopher Lee, Vivien Leigh, Anya Linden, David Litvinov, Annie Llewellyn, Michael Luke, Peter Lumley, Anna Lund, Richard Lund, Barbara Lygon, Juliet Lygon, Margaret Lygon, Julia Lymington, David Lyon-Maris, David McCallum, Gloria MacGowran, Colin McIvor, Sheila McIvor, Lance Macklin, Nicholas Maclean, Christopher MacLehose, Edward Maguire, John Maguire, Christopher Mallaby, Louis Malle, Tom Maschler, John Meade, Maxine Meade, George Melly, Jo Menell, Clarissa Merton, Colly Messai Andargatchew, Molly Messai Andargatchew, David Milford Haven, Hugh Millais, Suzy Millais, Jonathan Miller, Linda Mindel, David Mlinaric,

Michel Molinare, David Montgomery, Beecher Moore, Bobby Moore, Christopher Moorsom, John Morgan, Charles Morland, Jenny Morland, Martin Morland, Bill Morton, Johnny Moynihan, Andrew Mulligan, Sue Murray, Venetia Murray, Ilhan Nebioglu, John Newton, Joan North, Ken Obank, Christopher Columbus O'Donnell, John Osborne, David Owen, Debbie Owen, Tony Page, Elizabeth Paget, Nicky Paget, Antonia Pakenham, Tom Pakenham, all the Pakenhams, Anita Pallenberg, Michael Parkin, Tinka Paterson, Isabel Patino, Sandra Paul, Daphne Peacock, Michael Peacock, Clare Peploe, Cloe Peploe, Mark Peploe, Willy Peploe, Lance Percival, Michael Percival, Dorli Percival, Jon Pertwee, Tim Phillips, Caroline Phipps, Nicholas Phipps, Vivian Pickles, Alexander Plunket Greene, Alexei Poklewski-Koziell, Basha Poklewksi-Koziell, Vincent Poklewski-Koziell, Yash Pomian, James Pope-Hennessy, Davina Portman, Suna Portman, Bronwen Pugh, David Puttnam, Mary Quant, David Queensberry, Michael von Raben, Joyce Rackham, Enzo Ragazzini, Gerald Reddington, Clare Rendlesham, Tony Rendlesham, Jeremy Renton, Tony Richardson, Nicholas Ridley, Diana Rigg, Nicholas Roeg, Giles Romilly, Jake Rothschild, Marye Rous, Anthony Rous, Jonathan Routh, Ethne Rudd, Tony Rudd, Mali Safer, Barry Sainsbury, James Sainsbury, many Sainsburys, John St Aubyn, Julian St Leger, Nadia Sakal, David Salmon, Robert Sanders, Celia Sandys, Edwina Sandys, Peter Saunders, Philip Saville, Victor Saville, Peter Scaramanga, Nena von Schlebrugge, Mark Schreiber, Frances Schuster, Henry Schuster, John Scott, Anne Seaton-Reid, Harold Sebag-Montefiore, Hussein Shariffe, Michael Shea, Mona Shea, Jane Sheffield, Shura Shivarg, Milton Shulman, Maurits Sillem, Gordon Simpson, Taffy Slapek, David Spanier, Lizzie Spender, Kazimir Stamirski, Ray Stark, Jonathan Stedall, Alex Sterling, Johnny Sterling, Jocelyn Stevens, Susan Stocken, Charlotte Strachey, John Strachey, Arabella Stuart, Iain Sutherland, Jeanne Sutherland, Henriette Swanzy, Henry Swanzy, Gloria Taylor, Jimmy Taylor, Colin Thubron, Nicholas Tomalin, Feliks Topolski, Elizabeth of Toro, Polly Toynbee, Annie Trehearne, Violet Tree, Carly Tufnell, Rosie Tufnell, Sarah Tufnell, Bill Turner, Kenneth Tynan, Mary Ure, Harvey Usill, Malcolm Valentine, Anne Valery, James Verner, Claude Virgin, Jillie Virgin, Roz Watkins, Mark Watney, Veronica Waugh, James Wells, John Wells, West de Wend Fenton, Audrey West, Christine West, Michael West, Paul Weychan, Wanda Weychan,

Rita Wheatley, Timothy Whidbourne, John White, Xenia White, Sarah Wignall, Desmond Wilcox, Alan Williams, Emlyn Williams, Audrey Withers, Giles Wontner, Hugh Wontner, Julian Wontner, Deborah Wood, Peregrine Worsthorne, Anne Wyndham, Francis Wyndham, Hugh Wyndham, Joan Wyndham, John Wyndham, Mark Wyndham, David Wynne Morgan, Charlotte Zapary, Carolyn Zervudachi, Nolly Zervudachi.

Index